Getting Out of Debt

by Steven Bucci, et al.

A Wiley Brand

Getting Out of Debt For Dummies®

Published by: **John Wiley & Sons, Inc.,** 111 River Street, Hoboken, NJ 07030-5774, www.wiley.com

Copyright © 2024 by John Wiley & Sons, Inc., Hoboken, New Jersey

Published simultaneously in Canada

For general information on our other products and services, please contact our Customer Care Department within the U.S. at 877-762-2974, outside the U.S. at 317-572-3993, or fax 317-572-4002. For technical support, please visit https://hub.wiley.com/community/support/dummies.

Wiley publishes in a variety of print and electronic formats and by print-on-demand. Some material included with standard print versions of this book may not be included in e-books or in print-on-demand. If this book refers to media such as a CD or DVD that is not included in the version you purchased, you may download this material at http://booksupport.wiley.com. For more information about Wiley products, visit www.wiley.com.

Library of Congress Control Number: 2024933667

ISBN 978-1-394-25033-2 (pbk); ISBN 978-1-394-25034-9 (ebk); ISBN 978-1-394-25035-6 (ebk)

SKY10070183_032224

Contents at a Glance

Table of Contents

Introduction

So you're concerned about how much you owe to your creditors. Join the crowd! You shouldn't even try to guess how many people are worried about their debts. Suffice it to say the number is staggering, and it keeps on growing.

Whether you picked up this book because you're drowning in debt and looking for a financial life raft or because you're just feeling uncomfortable about the amount you owe to your creditors, this book is here to help. You find out how to assess the state of your finances, put together a budget, understand credit reporting, get your debts paid off as quickly as possible, and deal with high-risk debts like your mortgage and student loans.

When your financial problems are behind you (which *will* happen if you put the advice in this book into action), you then get advice for your financial future. You discover the credit rebuilding process and find the basics about money management.

About This Book

If you follow the advice in this book, your debt will diminish. Eventually, you'll have more disposable income, and you'll start to gain financial peace of mind. You'll even be able to put money away for your family's financial future and work toward such goals as buying your own home, taking a vacation, helping pay for your kids' college educations, and funding your retirement.

You won't find any fake how-to-get-out-of-debt-overnight advice in *Getting Out of Debt For Dummies*. You can no more get rich overnight than you can get out debt overnight. Those who have accomplished either know that slow and steady wins the race. Getting out of debt can be done, but it takes time — months or even years, depending on how much you owe relative to your income. Despite what some ads claim, there are no shortcuts to debt reduction.

Getting out of debt may also require lifestyle changes and even some sacrifice. For example, for your family to meet its financial obligations without using credit, you may have to slash your spending to the bare bones and work at a second (or even a third) job.

As you already know, getting into debt is easy. Getting out is not. This book provides everything you need to meet that challenge.

A quick note: Sidebars (shaded boxes of text) dig into the details of a given topic, but they aren't crucial to understanding it. Feel free to read them or skip them. You can pass over the text accompanied by the Technical Stuff icon, too. The text marked with this icon gives some interesting but nonessential information about getting out of debt.

One last thing: Within this book, you may note that some web addresses break across two lines of text. If you're reading this book in print and want to visit one of these web pages, simply key in the web address exactly as it's noted in the text, pretending as though the line break doesn't exist. If you're reading this as an e-book, you've got it easy — just click the web address to be taken directly to the web page.

Foolish Assumptions

We assume that because you're taking the time to read these words, you're serious about wanting to get out and stay out of debt, and you're willing to do whatever it takes to achieve that goal. That's great, because the road to financial health is not always smooth.

We also assume that you don't know very much about money management. Don't be embarrassed, and don't let that fact prevent you from taking action against your debt. Most U.S. consumers need help with basic money management, and this book offers exactly that.

Icons Used in the Book

Throughout this book, you find eye-catching icons that call your attention to especially important or helpful information. Here's what each icon indicates.

REMEMBER

The Remember icon highlights information about getting out of debt that's crucial. Be sure to make an effort to tuck it into your mental filing cabinet for future use.

TIP

The Tip icon alerts you to advice that can save you time, money, and legal hassles.

WARNING

Make sure you read the text next to each Warning icon! If you don't, you could face some serious consequences.

TECHNICAL STUFF

This icon flags information that delves a little deeper than usual into a particular topic related to getting out of debt.

Beyond the Book

In addition to the material in the print or e-book you're reading right now, this product comes with some access-anywhere goodies on the web. Check out the free Cheat Sheet for info on compiling a list of your debt, handling a debt repayment plan, and finding free help. To get this Cheat Sheet, simply go to www.dummies.com and enter **Getting Out of Debt For Dummies Cheat Sheet** in the Search box.

Where to Go from Here

Your debt situation may be daunting, but don't be daunted by this book. What this book explains isn't tough to understand. You only need to bring your time and resolve to try what works to get your debts in the rearview mirror.

So plunge in. Why not get your feet wet by starting at the very beginning of the book in Chapter 1? There you find the basics of eliminating debt.

But if there's a particular type of debt keeping you awake at night, or if you're haunted by never-ending phone calls from debt collectors, jump right to the chapters that deal with those subjects. You can always back up and read earlier chapters that provide the basic tools for debt management.

Wherever you start reading, know this: If you follow the advice in this book and stay focused and disciplined, you *will* overcome your debts and emerge confident and with a brighter financial future.

1

Getting Started with Getting Out of Debt

Discover the different types of debt you can incur, determine the right debt payoff method for you, and find out how to stay debt-free.

Ask some important questions about your relationship with money. Review what a budget is, figure out why you can't seem to make one work, and assess your overall financial picture.

Examine the parts of a budget to successfully align your spending with your income.

Check out categories, the right tools, and strategies to create your new spending plan.

Survey strategies and tactics to spend less and get more value.

Chapter **1**

Eliminating Debt: The Basics

Everyone hates having debt, but think about it: 99 percent of the population just can't feasibly make a significant purchase or tackle a crisis without taking on some kind of debt, like student loans, auto loans, and credit cards. However, that doesn't mean you can't do anything about it.

This chapter looks at the different types of debt to help you create a budget for paying it off. You find out how to rank the importance of each debt so you can create a payoff plan that works with your budget, and you get tips anyone can use to keep themselves from accumulating more debt. It's all fun and games when you come home with something shiny until you have to pay it back.

REMEMBER

The illusion that you're a terrible person if you have debt is a common misconception. In fact, many personal finance gurus even suggest that if you have debt, you shouldn't enjoy your life until you pay that debt off in full. Ignore them. Debt happens to everyone at one time or another, and you don't deserve a lower quality of life than the person down the street.

Looking at the Different Types of Debt

You acquire *debt* when you borrow a certain amount of money intending to pay it back. People can take on debt, but so can companies, corporations, and even countries. Heck, as of this writing, the United States is more than $33.7 trillion in the hole, according to U.S. Debt Clock.org.

Different types of debt affect your credit score in different ways, as you find out in Part 2. You want different types of debt paid off in full on your credit report so lenders can see that you're a trustworthy applicant capable of paying off more than one type of loan. You *do not* want too many open or any delinquent accounts. The following sections review the different types of debt so you can get organized and pay these monsters off.

REMEMBER

You often see people refer to debt as being "good" debt or "bad" debt:

>> *Good debt* typically provides a return on your investment. Student loans are considered good debt because you're using them to secure a college degree, which helps increase your earning potential. Another example of good debt is a home loan because your home can appreciate in value over time, allowing you to sell for a profit.

>> *Bad debt* is anything you've borrowed that doesn't further your finances; you can think of bad debt as anything that decreases your net worth over time, usually with depreciating assets. This type of debt includes auto loans (because cars lose their value) and credit cards.

Student loans

Student loan debt is money you borrow for costs associated with higher education, such as tuition, textbooks, laptops, and living expenses. If you attend a trade school or vocational school, additional expenses can apply. For example, you may need specific tools if you go into automotive repair or a stethoscope if you're a medical assistant.

These types of debts are considered *unsecured installment loans*. When a debt is *unsecured*, you aren't providing any collateral to the financial institution (or lender). An *installment loan* means that you'll pay back the loan at regular intervals, but the payment amount may change based on the type of interest rate you have (that is, a fixed rate versus an adjustable rate).

Student loan debt can be recalculated depending on the type of loan and repayment plan. The interest rates on a student loan can be fixed or graduated (the rate increases as income increases). The lender determines the frequency of payments, which can vary but usually occur once a month over several years. Repayment starts six months after graduation, a span known as a *grace period.*

You can receive either a federal loan from the U.S Department of Education or a private loan through a bank or alternative lender. Private loans are much harder for a younger student to obtain because these loans are typically based on your credit score and credit history. Federal loans, on the other hand, require you to complete the Free Application for Federal Student Aid (FAFSA). Each of these types of loans has different requirements as well as pros and cons, such as income-based repayment options or the ability to refinance at a lower rate.

TIP

Everyone who hasn't started their higher ed journey yet should at least fill out the FAFSA. A lot of schools award grants and scholarships based on the information you provide. You can find the online application at https://studentaid.gov.

Credit cards

Credit card debt is money you borrow from a financial institution or company through a line of credit. A *line of credit* is a preselected amount of money you can access at any time as long as you don't exceed the available credit limit. The length of time to pay back the money is typically a month. After the month is over, the funds you borrowed acquire interest, which means you have to pay back more than what you had initially borrowed in the first place.

Credit cards, like student loans (see the preceding section), may be unsecured. If a credit card is secured, the lender wants you to put some skin in the game by providing some collateral such as paying a hefty fee or providing a cash deposit when you open the account. The lender doesn't keep the collateral forever — usually a year, sort of like a deposit. After you've established a history of making your payments on time, it refunds your collateral and moves you to an unsecured line of credit.

Along with being unsecured or secured, credit cards are also known as revolving debt. *Revolving debt* allows you to borrow money and pay it back, only to repeat the cycle again and again with no end date. Credit cards can also come with perks such as free travel, cash back, and discounts meant to keep you using your credit card again and again. When you use credit cards responsibly, you can take advantage of these perks without spending additional money if you pay your card off in full every month. Many travel bloggers haven't paid for a room or flight in years!

Home and auto loans

Unlike the student loan and credit card debt in the preceding sections, which can slowly creep up on you, purchasing a home or automobile can cause you to acquire a large amount of debt at one time. New cars can start at $20,000 and go up from there. Homes typically go for hundreds of thousands of dollars and, depending on the location, sometimes even more! We don't have that type of cash lying around, and you probably don't either.

Home loans

Mortgages, like student loans, are considered installment debt. When you're approved for a mortgage, the bank that has approved your financing sets up an arrangement with you to pay back the loan over time — usually 15 or 30 years. Still, the exact arrangement depends on your lender and other factors, such as what type of loan you're approved for, interest rates, and whether you have a down payment.

Mortgages are considered secured debt. A lender knows it's getting its money back no matter what when helping you finance a home. So if you end up short one month and can't pay your mortgage, no sweat — to the lender, not you. You'll have to pay when it shows up on your credit report. However, after you're 120 days late, the lender will start the foreclosure process and take the house back. Sure, it would've made more money if you had fulfilled the loan's terms, but it's still getting something out of the deal.

WARNING

You find out how to prioritize your debt within your budget later in this chapter, but please pay your mortgage. You don't want a foreclosure on your credit report! Foreclosures can prevent you from finding a new place to live, even when you're just looking to rent. This costly mistake can cost you thousands of dollars for years to come.

Auto loans

If you don't have enough cash to purchase a vehicle outright, you need a bank or credit union to finance you with an auto loan. Suppose you're buying a car through a dealership. In that case, its finance department reviews options with you based on your credit history and whether you're providing a down payment or a trade-in. Dealerships usually have preferred lenders they work with. You can choose to finance with them or look at your bank for finance options.

Auto loans are secured loans you pay off in installments. Because it's an installment loan, you make monthly payments over a timeline, usually no more than six years. Six-year loans are more common when you're purchasing a brand-new car versus an older model because the loan amount tends to be more significant. Auto loans also come with collateral, which is why they're secured. If you don't make your payments, the lender can take the vehicle in a process called *repossession*. It finds someone else to buy your car and then sticks you with the difference of what's still left on your loan. This process happens in a much shorter time frame than a home foreclosure (see the preceding section), but can you imagine? You're getting up to get a coffee one day, and then *bam!* Your car is gone!

Miscellaneous debt

If you've read the preceding sections, you may be thinking, "I owe someone money, but you haven't even mentioned it yet!"

Never fear, for this section talks about other types of debt you may need to include in your budget.

Government agencies

Child support, outstanding taxes, any debt owed to agencies besides the IRS, and any excess unemployment payments are all debt that falls into this category. Debt owed to the government is serious business. In fact, unpaid debt can lead to many reper-cussions, such as having your paycheck garnished or, in some cases, losing your driver's license.

The United States Department of Treasury's Financial Manage-ment Service operates the Treasury Offset Program, also known as the TOP. The TOP allows federal and state agencies to collect money however they see fit, such as by garnishing your wages through your employer or taking the money out of your tax refund. Your employer has no choice but to abide, which means a relatively smaller paycheck.

WARNING

Don't forget your property taxes. This bill is just as important as paying your mortgage. When your property taxes become delin-quent, the state where the property is located can sell your prop-erty even if you own the home that's located on it. If you need assistance, ask your mortgage lender if you can open an escrow account.

Court-ordered debt

Specific crimes like unpaid parking tickets, breaking traffic laws, and more severe ones like misdemeanors and felonies carry a fine. Fines cost money and hopefully discourage you from com-mitting the crime again. You usually pay this type of debt to the court, where a judge presides over your case. You may also be asked to pay court fees and, if applicable, restitution toward a victim.

Overdue bills turned over to collection agencies

Unpaid bills that go to a collection agency show up on your credit report to haunt you. Evictions, utility bills, and outstanding lines of credit from places like department stores all fall in this bucket.

Bills you'd rather ignore don't go away, as much as you want them to, which is why your budget helps you figure out where the money to pay them comes from.

Medical bills

Recently, the Consumer Financial Protection Bureau reported that consumers collectively had $88 billion of medical debt. *Medical debt* includes any services you receive from your provider, testing, bloodwork, and hospital stays. It can even include medication and transportation to receiving medical care, like a ride in an ambulance. Many insurance companies charge high premiums, and despite the 2010 passage of the Affordable Care Act (or ACA), many Americans still struggle to afford healthcare coverage. Some employers cover part of the insurance premiums, but others don't. Even if you have health insurance, you're expected to pay what's known as a deductible before your health insurance provider covers any of the bill.

Personal loans

You can also take out what's known as a personal loan from a bank or another financial institution. *Personal loans* are unsecured loans from a lender that you pay back in monthly payment or installments. Weddings, trips, and holidays are some reasons people take out personal loans.

Loans from friends or family

Sometimes loans don't come from a bank but from a friend or family member. These loans typically have no interest rate or payment schedule because the lender provides the money in good faith that you'll eventually pay them back.

Paying Off Your Debt

Your debt may seem overwhelming, and you may wonder what the purpose of creating a budget is when you have so many other bills to pay. But a budget is a money plan that tells your money where to go, not the other way around. If paying off debt is going to be a part of your budget, pull up a seat. The following sections discuss how to pay off your debt so you can eventually start putting your money toward your other financial goals.

REMEMBER

There's no right way to pay off your debt. Just like everything else about you, your debt is unique. You have different financial responsibilities than others do and vice versa. Your debt repayment plan will be different if you have kids or take care of an older family member. It will also look different based on your income and current expenses. That's why mapping out where your money goes, as Chapter 3 explains, is so important. After you've aced that step, you can strategize toward making your debt repayment plan.

Compiling a list of your debt

The first step to tackling debt repayment is to compile a debt assessment by making a list of the different types of debt you currently have. You need to see all this information in front of you so you aren't forgetting anyone you owe money to. You can include an amount as small as owing your spouse $5 for a coffee or as large as your mortgage. For each debt, log into your account online to make a note of the following things:

>> **The company the debt is owed to, the amount owed, and the due date for payment:** If you haven't made payment arrangements, make a note of that, too.

>> **Type of debt:** Is this debt your mortgage, car loan, or an unpaid bill? Look over the list in the earlier section "Looking at the Different Types of Debt" if you're unsure how to categorize it. You can also leave a reminder to ask someone or even call the company to which you owe the debt.

>> **Secured or unsecured debt:** Both can be harmful to your credit report if you don't pay, but this information is important because secured debt usually means that you have some type of collateral the lender can confiscate if you don't pay the debt on time. The collateral can be vital to your and your family's survival if it's an auto or home loan. Unsecured debt has no collateral at stake.

>> **Revolving loan or installment loan:** With an installment loan, you already have a payment arrangement in place. After you've paid off revolving debt, you can always borrow more.

>> **Any pressing circumstances related to the debt:** A pressing circumstance may be a garnished paycheck or the threat of a suspended driver's license. You can even go so far as to say that any tension between you and a friend or family member over a loan is a pressing issue.

Next, you should reorganize the information in either a spreadsheet or in a notebook. First, list the name of the creditor, the type of debt, the payment amount, the due date, the interest rate or APR (annual percentage rate), and the total amount still owed. If an account has a payoff amount listed anywhere, you can add it as a note. Figures 1-1 and 1-2 are two formatting examples of a debt assessment.

	A	B	C	D	E	F
1	Creditor	Type of Debt	Payment Amount	Due Date	APR	Amount Still Owed
2	Bank of America	Mortgage	$1,978.55	1st of every month	4.50%	$345,231
3	Credit Union	Personal Loan	$150	5th of every month	3%	$2,450
4	Credit Union	Auto Loan	$497	10th of every month	3%	$16,679
5	SoFi	Student Loan	$358	15th of every month	7%	$28,766
6	Capital One	Credit Cards	$179	20th of every month	19%	$2,023
7	American Express	Credit Cards	$67.44	25th of every month	15%	$786
8	Mastercard	Credit Cards	$97	30th of every month	18%	$877
9	Dr. Smith	Medical Bill	$50	30th of every month	0%	$350

FIGURE 1-1: A debt assessment spreadsheet.

© John Wiley & Sons, Inc.

Debt Total, January		
Creditor (Debt Type)	Payment Amount / Due Date / APR	Amount Still Owed
BOA (Mortgage)	$1,978.55 / 1st every month / 4.50%	$345,231
Credit Union (Personal)	$150 / 5th every month / 3%	$2,450
Credit Union (Car)	$497 / 10th every month / 3%	$16,679
SoFi (Student)	$358 / 15th every month / 7%	$28,766
Capital One (CC)	$179 / 20th every month / 19%	$2,023
Amex (CC)	$67.44 / 25th every month / 15%	$786
Mastercard (CC)	$97 / 30th every month / 18%	$877
Dr. Smith (Medical)	$50 / 30th every month / 0%	$350

FIGURE 1-2: A debt assessment compiled on a notebook page.

© John Wiley & Sons, Inc.

Considering different payoff methods

What does a debt payoff plan even look like? Well, you can keep doing what you're doing now and pay your monthly payments. Or you can try one of these three main debt payoff methods:

>> The snowball method

>> The avalanche method

>> The fireball method

REMEMBER If making the minimum payments is where you are right now in your money journey, that's okay. You'll eventually work your way to where your financial goals allow you to pay off more of your debt. For example, you may pay your monthly car payment without trying to pay it off because you have other priorities. You're not a bad person for not wanting to pay off your debt faster than you have to.

The snowball method

The *snowball method* works like this: You pay your regular debt payments, and then anything extra you can come up with to pay on your debt goes toward the smallest one first. You then continue this process until your smallest debt is paid off. The goal of the snowball method is to keep you consistent with your debt repayment by motivating you with small wins. When you continually succeed in any area of your life, it's easier to stay on track consistently. Consistency is what's going to enable you to achieve your goals.

Using your debt assessment from the previous section, arrange your debts from smallest amount owed to largest amount owed. It may look like Figure 1-3 or Figure 1-4.

For example, say your first smallest debt is a bill you owe the dentist. It's $350, and you're currently paying $50 a month. Your next smallest bill is a credit card for $786, and you're paying $50 on this one as well.

FIGURE 1-3:
A debt spreadsheet organized by the amounts still owed.

	A	B	C	D	E	F
1	Creditor	Type of Debt	Payment Amount	Due Date	APR	Amount Still Owed
2	Dr. Smith	Medical Bill	$50	30th of every month	0%	$350
3	American Express	Credit Cards	$67.44	25th of every month	15%	$786
4	Mastercard	Credit Cards	$97	30th of every month	18%	$877
5	Credit Union	Personal Loan	$150	5th of every month	3%	$2,450
6	Capital One	Credit Cards	$179	20th of every month	19%	$2,023
7	SoFi	Student Loan	$358	15th of every month	7%	$28,766
8	Credit Union	Auto Loan	$497	10th of every month	3%	$16,679
9	Bank of America	Mortgage	$1,978.55	1st of every month	4.50%	$345,231

© John Wiley & Sons, Inc.

FIGURE 1-4:
Debt compiled on a notebook page, organized by the amount still owed.

Debt Total, January		
Creditor (Debt Type)	Payment Amount / Due Date / APR	Amount Still Owed
Dr. Smith (Medical)	$50 / 30th every month / 0%	$350
Amex (CC)	$67.44 / 25th every month / 15%	$786
Mastercard (CC)	$97 / 30th every month / 18%	$877
Credit Union (Personal)	$150 / 5th every month / 3%	$2,450
Capital One (CC)	$179 / 20th every month / 19%	$2,023
SoFi (Student)	$358 / 15th every month / 7%	$28,766
Credit Union (Car)	$497 / 10th every month / 3%	$16,679
BOA (Mortgage)	$1,978.55 / 1st every month / 4.50%	$345,231

© John Wiley & Sons, Inc.

You're able to cut some expenses in your budget, which frees up $100 per month (good job!), and you've decided to put this money toward debt. Throw the extra $100 on top of the regular $50 payment and pay the dentist bill in full within two months.

Now you have an extra $150 a month in your budget to use toward debt repayment (the $100 you freed up in expenses, plus the $50 you were putting toward that dentist's bill). You can apply this $150 toward your next smallest debt, your credit card. When your next payment is due, you pay $200 rather than the regular payment of $50. You've snowballed your old debt payment amount toward another debt payment amount. This approach is going to enable you to pay off this debt faster, too.

The one con with this debt repayment strategy is that you pay more interest over time. Paying more in interest and other fees means you're paying more money in the long run than you would with something like the avalanche method, which is discussed in the following section. But if using the snowball method means you're motivated to actually stick to your debt repayment strategy, that trade-off may be okay for you.

The avalanche method

If you'd rather save money and possibly get out of debt faster, then the avalanche method may be a better fit for you than the other methods in this chapter. The *avalanche method* requires you to focus on paying down your debt by homing in on your interest rather than the amount owed. The longer you take to pay a creditor back, the more interest your loan accrues. Depending on the type of debt you have, the interest can fluctuate and collect on different amounts of money at different times.

Using your debt assessment from earlier in the chapter, organize your creditors from the highest to lowest interest. Figures 1-5 and 1-6 show two formatting examples that use the avalanche method.

	A	B	C	D	E	F
1	Creditor	Type of Debt	Payment Amount	Due Date	APR	Amount Still Owed
2	Capital One	Credit Cards	$179	20th of every month	19%	$2,023
3	Mastercard	Credit Cards	$97	30th of every month	18%	$877
4	American Express	Credit Cards	$67.44	25th of every month	15%	$786
5	SoFi	Student Loan	$358	15th of every month	7%	$28,766
6	Bank of America	Mortgage	$1,978.55	1st of every month	4.50%	$345,231
7	Credit Union	Personal Loan	$150	5th of every month	3%	$2,450
8	Credit Union	Auto Loan	$497	10th of every month	3%	$16,679
9	Dr. Smith	Medical Bill	$50	30th of every month	0%	$350

FIGURE 1-5:
A debt spreadsheet organized by APR.

© *John Wiley & Sons, Inc.*

Debt Total, January

Creditor (Debt Type)	Payment Amount / Due Date / APR	Amount Still Owed
Capital One (CC)	$179 / 20th every month / 19%	$2,023
Mastercard (CC)	$97 / 30th every month / 18%	$877
Amex (CC)	$67.44 / 25th every month / 15%	$786
SoFi (Student)	$358 / 15th every month / 7%	$28,766
BOA (Mortgage)	$1,978.55 / 1st every month / 4.50%	$345,231
Credit Union (Personal)	$150 / 5th every month / 3%	$2,450
Credit Union (Car)	$497 / 10th every month / 3%	$16,679
Dr. Smith (Medical)	$50 / 30th every month / 0%	$350

FIGURE 1-6: Debt organized by APR on a notebook page.

© John Wiley & Sons, Inc.

Let's look at the creditors with the highest interest rates, which looks like this:

1. Credit card 1 at 19 percent with a $179 monthly payment

2. Credit card 2 at 18 percent with a $97 monthly payment

3. Credit card 3 at 15 percent with a monthly payment of $67.44

You've cleared up an extra $100 in your budget for debt repayment. Because you're paying the most interest on your credit card, you focus on that bill first. Rather than paying $179 on credit card 1, you're now paying $279. After you pay off that credit card, you then move onto the next credit card. You take that $279 and apply it to the monthly credit card payment until that debt is gone. Then you continue onto your student loan and so on until you've paid everything off.

If you don't have a problem with consistency, this payoff method may work for you. You're paying off your debt at a much faster rate than before while also paying less money overall. Depending on the type and amount of loan, you don't always have small wins along the way, so this debt payoff method requires you to be patient. But saving money is always a win because you can then apply that cash to your budget somewhere else.

The fireball method

Though debt is still debt at the end of the day, the fireball method, coined by SoFi, allows you to categorize your debt to pay it off on a timeline that works for you. This method plays off the snowball method covered earlier in the chapter.

First, refer to your debt assessment from earlier in the chapter and categorize your debt as either good or bad. (Check out the earlier section "Looking at the Different Types of Debt" for more on this distinction.)

Figures 1-7 and 1-8 show the two formatting examples to categorize good and bad debt.

	A	B	C	D	E	F
1	**Good Debt**					
2	**Creditor**	**Type of Debt**	**Payment Amount**	**Due Date**	**APR**	**Amount Still Owed**
3	SoFi	Student Loan	$358	15th of every month	7%	$28,766
4	Credit Union	Auto Loan	$497	10th of every month	3%	$16,679
5	Bank of America	Mortgage	$1,978.55	1st of every month	4.50%	$345,231
6						
7	**Bad Debt**					
8	**Creditor**	**Type of Debt**	**Payment Amount**	**Due Date**	**APR**	**Amount Still Owed**
9	Capital One	Credit Cards	$179	20th of every month	19%	$2,023
10	Mastercard	Credit Cards	$97	30th of every month	18%	$877
11	American Express	Credit Cards	$67.44	25th of every month	15%	$786
12	Credit Union	Personal Loan	$150	5th of every month	3%	$2,450
13	Dr. Smith	Medical Bill	$50	30th of every month	0%	$350

FIGURE 1-7: A spreadsheet separating good and bad debt.

© John Wiley & Sons, Inc.

Then arrange each list debt from smallest amount owed to the largest amount owed. Figures 1-9 and 1-10 show two formatting examples that use the fireball method.

Debt Total, January - Good

Creditor (Debt Type)	Payment Amount / Due Date / APR	Amount Still Owed
Credit Union (Car)	$497 / 10th every month / 3%	$16,679
SoFi (Student)	$358 / 15th every month / 7%	$28,766
BOA (Mortgage)	$1,978.55 / 1st every month / 4.50%	$345,231

Debt Total, January - Bad

Creditor (Debt Type)	Payment Amount / Due Date / APR	Amount Still Owed
Dr. Smith (Medical)	$50 / 30th every month / 0%	$350
Credit Union (Personal)	$150 / 5th every month / 3%	$2,450
Capital One (CC)	$179 / 20th every month / 19%	$2,023
Mastercard (CC)	$97 / 30th every month / 18%	$877
Amex (CC)	$67.44 / 25th every month / 15%	$786

FIGURE 1-8: A written list separating good and bad debt.

© John Wiley & Sons, Inc.

	A	B	C	D	E	F
1	**Good Debt**					
2	**Creditor**	**Type of Debt**	**Payment Amount**	**Due Date**	**APR**	**Amount Still Owed**
3	Credit Union	Auto Loan	$497	10th of every month	3%	$16,679
4	SoFi	Student Loan	$358	15th of every month	7%	$28,766
5	Bank of America	Mortgage	$1,978.55	1st of every month	4.50%	$345,231
6						
7	**Bad Debt**					
8	**Creditor**	**Type of Debt**	**Payment Amount**	**Due Date**	**APR**	**Amount Still Owed**
9	Dr. Smith	Medical Bill	$50	30th of every month	0%	$350
10	American Express	Credit Cards	$67.44	25th of every month	15%	$786
11	Mastercard	Credit Cards	$97	30th of every month	18%	$877
12	Capital One	Credit Cards	$179	20th of every month	19%	$2,023
13	Credit Union	Personal Loan	$150	5th of every month	3%	$2,450

FIGURE 1-9: A spreadsheet arranging bad and good debt by amount owed.

© John Wiley & Sons, Inc.

Now focus on your bad debt, paying off your smallest loan first. Like the snowball method, you'll still be making your minimum payments, but any extra money goes toward eliminating your smallest debt first. After you pay it off, you apply that payment amount to your next highest debt. Unlike the snowball method, you're focused on only your bad debt for now.

Debt Total, January - Good		
Creditor (Debt Type)	Payment Amount / Due Date / APR	Amount Still Owed
Credit Union (Car)	$497 / 10th every month / 3%	$16,679
SoFi (Student)	$358 / 15th every month / 7%	$28,766
BOA (Mortgage)	$1,978.55 / 1st every month / 4.50%	$345,231

Debt Total, January - Bad		
Creditor (Debt Type)	Payment Amount / Due Date / APR	Amount Still Owed
Dr. Smith (Medical)	$50 / 30th every month / 0%	$350
Amex (CC)	$67.44 / 25th every month / 15%	$786
Credit Union (Personal)	$150 / 5th every month / 3%	$2,450
Mastercard (CC)	$97 / 30th every month / 18%	$877
Capital One (CC)	$179 / 20th every month / 19%	$2,023

FIGURE 1-10: A written list arranging bad and good debt by amount owed.

© John Wiley & Sons, Inc.

After you've taken care of the bad debt, you then turn to your good debt. But instead of throwing all the money you were applying toward your bad debt to the good debt, you put it toward your savings goals, such as paying for a down payment on a house. Essentially, you're starting a new snowball for your good debt. Because you're still paying off your good debt, this method encourages you to work on your other goals simultaneously. Most people take advantage of this time to work on catching up on retirement. Wherever you put the money, this method can help you determine what debt you should take care of first while motivating you with small wins.

REMEMBER

The only issue we have with this method is the significance of designating something as good or bad. People often associate the word *bad* with shame, and personal finance shouldn't be shameful. You don't always choose to take out bad debt; sometimes things happen, like medical emergencies, car repairs, and sick pets.

THE DEBT CONSOLIDATION METHOD

We don't actually recommend the debt consolidation method, but we feel you as a consumer deserve to know all your options to make the best choice for you.

Debt consolidation is when you combine multiple debt repayments into one. So instead of paying everything to multiple creditors separately, you only have one to pay. Many debt consolidation companies allow you to consolidate only lines of unsecured debt.

You find three different types of debt consolidation:

- **Credit counseling:** Various nonprofits offer credit counseling services as well as debt consolidation programs. These outfits are strictly regulated by law in what they can and can't do when serving you. Because they must act in your best interest, that means providing you with financial education and discussing what your debt relief options are, including debt consolidation or bankruptcy. It also means debt relief options that are free or low-cost. *Note:* With credit counseling, you can get budgeting help and options for getting out of debt for free, with no obligation to consolidate. If you're considering consolidation, but you aren't sure, credit counseling can be a good option.

- **Debt relief or settlement companies:** Instead of looking at your individual situation to provide you with helpful and productive solutions, a debt relief or settlement company offers to negotiate with your creditors when you enroll in a debt management plan through its organization. Along with requiring additional fees on top of your monthly payment, it directs you to stop paying your creditors so it can negotiate a better rate on your behalf.

  Not paying your creditors does more harm than good. Being delinquent on one account can harm your credit score, but being delinquent on several is truly bad news. This type of debt consolidation can prey on you as a consumer and ruin

(continued)

(continued)

your credit score without your knowledge. Ruining your credit score can make your financial situation even worse.

- **Debt consolidation loans:** A debt consolidation loan through a financial institution allows you to borrow an amount of money that covers the amount you owe your creditors for your current debt. If approved for the loan, you may receive the funds to pay off your creditors, or the financial institution may offer to pay them off directly. You then get a monthly payment plan to repay the loan with a fixed interest rate.

You can do a lot of the work that debt relief management companies charge you for. This approach allows you to save money and also your credit score. You don't have to sign up for a debt repayment plan, because you can pay the debt independently. Companies just want you to think that you can't.

The idea of one monthly payment can sound tempting, especially if you have tons of debt to pay. And you can make debt consolidation loans work if you use them appropriately. But debt consolidation loans aren't a quick fix.

If you choose this route, you may not be addressing the root issue of your debt. You can also get into more debt because you're making your credit cards and other lines of credit available again. Telling yourself you'll just use the card once and pay it back, only to find yourself right where you started, is so easy.

Applying additional strategies

You can implement a variety of other strategies to help pay your debt off even faster.

Make a debt payoff settlement

When you fall behind while paying your debt, you become delinquent. Your creditor may work with you to get back on track, but if it sees no progress, it eventually gives up and, in the case of unsecured debt, sells your debt to a collection agency.

Debt sold to collection agencies shows up on your credit report, so you want to avoid this scenario as much as possible. But if you're stuck with a collections bill, call the agency and see whether you can settle for less than the amount you owe. Collection agencies don't really have people banging down their doors to pay their debt, so they're more likely to work with you and accept an amount less than you owe.

A collection agency will most likely accept half of what you owe. Say you have a creditor $500 debt in collections. When you have $250 to part with, call the agency and ask to speak to someone about a settlement offer. First, kindly thank them for taking your call and for being patient with you while you get your financial affairs in order. Next, acknowledge the fact that you do owe them money and ask whether they'd be willing to settle your account today if you could make a cash payment.

If they say yes, great! Ask them for an amount they're willing to accept and then go from there. *Tip:* You always ask what they can do first because they may come back with a lower amount than you had originally thought to offer. After you agree on a payoff amount, ask to receive it in writing via email so you can pay while still on the phone.

REMEMBER

After you've received confirmation in writing, go ahead and make your payment. Make sure to ask for a receipt via email and also by mail. Keeping detailed records of payment is important; selling someone's debt from collection agency to collection agency is a common practice, and you don't want to have to pay for the same debt mistake twice.

Negotiate with creditors

You don't have to wait for your debt to end up being turned over to collections to negotiate with your creditors. If you have a bill like medical debt, call the medical provider to see what it can do. A lot of doctor's offices will allow you to settle your bill for an agreed-upon portion because getting a small guaranteed payment is better than never receiving any payment.

Some medical providers, like hospitals, have financial relief departments. The financial relief department assigns a case worker to look over your medical bills along with your finances to see whether you qualify for assistance. Depending on the amount, they may agree to put you on a payment plan or waive the debt entirely.

TIP

To find a nonprofit hospital located closest to you, type "non-profit hospital (city you're currently located)" into an online search engine. You can then filter results to find one that meets your needs.

When you have medical emergencies, try to seek medical care at a nonprofit hospital. By law, nonprofit hospitals must offer financial assistance programs. You can also call your local community resource center to see whether any other organizations in your area can help with medical assistance.

Ask about hardship programs

If you have credit card debt that you need assistance with, ask your creditor whether it offers any payment assistance. Some credit card companies have hardship programs that can allow you to go on a monthly repayment plan with more affordable payments. They may also lower any fees or interest you currently pay for a few months. Circumstances that can qualify for hardship include but aren't limited to divorce, death of a loved one, loss of job, or health issues.

TIP

Your other creditors may offer financial assistance programs as well. Some creditors offer a pause on payments by extending the length of your loan. Other options can include moving your payment due date into the future to give you some time to catch up.

REMEMBER

Asking for help can hurt your pride. But you know what? It shouldn't. Instead of being sad or ashamed you had to ask for help, be proud. It takes a strong person to know when they need help, and it takes an even stronger person to ask out loud. Needing help is okay, and your finances will be better off too!

Use balance transfers

Another strategy you can look into is opening a new credit card for a balance transfer. A *balance transfer* is when you move your debt from one creditor to a new creditor for a lower interest rate. Sometimes the interest rate on a balance transfer is as low as

0 percent. The goal of the balance transfer is to save you money in finance fees by offering you a low rate for a predetermined time period. You may also be able to move other types of debt with the balance transfer, such as an auto or personal loan.

To apply for a credit card that offers a balance transfer, you most likely need to have a credit score of 670 or above. You find out more about credit scores in Part 2, but for now, know your credit score can range from 300 to 850. The higher the credit score you have, the better.

WARNING

Make sure you're aware of the terms and conditions of your new balance transfer credit card. With balance transfers, your 0 percent APR typically only lasts 12 to 18 months. After that, your credit card balance starts collecting interest on the debt you've transferred over. The whole point of a balance transfer is to save money on fees and interest, so take advantage of it as much as possible. Also, make sure you know what if any circumstances, such as making a late payment, may cause you to lose your 0 percent interest rate.

If you're approved, double-check how the debt will be transferred over. A creditor may contact the other creditors directly on your behalf to pay your debt off, or it may expect you to take care of it on your own. Make sure to transfer the debt incurring the highest interest rate first so you can take advantage of the lower interest rate as much as you can.

Make extra payments

If, after creating your budget, you find yourself with extra money, consider using it to make extra payments on your debt. One way to approach this strategy is by making a payment that's applied to the loan principal, such as on a mortgage.

When you pay extra on your mortgage, you can ask your loan provider to apply the money to your loan principal. Every time you pay additional money to your loan principal, you're paying less interest. By lowering the amount you owe directly, you lower the amount you pay over time in financing fees. You can even accomplish this goal by splitting up your monthly mortgage payment and applying half every two weeks. By using this tactic, you're making 13 payments a year rather than 12. *Note:* Not all creditors allow extra payments to go to the loan principal, so always research the terms of your loan.

TECHNICAL STUFF

If you're interested in seeing how you can apply this strategy to your situation, check out the extra payments calculator from Freddie Mac. This calculator allows you to input different payment amounts across different scenarios. It allows you to see that even small additional payments here and there can add up over time. Find the calculator at myhome.freddiemac.com/ resources/calculators/extra-payments.

Use financial windfalls

Using any *windfalls* (unexpected money) you receive can help you get out of debt faster. Because you've already covered your expenses, put that extra money to work. If you get a bonus or overtime pay, put it on your car loan. Taking advantage of extra money you weren't expecting can help get you ahead further than you think.

TIP

If you feel the urge to use that windfall to treat yourself, consider the 80-20 rule. Apply 80 percent of your windfall toward your debt and then keep the remaining 20 percent for fun. With this approach you're taking care of business, but you're still making fun a priority. Prioritizing fun is one way to keep you motivated on your debt journey.

Avoiding Accumulating More Debt

Paying your debt off is important, but so is keeping yourself from getting into more debt. Incurring more debt is easy to do and can happen quickly. However, you can be proactive while keeping your budget intact.

Here are a few tips to keep in mind when you're reviewing your debt and debt repayment:

>> **Know your rights.** Before you speak to any debt collector or creditor, be aware of the questions they can and can't

ask. Also beware of illegal debt collection practices, such as contacting you by phone after you've asked them to stop. Check out the Fair Debt Collection Practices Act for more information: www.federalreserve.gov/boarddocs/supmanual/cch/fairdebt.pdf.

>> **Check your budget to ensure the amount you can pay toward your debt.** Don't promise an amount you can't pay.

>> **Make a list of debts you want to negotiate.** Refer to the earlier section "Considering different payoff methods" for information on compiling a debt assessment.

>> **Call your collector.** Use the following phone script for reference:

> *"My name is [insert your name], and I am calling to discuss my current account status. I know I'm late, but I am currently facing an unforeseen financial hardship that has affected my finances, including this account. I would like to see what we can do to help bring my account to good standing. Can we discuss what my options are? Is it possible to arrange a payment plan?"*

REMEMBER

If you're arranging a payment plan, always be sure to get it in writing and do not offer to pay more than you can realistically afford based on your current budget.

>> **Make sure you get the settlement agreement in writing.** Before you hand over the case, ensure you've received the debt repayment agreement in writing, even if that's email, from the debt collector. Also document what time your phone call took place and to whom you spoke.

REMEMBER

>> **Stick to the repayment plan.** Follow through with your end of the agreement. If you don't, the collector can then decide that you must pay the full amount, and it probably won't be willing to work with you on a settlement again.

Look into refinancing options

If your student, auto, or mortgage loan has a high interest rate, consider refinancing to save money. When you *refinance* a loan, you take out a newer loan with better terms and conditions to pay off an old loan. By refinancing a loan, you can have smaller monthly payments while paying less money overall with a better interest rate. This option is great if you have a good credit score.

TIP

If you don't have a high credit score, look to see what you can do to improve your rating. Make sure you pay your debt on time and work hard to lower your *credit utilization rate* (how much of your available credit you're using).

As you improve your credit score, more financial products become available. Eventually, you'll be able to find a loan with better terms than what you're currently paying.

Save an emergency fund

Emergency funds are crucial to keeping you out of debt. When people don't have the money to cover a financial emergency, they often charge it to a credit card or take out a loan. This scenario can turn into a nasty cycle of endless debt repayment that keeps you from achieving your financial goals. Having an emergency fund allows you to have the money available to keep emergencies from derailing your budget.

You can also avoid some emergencies if you plan ahead in your budget and take time for regular maintenance and screenings.

Say no to credit card offers

REMEMBER

If you're trying to pay off debt, stay away from store credit cards and other in-house financing options. This type of consumer financing can keep you stuck in the cycle of charging for an item you don't need because you're "saving" money. If saving money is what you're after, look up discount codes on the internet. You can find a coupon for just about everything out there if you search hard enough.

Another great way to stay away from credit when working on debt repayment is to pay in cash from your bank account. Instead of using your credit card, pay with your debit card, which is deducted from your account. Go through any online retailers you use and update your payment information. This step ensures you're using your budget to pay for your purchases and not relying on credit.

Please keep in mind that there is a higher fraud risk when using your debit card. Banks can only offer so much in terms of fraud protection, unlike credit card companies.

Invest in the right insurance

One way to keep yourself out of debt is to have adequate insurance for your health, car, and home. Insurance is an important tool for protecting both you and your finances. Instead of your having to take care of a financial emergency all on your own, an insurance policy can help you weather the cost (after you pay a deductible or co-pay). Insurance doesn't have to be expensive, either. Both online and in-person insurance brokers can offer you great deals and rates.

Health insurance is expensive, but going without insurance can cost more. Medical bills are one of the main reasons people declare bankruptcy. If you don't have health insurance and need major surgery, you can be hundreds of thousands of dollars in debt before you even know it. A lack of health insurance can also cost you your quality of life. Without health insurance, you may not have adequate preventive care — care that can help you avoid having serious medical issues in the future — or be able to fill the prescriptions you need.

You should also consider life insurance, short-term and long-term disability insurance, and long-term care if you're close to or in retirement.

Chapter **2**

Facing Financial Facts

You're reading this book, so you're likely at least a little worried, maybe *really* worried, about your debts, and you're not sure what to do about them. You're probably not reading this book just for the fun of it!

Here's another assumption about you: You probably don't have a good handle on the true state of your finances. After all, it's human nature to try to avoid bad news.

Facing financial facts can be unsettling and even scary. Also, when you know the state of your finances, you probably can't ignore the fact that improving your financial situation requires changing your lifestyle and making some big sacrifices.

But no matter how scary it is, confronting the reality of your financial situation is essential. You have to take that first step before you can create an effective plan of action for dealing with your debts. Unless you know where you are, it's hard to know where you need to go. And until you come face to face with the facts of your finances, you may find it impossible to develop the resolve and self-discipline you need to implement your plan of action.

This chapter guides you through a series of financial fact-finding exercises. They include answering some questions about your money situation and how it's affecting your life, evaluating your relationship with money, and taking stock of your assets, liabilities, and spending.

The more bad news you get as you complete these exercises, the more critical it is that you get serious about dealing with your debts. The sooner you do, the quicker and easier it will be to improve your finances and the less likely that your creditors will take some of your assets or that you'll have to file for bankruptcy. So let's get going!

Answering Some Questions

REMEMBER

You'll get a general sense of the severity of your debt problem by honestly answering the following questions. The more often you answer "yes," the more you have cause for concern.

>> Are you clueless about how much money you owe to your creditors?

>> Over time, is a growing percentage of your household income going toward paying your debts?

>> Do you ever pay your bills late because you don't have enough money?

>> Have you stopped paying some of your debts?

>> Are you paying only the minimum due on some of your credit cards because you can't afford to pay more?

>> Are you using credit and/or credit card cash advances to help pay debts and/or your basic living expenses, like groceries, rent, utilities, and so on?

- » Have you maxed out any of your credit cards, or have any of your cards been cancelled for nonpayment?

- » Do you have little or nothing in savings?

- » Have you borrowed money from friends or relatives to pay your bills?

- » Have debt collectors begun calling you, and/or are you receiving threatening notices from some of your creditors?

- » Are you having a hard time concentrating at work because you are worried about money?

- » Are you losing sleep because of your finances?

- » Have you and your spouse or partner begun fighting about money?

- » Are you drinking more or using illegal drugs in order to try to cope with your money worries?

Evaluating Your Relationship with Money

Some serious soul-searching is in order if you're worried about how much you owe to your creditors, and the following sections can help. If you are really honest with yourself, you may conclude that *you* are the reason you've got a debt problem.

TIP

Here are two good books that can help you honestly evaluate your relationship with money and change the way you think about it:

- » *Your Money or Your Life: Transforming Your Relationship with Money and Achieving Financial Independence* (Penguin) by Joe Dominguez and Vicki Robin. This personal finance classic helps you evaluate the role that money plays in your life, reorder your priorities, and live on what you make.

>> *The Financial Wisdom of Ebenezer Scrooge: 5 Principles to Transform Your Relationship with Money* by Ted Klontz, Rick Kahler, and Brad Klontz (Health Communications, Inc.). This book combines quotes from Charles Dickens's *A Christmas Carol,* real stories of people with money problems, and the authors' own advice to help you figure out how your attitudes about money affect your life and to help you change destructive patterns.

Equating stuff with success

You may have the misconception that you are what you buy, which means the more you spend, the more successful and important you are. It's easy to develop that mindset because we are bombarded with messages that equate money and stuff with success. How often do you see ads promoting frugality, saving, or self-denial?

If you're hanging with a fast set and struggling to keep up, it may be time to reevaluate your friendships. Trying to keep up with the Joneses may be driving you into the poor house.

Recognizing emotional spending

Maybe you spend money for emotional reasons. For example, think about what you do when you feel sad or disappointed, or when you want to celebrate a success. Do you head to the mall or click on your favorite retail website? Do you treat yourself to an expensive meal or enjoy a weekend getaway even though you really can't afford it?

TIP

If this describes your behavior, you need to get a handle on why you're overspending. Meet with a mental health professional; you may qualify for help from a low-cost/no-cost clinic in your area. Or get involved with Debtors Anonymous (DA). DA uses the time-tested methods of Alcoholics Anonymous to help people understand why they spend and to gain control over their spending. To find a DA chapter in your area, go to www.debtors anonymous.org, or call 781-453-2743.

Living for the moment

Maybe your problem is that you live for today and don't think about tomorrow. In some ways, living in the moment is great, but not if you turn a blind eye toward your future. How do you know if you've got this attitude toward money? You probably

>> Use credit too much.

>> Don't try to pay off your credit balances as quickly as possible, using the rationale that there will be plenty of time to do that later.

>> Save little, if anything.

>> Rarely if ever take time to balance your checkbook and check out your credit reports and credit score, much less develop and use a household budget.

These money attitudes are self-destructive, and they do catch up with you eventually. Since you're reading this book, they probably already have.

Taking Inventory of Your Finances: A Spending Analysis

The first part of a new financial you is taking inventory of your finances. You're going to want to know where you're coming from so you can track your progress and pat yourself on the back when you start making actual financial moves.

REMEMBER

By taking inventory of your finances, you can clarify where you stand financially — both good and bad. Here are just a few of the benefits:

>> **You have financial data to review anytime.** When you have actual numbers in front of you, you can assess where you're in good standing and where your finances may need a little work. Maybe you've been a rock star with that employer-matched 401(k) but have done little to pay down your student loans.

» **You can set realistic monetary goals.** When you know your income and expenses, you know how much is left for things like debt repayment or saving for a vacation. It makes it possible to set a timeline for reaching those milestones.

» **You notice when accounts don't serve your current needs.** You may discover you're paying credit card fees for a card you don't use. An account like a 529 Savings Plan may no longer be necessary because your child has changed their career goals. Maybe you're not earning enough in an investment vehicle, and that money can better serve you elsewhere. All these small things can add up to money lost.

» **You can try to pay off debt faster, which can save you money.** By looking over your current liabilities, you may find that you can cut years off your payment timeline by making an additional payment or two. You may also realize that you can consolidate a current loan for a better interest rate.

» **You can save time with organized finances.** Having all your accounts in one general place you can see, such as a spreadsheet or an online tool, can save you time and stress from having to always track them down individually. You can monitor due dates for debt repayments and check balances in accounts before any significant financial purchases are made. You also know which financial institution is in charge of what. You may uncover a forgotten bill or two that can still be saved from going into collections. And when any new accounts or bills come in, you can plug them in with the rest. Discover ways to organize your records in the later section "Record-keeping systems."

The following sections are an overview of the first steps of creating your budget.

Make a list of your financial assets and liabilities

Spoiler alert: This step may take a bit longer if you don't already have some kind of net-worth tracker or don't currently have all your financial accounts in one place. The following sections give you an overview of assets and liabilities and your options for corralling your financial info in one place.

Assets

Financial assets are anything with a positive financial value. Lots of things can qualify, as shown in Figure 2-1:

>> Checking and savings accounts, the cash you have under the mattress, and any checks you've been meaning to cash.

>> Money market accounts, your retirement fund at work, pensions, brokerage accounts, company stock shares, treasury bills, and bonds.

>> Some life insurance policies.

>> Physical items you can *liquidate* (convert into cash), such as your home; your car or other vehicles like ATVs, motorcycles, or boats; jewelry; collectibles; and anything else that you can sell for a profit. (That fancy purse you keep in a dust jacket that you can sell tomorrow for a few hundred dollars? Put that on the list, too.)

TIP

Make sure accounts such as financial assets have a beneficiary listed so your heirs have easy access. Having a will or trust is highly recommended because you never know what tomorrow will bring. Still, these can go to probate and can make your assets inaccessible to your beneficiaries for an extended period of time. You also want to ensure that will is detailed so there's no question of who inherits what. A clear and precise estate plan helps your loved ones focus on healing instead.

Financial Asset Checklist

Traditional Banking
- ☐ Checking account
- ☐ Premium checking account
- ☐ Business checking account
- ☐ Rewards checking account
- ☐ Savings account
- ☐ High-yield savings accounts
- ☐ Money market account
- ☐ Certificates of deposit (CD)
- ☐ Prepaid cards
- ☐ Cash on hand

Retirement
- ☐ Traditional IRA
- ☐ Roth IRA
- ☐ 401(k)
- ☐ SIMPLE 401(k)
- ☐ 403(b)
- ☐ SIMPLE IRA plans
- ☐ SEP Plans (employee pensions)
- ☐ SARSEP Plans
- ☐ Federal government pension
- ☐ 457 plans

Brokerage
- ☐ Stocks
- ☐ Mutual funds
- ☐ Index funds
- ☐ Exchange-traded funds (ETFs)
- ☐ Government-issued bonds
- ☐ Corporate bonds
- ☐ Commodities
- ☐ Real Estate Investment Trusts (REITs)

College
- ☐ 529 Savings Plan
- ☐ Coverdell account
- ☐ Uniform Gift to Minor Accounts (UGMA)

Physical
- ☐ Real estate (primary residence)
- ☐ Real estate (rental properties)
- ☐ Vehicles (both primary and other)
- ☐ Jewelry
- ☐ Art and collectibles
- ☐ Life insurance policies
- ☐ Gold and other precious metals

FIGURE 2-1: A few suggestions of what can be considered a financial asset.

© John Wiley & Sons, Inc.

Liabilities

Your *financial liabilities* are anything you owe money on. Your home is considered a positive financial asset (see the preceding section), but the mortgage you owe isn't. Other types of housing debt can include a second mortgage, a rental agreement, or property taxes.

Other financial liabilities include the following:

>> Loans on other items you've financed, such as your car or education

>> Personal loans from a financial institution or family friend

>> Credit cards that currently have a balance

>> Other outstanding debt like medical bills

Even unpaid taxes, fines you owe a court, or child support can be considered financial liabilities.

Record-keeping systems

After you've made a list of all assets and liabilities off the top of your head (see the two preceding sections), track down any paperwork and/or information necessary to create an online account so that you can log into the accounts. Next, you need to decide how you want to keep all your financial documentation where it's not only safe but also accessible in case of an emergency.

You may choose to save your information in a spreadsheet program such as Microsoft Excel or enter all your information into an online tool like Empower (www.empower.com/). Empower is a net-worth tracking tool that takes your liabilities and subtracts them from your assets to determine your net worth. You aren't determining your net worth quite yet for this exercise, but this resource can be a neat tool to help get you started.

Another part of your record-keeping system should involve taking care of your physical paperwork. Having stacks of paper everywhere isn't helpful. You can store your paperwork in folders within a file box or filing cabinet; if you prefer a more minimalist approach, you can purchase a scanner, upload your paperwork to your computer, and discard the documents in a safe and secure manner.

Review your spending for the past three months

Anytime you're attempting a new goal, doing some research is a great idea. So for the second step to creating a budget, you need to review (research) the past three months of your spending habits. Where do you even start? Easy: your bank statements. Your bank has a lot of helpful information, including the option to see where your money is coming from and where it's flowing out.

TIP

Check whether your bank has a spending analysis tool. This kind of resource can be a great place to start to see your spending in action.

Open a new spreadsheet on your computer or grab a pen and a piece of paper. Start to look over every expense you have. First, write down any expenses that are the same amount every month, such as your rent, internet bill, car payment and insurance, streaming services, and any other expenses that rarely change unless you make a specific change to your service, such as upgrading a tier.

Next, look over your spending that can vary from month to month. Items under this type of spending can be groceries, dining out, gas for your car, and any entertainment expenses while having fun with your friends or family. You can list them individually by category. If this approach seems too overwhelming, or you buy different types of items in one general place, group the transactions by store (see Figure 2-2).

	A	B	C	D	E
1	**Expense**	**Category**	**Amount**		
2	Rent	Living Expenses	1200		
3	Target	Groceries	57.43		
4	Netflix	Entertainment	14.99		
5	Gas	Transportation	20		
6	Target	Household Items	14.87		
7	Amazon	Clothing	35.78		
8	Chewy	Pet Items	40.99		
9	Uber Eats	Dining Out	25		
10					

FIGURE 2-2: A spreadsheet that displays how you track your spending.

© John Wiley & Sons, Inc.

TIP

When looking over your spending, don't forget to look at where you're using your credit cards and any apps you use to transfer money, like Venmo or PayPal. You can easily see these transactions while reviewing your bank statements, but they often don't list the retailer or item. For example, you may use your PayPal account when you buy anything through your favorite food delivery service. Your checking account then has a lot of PayPal transactions but doesn't categorize them automatically into "dining out." You have to review the transaction in your actual PayPal account.

After you've gone over the past three months of your spending habits, you notice trends. You may see that you've spent more money than you imagined on dining out or mindlessly shopping online. You see how those $5 transactions here and there add up over time, and probably to an amount you didn't realize. You may also be pleasantly surprised at how little you've spent and be able to congratulate yourself on keeping your expenses down.

REMEMBER

Money can be emotional, and when you realize you've wasted some of it, you can quickly feel like crap. But guess what? Money flows in and out. It's not gone forever and can find its way back to you. It's up to you where it goes next.

Chapter 3

Breaking Down the Parts of a Budget

When you're *financially aware*, you know how much is in your checking account, whether you're on track to meet your goals, and whether you can afford to go eat sushi with friends. Anytime you become aware of an area of your life, it benefits you and those around you. People often don't realize that what's happening inside them affects what's happening outside them. When you become financially aware, your life can change in ways you haven't even begun to imagine. You can make room for things that matter so you're living life on your terms.

But before becoming financially aware in all areas of your life, including your budget, you must recognize the different types of income, expenses, and financial goals. These items are all critical parts of your budget. Understanding the difference is key to budgeting correctly, and this chapter can help.

TIP

Grab a notebook and write out what your life would look like if you were financially aware. Maybe you'd be more generous with your time or pursue a new hobby you've always wanted to try. Perhaps you'd sleep better at night because you'd know where you financially stood at any time. When you see what financial awareness looks like, you can become it.

Seeing Where Your Money Goes: Your Expenses

Your money goes to various places, and hopefully, you've done a spending analysis (see Chapter 2) to show you where. You've most likely discovered spending patterns. Some of the patterns may have surprised you, while other patterns didn't. Perhaps you've realized you've spent way too much in a category, like takeout coffee. (Mmm, lattes.) That's okay.

TIP

If you haven't already completed the spending analysis we lay out in Chapter 2, hit pause on this section and go do that. The info from your analysis will make breaking down your personal expenses so much easier.

REMEMBER

Just know that your new budget has three components:

>> Expenses (how much money you're spending)

>> Income (how much money you have coming in)

>> Financial goals (things you want to accomplish, such as paying down debt or saving for something in the future)

All three are imperative to how your new future budget will affect your financial life. In fact, they're equally important to be financially aware of. Your expenses can affect how much income you need to bring in, which determines whether you can accomplish your goals by working one regular full-time job or whether you also need to get a part-time job or a side gig. Your income determines how much money you can spend on your lifestyle or put toward your future, like retirement. It's all related, so the sooner you figure out what you need to pay and what you want to accomplish, the faster a budget will work for you.

REMEMBER

Like anything in life that you're trying to improve, things may get worse before they get better. Finding where you are in life can be discouraging. Who in their right mind wants to feel discouraged? But keep this in mind: You're taking positive steps to change your finances. These steps will have a cascading effect and change all areas of your life for the better.

Identifying fixed expenses

Fixed expenses are expenses that are the same amount of money every billing period, such as paying your rent or mortgage. Most fixed expenses are paid monthly, but some are weekly, quarterly, or annually. For example, you may pay for your car registration every year, but you may pay monthly for your car insurance. Weekly fixed expenses may include things like a parking pass. Figure 3-1 shows various examples of fixed expenses.

When you understand what a fixed expense is, you're ready to evaluate what you need to spend money on every month.

1. **Complete a spending analysis (see Chapter 2).**

   Because you divide your spending into categories, you should see a recurring theme with how much you spend each month on certain items or necessary expenses.

2. **Make a list of your fixed expenses.**

   Examples can include your rent, utilities, gym memberships, or fun things like subscription boxes or streaming services.

3. **Add up the total costs for these fixed expenses each month over the previous three months.**

   You now clearly see how much you spend every month on your fixed expenses. You can even divide this amount per paycheck if you feel like getting creative. (That may hurt your feelings, so be careful how far you want to dig.)

4. **Evaluate whether you need those fixed expenses.**

   Now's the time to see whether all your fixed expenses are necessary. Do you need to be spending money on a gym membership every month, or can you find a cheaper way to work out, such as utilizing local running trails? If you've signed up to get monthly items or deliveries, do you have the option to pause them and work through your current supply instead?

REMEMBER

Make sure you ask questions about your larger fixed expenses, too — not just the minor ones. Rent may be costing you more of your take-home pay than you realize you're comfortable with. Moving can be expensive, so you don't need to randomly decide to change apartments, but do make a note to research other living arrangements when you get closer to the end of your lease.

Fixed Expenses

Household

- [ ] Rent
- [ ] Mortgage
- [ ] Property taxes
- [ ] HOA fees
- [ ] Rental or Homeowners insurance
- [ ] Internet
- [ ] Electricity
- [ ] Water
- [ ] Cellphone
- [ ] Gas

Debt

- [ ] Auto loan
- [ ] Student loans
- [ ] Personal loans
- [ ] Debt settlements
- [ ] Medical bills
- [ ] Government agencies
- [ ] Court-ordered debt

Financial

- [ ] Automobile Insurance
- [ ] Life Insurance
- [ ] Disability Insurance
- [ ] Retirement contributions
- [ ] Banking fees

Medical

- [ ] Health insurance premiums
- [ ] Insurance co-pays
- [ ] Flexible Spending Account
- [ ] Health Saving Account
- [ ] Therapy
- [ ] Prescriptions

Work

- [ ] Public transportation
- [ ] Parking
- [ ] Professional association fees
- [ ] Professional development classes
- [ ] Conferences/networking events

Personal

- [ ] Gym
- [ ] Subscriptions
- [ ] Memberships
- [ ] Streaming services

Children

- [ ] Childcare
- [ ] Tuition
- [ ] 529 and Coverdell savings accounts
- [ ] After school activities

© John Wiley & Sons, Inc.

FIGURE 3-1: Spending categories that are considered fixed expenses.

Just because an expense is fixed doesn't mean you can't find a way to lower the costs.

>> See whether you can save money by switching to purchasing items quarterly rather than monthly.

>> Call your providers, such as cellphone or internet, to see whether you qualify for any discounts or loyalty rates.

>> Research competitors for insurance policies: healthcare, automobile, renters or homeowners, and life.

>> Consider switching to different tiers of subscription services, such as home streaming networks.

>> Take advantage of apps that provide coupons, cash back on your purchases, and price match for the best deal.

>> Install web browser extensions that help you shop a bit more savvily and save you some extra cash.

>> Check to see whether your bank offers you cash back for using your *debit card*.

Call your service providers to see whether they offer a loyalty rate or discount you may qualify for. Companies want to keep their customers, and if they know you're looking to jump ship, they'll be happy to assist. Some companies and service providers even offer discounts for students, public servants, or those in the military. If your current provider doesn't have anything for you, look to see whether another provider can better fit your needs. A switch may be a way to free up some additional room in your budget so you can breathe. It doesn't hurt to ask. The worst they can do is say no and have you keep paying what you already are.

You can even discuss options with your landlord or mortgage company. Nothing is off the table; the more money you can free up, the more you have to save for your goals or spend on things that bring value to your life.

Allowing for variable expenses

Variable expenses, or *variable costs*, are different from fixed expenses (see the preceding section). Variable expenses are different from month to month and may be items you regularly purchase or ones you buy only occasionally (see Figure 3-2). Common variable expenses include the following:

>> Groceries

>> Gas for your car

>> Food for your pets

>> Items for any hobbies

>> Personal care items like hygiene products or makeup

Variable Expenses

Food

☐ Groceries
☐ Dining Out
☐ Lunch (work and school)
☐ Coffee

Transportation

☐ Gas
☐ Tolls
☐ Oil changes and other car maintenance
☐ Car repairs
☐ Registration and other fees
☐ Rideshares

Entertainment

☐ Concerts
☐ Alcohol
☐ Books
☐ Hobbies
☐ Games for family
☐ Admission to movies or museums

Household

☐ Pet food
☐ Other pet expenses
☐ Cleaning supplies
☐ Decor
☐ Clothing
☐ Personal grooming
☐ Child expenses such as diapers or formula
☐ School field trips and other extracurricular activities

© John Wiley & Sons, Inc.

FIGURE 3-2: Spending categories that are variable expenses.

These types of expenses can be more challenging for you to track. Depending on the time of year or stage of your life, your spending in these categories can fluctuate. You may spend nearly nothing in a category like household items one month and then easily spend a few hundred dollars there the next month. You may spend a lot more money during the holiday season between purchasing gifts and travel-associated costs.

REMEMBER

Because variable expenses are less predictable, assigning a monetary value of what you should spend per month can be frustrating and challenging. You may have control over some of them but not for others, and that's okay. You may get easily flustered when a category spikes for you and initially throws everything you had planned off course. You're going to figure this all out, too, and this book is here to help every step of the way.

Needs and wants

Variable expenses include both needs and wants. You can't just opt out of a lot of your variable spending. You have to purchase things like medicine, and you have to eat.

Generally speaking, *needs* include food, gas to get to and from work if you commute, clothing, and so on. *Wants* are things like getting the newest cellphone when your current one is perfectly usable or spending money on experiences like concerts or dining out.

REMEMBER

Just because you can't avoid purchasing some items doesn't mean you can't still save money. One of the ways you can cut your variable expenses is to consider lower-priced alternatives to your usual purchases.

Say you're in the market for foundation because your old bottle is empty. Instead of going to an expensive makeup counter to purchase your usual foundation, try to find a similar product from a different brand that's a lower price. In this example, the high-end foundation is considered a want because you can find less-expensive brands of foundation. But regardless of what some may say, foundation can be a need based on your own comfort and personal preference.

The difference between needs and wants can get murky quickly, especially because one person's want may genuinely be another person's need (see Figure 3-3). Spending money on your wants is perfectly okay; you just need to figure out how to budget for them properly. The 50/30/20 budgeting method allows you to categorize most of your expenses based on your needs (50 percent of your income) and wants (30 percent of your income); the remaining 20 percent goes toward savings and debt.

FIGURE 3-3:
A list of what expenses are needs and wants.

REMEMBER

Voluntarily spending money on nonessential items or items that are categorized as wants rather than needs is called *discretionary spending.*

REMEMBER

Be realistic when determining your wants and needs. Suppose you have a specific life situation that requires you to spend a bit more on your variable expenses. Perhaps you have several chronic health conditions. Some things help you manage your quality of life on days when you can't get out of bed, like ordering takeout so you don't have to spend energy preparing a meal. You may hate sometimes admitting that you need to pay more in a specific budget category, like dining out, than people say you should. But guess what? If you're realistic, that will keep you under budget every month.

Value-based spending

One more idea to help save you money and curb your expenses is to evaluate whether your current spending is *value-based* (rooted in the things you value in life) or a result of trying to keep up with your friends and family. Maybe you didn't want to be the only one left out of a vacation, but you really don't want to visit that destination. Or maybe you've convinced yourself that life will be infinitely better if you just buy whatever product your favorite influencer recommends. (Perhaps you almost bought cool containers for your bathroom before you realized what you really needed was just to do a massive purge.)

TECHNICAL STUFF

If you don't know what your values are, that's okay. A lot of free and paid surveys online can help you figure it out. The Barrett Values Centre provides a Personal Values Assessment quiz online, found at www.valuescentre.com/pva.

Knowing Where Your Money Comes From: Your Income

Your *income* is an essential component of your budget. Knowing how much money you have coming in can ensure your expenses don't exceed your income. It can also help you set realistic goals for all areas of your life that relate to your finances and perhaps even quality of life. You may realize you have more income than you initially thought you had, or a spending deficit that means you need to find ways to either cut back or earn more.

REMEMBER

When discussing your income, one dollar amount you need to keep in mind is your *net pay*, also referred to as *disposable income*. Net pay is the amount of money left over after any withholdings you may be subjected to, such as taxes (federal and state if your residence requires it), Social Security, Medicare, and any wage garnishments you may be paying off. It's important to consider because it's the amount of money you use to budget every month. It's the money you have to put toward your goals, pay your bills, and cover your variable expenses.

Depending on a monthly income

The first type of income you should consider is what you earn monthly to cover all your expenses. *Monthly income* can come from various sources. While it can be consistent dependent on your income type, it can also be different from month to month. Here's a list of different types of monthly income you can earn:

>> **Income from full-time and/or part-time employment:** This income you receive from an employer that has you on its payroll and that you regularly trade your time for money. Some jobs pay a flat amount of money per paycheck, known as a *salary*, and others may pay an hourly *wage*. Hourly income can fluctuate because the hours you work may vary, while a salary doesn't.

>> **Income as a self-employed freelancer or consultant:** Freelancers and contractors make variable income depending on what's on their roster. Both are considered self-employed, but the main difference is the number of clients and the type of projects they're currently working on. *Freelancers* balance more than one client and work on projects with a short timeline. *Contractors* take on more significant projects with one main client and do smaller work for several.

TIP

At different times in your life, you may prefer different compensation structures, and no one approach is right or wrong.

>> **Pensions and other paid retirement plans:** A *pension* is a type of retirement program that an employee, an employer, or both pay into. The plan pays a fixed sum to the employee at regular intervals on retirement. Each employer decides on a compensation formula approved by the U.S. Department of Labor (see Figure 3-4). Some pensions require you to work for the company for a certain number of years before you're eligible (or *vested*). Federal, state, and local government or other public sectors also allow for paid retirement plans.

>> **Retirement plans:** Outside of traditional pensions or government-paid retirement plans, you can still receive payments from your retirement accounts if you've previously planned. These types of retirement accounts allow you to save for retirement by investing. The most popular ones are 401(k), 403(b), and Roth IRAs, but you can find a complete list on the IRS website (www.irs.gov/retirement-plans/plan-sponsor/types-of-retirement-plans).

>> **Social Security retirement benefits:** When people talk about receiving Social Security, they're usually referring to retirement benefits. Every year you remain in the workforce, you can receive up to four work credits. In 2024, you must earn $1,730 to earn a work credit. This means that you must make at least $6,920 per year to earn all 4 credits you're eligible for. After you've earned 40 credits (which you could do over the course of 10 years), you're eligible to collect partial benefits at age 62 and full benefits at age 67. For up-to-date information, please visit www.ssa.gov/retirement.

>> **Social Security Disability Benefits, Supplemental Security Income, and survivors benefits:** Social Security has three other benefits. If you're disabled, you can receive two different types of benefits.

- *Social Security Disability Insurance (SSDI)* benefits are granted when you match the Social Security Administration's definition of having a disability and have earned enough workforce credits, depending on the age you become disabled.

- If you've never worked due to a disability, you can qualify for *Supplemental Security Income (SSI)*.

Last but not least, if you're a child, a spouse, or a parent who relies on someone in the workforce to support you and they die, you can get *survivors benefits*.

>> **Cash benefits from the state:** You may qualify for cash assistance in some states, depending on your situation. Temporary Assistance for Needy Families (TANF) is one example. Along with cash assistance, other benefits you may be eligible for are work assistance, specific training to enter back into the workforce, and help with childcare. Go to www.benefits.gov/benefit/613 to find out more.

>> **Court-ordered payments:** For specific life situations, you may receive court-ordered benefits. Alimony and *court-ordered acceptable for processing (COAP),* which gives a former spouse the rights to retirement annuities, are benefits you may get during a divorce. Other court-ordered benefits include child support and restitution if you were a victim of certain crimes.

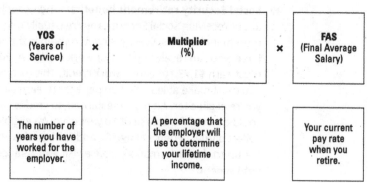

Pension Formula

| YOS (Years of Service) | × | Multiplier (%) | × | FAS (Final Average Salary) |

| The number of years you have worked for the employer. | | A percentage that the employer will use to determine your lifetime income. | | Your current pay rate when you retire. |

FIGURE 3-4: The formula used to determine an employer-sponsored pension.

Example: 25 years of service × 2% × $60,000 final salary
25 × 2% × $60,000 = $30,000 lifetime yearly pension payment

© John Wiley & Sons, Inc.

TIP

Take time to create a Social Security account at www.ssa.gov/myaccount. Doing so allows you to check your workforce credits, the money you've paid into Social Security, and an estimate of your retirement benefit payment. You can also check to see what other benefits may be available to you, such as disability or survivor, along with the amount you or a loved one would qualify for. This information can help you budget better for life circumstances and save for retirement.

Identifying additional sources of income

Just like your variable expenses (check out the earlier section "Allowing for variable expenses"), *variable* or *irregular income* means that your wages fluctuate every month. You can make this type of income yearly, monthly, weekly, or even daily. Variable income, for example from a side gig, is an excellent way to catch up on financial goals or supplement your income. *Side gigs* or *side hustles* are usually jobs that are dependent on task completion. You can freelance for a client or clients, using the skills you've learned from current or previous jobs.

After you start budgeting, you may find that your net pay doesn't cover all your monthly expenses or the goals you've set for yourself. In this case, you have to either cut your spending or earn more money. Some folks prefer to earn more money because it's easier for them than cutting expenses.

We feel everyone should have additional income streams. The economy can be downright volatile sometimes. A job may be here one day and outsourced the next. Things happen, which is why being able to budget with the best of them is more important than ever. The following is a short list common side gigs:

>> Become a *ride sharer,* a person who drives others in their vehicle for a fee

>> Doing/delivering grocery shopping or delivering food purchased through a restaurant

>> Selling items you have lying around or buying items for a lower price and then selling them for a profit on sites like eBay and Amazon

>> Creating content online as a writer

>> Making and selling crafts on a site like Etsy or on social media

Variable income from a side gig can still be considered earned income depending on the source, so check with the IRS to see whether you need to put money aside for taxes. Try to put 25 to 30 percent of any income earned from side gigs aside in a checking account. Pay your estimated taxes quarterly and save anything additional for business expenses. Even better, double-check to ensure you aren't missing expenses that you can use for tax deductions. Software fees, utilities such as internet, and inventory are all expenses that may be potential tax write-offs. For more information on self-employment taxes, go to the IRS official website at www.irs.gov.

You Gotta Have Dreams: Financial Goals

Setting goals allows you to work toward something you want in your life with the end goal of eventually achieving it. Goals can be simple, like brushing your teeth at night. They can be moderate, like learning a new language or losing some weight. They can also seem unattainable, like climbing Mount Everest. After you're clear on where you want to go, figuring out the steps to get you there is easier. (If Mount Everest is your goal, please send us lots of pictures.)

Having a financial goal can help ensure your budget tells your money where to go. It causes you to look at your spending and evaluate your current lifestyle. It helps you not eat cat food in retirement. It can help you live a life you love and are proud of.

REMEMBER

Setting financial goals can help you live a better quality of life, which can mean the difference in where you can afford to retire or whether you can take a leave of absence from an employer or have a life-changing emergency that causes you to pivot, such as an unexpected death. A budget can be flexible to meet the stage of life you're in, but having a bucket of money can shake things up. Oh, and make your overall life easier.

GOAL SETTING: A STEP IN THE RIGHT DIRECTION

You can compare goal setting to relying on directions to get where you're going rather than trying to wing it. Without being told where to go, you may not be able to reach your destination because you don't know the directions yourself. If you're semi-familiar with where you're driving, you may get there eventually, but directions make it so much easier. After you enter the address into your map app, your phone quickly starts to boss you around and has you taking U-turns in a hurry to get to where you want to be much more efficiently.

Saving for your future

Life is short, and every day you don't put money aside for your future is a day you're setting yourself up for risk and, even worse, failure.

You know stuff will eventually happen. You may need a new car for transportation to and from work. The perfect bungalow of your dreams may hit the housing market, and you see yourself establishing some roots! You may even have kids heading off to college — or, better yet, you may want to go back to school yourself to make more money so you can have an even better budget than before. "Someday" can turn into your current day, so you may as well plan for it.

Saving for the future isn't just about retirement or replacing things that break. It can also include fabulous trips you want to experience, like going to Europe or wine tasting in Napa. Maybe it's establishing a scholarship fund in someone's name at a local nonprofit, redecorating your house in whatever the cool new style is, or buying a muscle car to restore. Your future needs to include fun, and your budget helps you do just that.

REMEMBER

Make sure your goal is actually yours. One of the everyday things in the personal finance world is people telling others to become their own bosses. Do you know how hard it is to be your own boss? It's not as easy as many claim. Many people quit their jobs to make money but didn't have a clear plan or realized they didn't want self-employment at all. They let someone's goal become theirs instead of listening to their intuition. Make sure whatever financial goal you choose is one that you want to achieve, so you'll put in the hard work to make it your reality.

Paying down your debt

Another financial goal you can set is paying down your debt. Debt isn't evil if you use it strategically. But having even strategic debt can still be problematic. Who wants to pay thousands of dollars in interest and financing fees?

Setting a financial goal to pay your debt down can help in the long run when budgeting. Because as soon as you pay that debt off, you have more cash flow to do things with, like saving for retirement or adopting a pet from a shelter. The whole goal of this book is to help you eliminate your debt, but you can get started with the tips in Chapter 1.

Putting your financial goals in place

TIP

Setting financial goals doesn't have to be complicated. Just follow these steps:

1. **Establish what your goals are.**

For example, maybe you want to buy a house.

2. **Make the goal as clear as can be.**

Decide precisely how much money you'll need to buy that house and when you want to be able to make the purchase.

3. **Take actionable steps toward completing it.**

Examples of actionable steps may be paying extra on your credit card so that eventual payment can go toward opening a high-yield savings account for the house you want. Every little bit adds up, so don't be discouraged if you have to start small. With every action, you move the needle closer to your goal.

Celebrate the small wins, and make sure you know you have your own back. We have it, too.

Chapter **4**

Creating a New Budget

udgeting is one of the key financial tools you need to understand to succeed financially. If you have no idea how much money you have coming in or where you're spending it, you can't make a budget work. Proper budgeting gives you more options for how you spend your money.

When you use a budget, you plan for your future. You're taking charge of your life and leaving fewer things to chance. We know, however, that being in control and taking charge of your money can be overwhelming if you've never done it before. Fear of the unknown can paralyze people, especially regarding their finances. Particularly when you grow up without great financial role models, knowing what you're supposed to do or even avoiding picking up those habits is tough.

In this chapter, you find some budgeting guidelines that have helped millions of other people live the lives of their dreams. These guidelines may not all apply to you or your situation, and that's okay, too. A great saying is "Take what you want and leave the rest." That works for all areas of your life, including personal finance. It's personal and yours to call the shots.

Introducing a Few Budgeting Methods

REMEMBER

You may already be budgeting without even realizing it. If you send money to your retirement account and live off the remainder of your income, that's the pay-yourself-first budget or the 50/30/20 budget. If you give yourself a cash allowance for lunch, that's the envelope budgeting method. And if you make a list of categories to track your spending, that's zero-based budgeting. Here are brief explanations of each:

>> **Zero-based budgeting:** A *zero-based budgeting system* is when you assign a job to every single dollar that comes your way. The overall goal of a zero-based budget is to leave no dollar unaccounted for. With this budgeting method, you should have a zero balance after you allocate funds to each category of your fixed and variable expenses. But that doesn't mean that you should spend *all* your money. That's not a wise move for anyone, ever. It just means that, in general, your income aligns with all your spending and doesn't leave you in a deficit.

>> **The 50/30/20 budget:** The *50/30/20 budget* allocates money for all your financial needs, wants, and goals in a simple formula: 50 percent of your income goes toward your needs, 30 percent goes toward your wants, and the remaining 20 percent goes toward your savings and debt. This budgeting guideline should make people feel less stressed about money management because it's easier than other budgeting methods such as the zero-based budget. It may also be a lot more flexible to follow and fun.

>> **The envelope budget:** The *envelope budget method* (also referred to as *cash envelopes* or *cash stuffing*) is an effective way to monitor your cash flow visually and interactively. Like the zero-based budgeting method, you assign a dollar amount to a list of categories that your expenses fall under. However, the envelope budget doesn't require you to sort through your checking account to track expenses or sit in front of a spreadsheet to determine how much you have left to stretch until the end of the month.

After you've determined the amount of money for each category, you withdraw the amount of cash you've budgeted for from your checking account and put it into envelopes assigned to those categories. Then you're allowed to spend the cash in your envelopes however you see fit. But that's it — no debit or credit card for everyday expenses. When your cash is gone, it's gone. You're out of money until the next payday, when you can refill your envelopes again.

>> **The pay-yourself-first budget:** The *pay-yourself-first budget,* sometimes known as *reverse budgeting,* makes your financial goals a priority by focusing on them first rather than focusing on your expenses. Whatever you have left is what you then use to cover your fixed and variable expenses. By zeroing in on your goals first, you make sure they get covered no matter what.

Determining Your Budget Categories

The categories you choose can make or break your budget. When you create categories for your spending, you're creating a spending plan. Creating a spending plan is what's going to get you where you want to be: making your money work for you rather than against you.

Planning ahead for the month

The first step to figuring out what spending categories to use in your budget is to plan ahead for your month. Planning keeps you from wasting time and money, two of your most precious resources. Forgetting events, appointments, or renewal fees can all derail a budget. When you plan, you're fully aware of what you have coming up and can allocate money accordingly. For example, if you have a lot of upcoming get-togethers with friends, you can plan ahead by putting additional money into your entertainment category and cut back elsewhere.

Meal planning is a great example of planning ahead. Every week you make a list of meals to cook and then write out the ingredients you need. You shop for everything at once, meaning you make fewer trips to the grocery store. Knowing what you're eating every night ahead of time also means less money spent dining out.

Similarly, when you know you have something on the horizon, such as a birthday gift, you can shop around for the best deals. Because you aren't making a last-minute purchase, you aren't paying for convenience and forfeiting quality. Bonus: Planning ahead for an event also allows you to save for it a little bit at a time rather than all at once.

TIP

Here's how to make sure you have an eye on everything you may need a category for:

1. **Make a list of your fixed expenses.**

   Consider investing in a planner you can write in or using a calendar app.

2. **Add each expense on the due date within the calendar.**

   Look over your expenses to account for any irregular ones you may have forgotten about.

3. **Write down any upcoming appointments, birthdays, and social events that will cost you money and note how much money you'll likely need.**

   The calendar entries give you an idea of how much money you'll need to spend during the month to compare with your monthly income.

REMEMBER

You need to be aware of how much income you'll have so that you can accurately budget your categories. If your categories add up to more than your income, you may need to cut back on your upcoming spending.

TIP

Keep a running list in your Notes app of gifts you need to buy. When you know you need to buy a particular gift ahead of time, you're more likely to spend less money. List each recipient (by name), things they like, and the occasion so you're not racking your brain for the details later. For example, suppose one of your best friends is obsessed with *Star Trek*. While shopping, you randomly found some *Star Trek* socks at the dollar store. Now your friend will have multiple pairs of *Star Trek* socks for Christmas, and you've avoided the stress of finding a last-minute gift.

Reflecting on fixed and variable spending

Figuring out where your money goes and seeing where you want it to go can be empowering when determining your budget categories. Your fixed and variable spending can tell you a lot about yourself: your habits, preferences, what you value the most. For example, if you value self-development, the proof is in your therapy expenses, medications for your mental health, and a few subscription boxes you use to take time out for yourself. If you value health, you probably spend money on healthy meals and maybe a gym membership. If your rent is a large percentage of your budget, that may be because where you live is important to you.

TECHNICAL STUFF

Speaking of rent, a good rule of thumb is to not spend more than 25 percent to 30 percent of your take-home pay. If you live in a big city with high rent, don't feel bad that you're spending more than "recommended." You need shelter and can always balance your budget differently. If you want to aim for less than 25 percent to 30 percent, consider living with a roommate.

REMEMBER

Spending your money on things you value can help make you happier and more fulfilled. To get a sense of how your money reflects your values and, by extension, what are likely good budget categories for you, consider asking yourself the following questions:

>> What am I spending my money on?

>> Is my spending productive or helpful?

>> Am I happy to see that I've spent money on _____?

>> What values does my spending reflect?

>> What is my money saying to me?

>> How do I feel about how much I've spent on certain items?

>> Do I get emotional when I think about my spending habits?

>> Do I shop to make myself feel better?

>> Do I hide my purchases from others?

>> Am I an impulsive shopper?

>> Do I spend more on wants than on needs?

>> Do I often pay for convenience?

>> Am I planning for my future?

>> Is anyone in my life receiving financial assistance from me?

>> Am I receiving financial assistance from anyone?

These are all great questions to get you started on your money reflection journey. Be sure to take breaks if you get overwhelmed thinking about where your money goes. Just trust the process. Work your way through so you can develop your financial categories appropriately to make your money work for you.

TIP

If you really want to get in touch with how you spend your money, start a spending journal. Every day, write down your expenses and any emotions or thoughts tied to them. You may be surprised at what feelings come up. For example, if you see a lot of Starbucks purchases in your budget, you may figure out that you're physically exhausted. You can use that information to cut back on your coffee purchases and take time to rest properly.

Compiling a list of budget categories

You can split your budget among many different categories. Here's a list of some general categories and the kinds of expenses that may fall into them to get you started.

REMEMBER

You don't have to make your budget complicated. The categories listed here are just the tip of the iceberg. You may find that this number of categories is too many and want to make it simpler. Do what feels right for you and your money. The important part is that you stick to it.

Home

- Mortgage or rent
- Property taxes and homeowners' association (HOA) fees
- Homeowners or rental insurance
- Warranties
- House maintenance such as landscaping, pool, and cleaning services
- House repairs
- Appliances
- Furniture
- Household decor
- Cleaning supplies
- Security camera services

Utilities

- Electricity
- Water
- Your home's gas bill
- Trash pickup
- Internet (you can consider this item a utility because many people need it for work and school)
- Cellphone

Transportation

- Gas
- Vehicle payment (if not listed under debt)
- Vehicle insurance
- Vehicle maintenance, such as oil changes and repairs
- Vehicle registration
- Public transportation
- Highway tolls

- Parking fees
- Rideshares such as Uber and Lyft

» Food

- Groceries
- Meal-prep services such as Blue Apron
- Personal shopping services like Instacart
- Meal delivery like DoorDash and Postmates
- Dining out

» Children

- Baby formula and food if outside of regular groceries
- Daycare
- Child support
- Diapers
- Clothing
- Personal hygiene items
- After-school care
- School fees
- School supplies
- Gifts
- Toys
- Club or sports fees

» Medical

- Medical, dental, and vision insurance
- Co-pays
- Flexible spending account or health savings account
- Doctor visits
- Dental exams
- Hospital stays
- Medical testing

- Medications
- Therapy sessions
- Medical supplies and equipment
- Supplements and other alternative medical visits

» Pets

- Pet food
- Veterinarian visits
- Medication and supplements
- Pet insurance
- Grooming such as nails and haircuts
- Boarding or pet sitting
- Cat litter
- Clothing and toys

» Personal

- Hygiene products
- Grooming services such as haircuts and aesthetician visits
- Massages and other spa visits
- Makeup and perfume/cologne
- Clothing
- Shoes
- Accessories

» Entertainment

- Streaming services like Netflix and Hulu
- Media subscriptions such as Kindle Unlimited and Spotify
- Alcohol
- Admission fees
- Concerts and other performance shows

- Subscription boxes
- Supplies for hobbies
- Social outings with friends
- Video games and gaming devices
- Movie theater tickets

》 Party planning, gifts, and donations

- Birthday gifts
- Gifts for special occasions such as weddings, baby showers, and graduations
- Holiday gifts
- Food and decorations
- Cards
- Wrapping paper
- Shipping materials
- Charitable giving
- Tithing
- Fundraising

》 Travel

- Plane tickets
- Baggage fees
- Hotel accommodations
- House rentals
- Rental cars
- Local transportation
- Food
- Special outings
- Souvenirs

》 Insurance/future-planning

- Life insurance
- Short-term and long-term disability insurance

- Long-term care insurance
- Caregiving
- Nursing or retirement home
- Estate and trust legal fees
- Burial expenses

» Savings

- Retirement contributions
- Brokerage accounts
- Treasury bonds
- College fund
- Emergency fund
- Moving expenses
- Automobiles
- House down payments
- Weddings
- Graduation (expenses not covered in other categories)

» Debt

- Vehicle payments (if not listed under transportation)
- Student loans
- Credit cards
- Personal loans
- Medical debt
- 401(k) loans
- Payday loans
- Title loans
- Debt settlements
- Court judgments such as restitution or alimony
- Legal fees
- Back taxes

Using the Right Tools

One of the key components of budgeting is to make sure you're using the right tools to track where your money goes. Whatever budgeting method you decide to use, you need to know in general where you're spending your money so you can allocate the proper funds for your categories. (For more on figuring out what categories to use, head to the earlier section "Determining Your Budget Categories.")

Tracking your money with budgeting software

An easy way to keep track of your budget is by using budgeting software that you download to your computer desktop or access online. When you use budgeting software, you can relax and have it do the calculations for you. Letting go of manually tracking every monetary transaction can help you free up mental space to focus on something else.

TIP

When picking out budgeting software, make sure it supports a budgeting method you want to try and will stick with in the long run. For example, if you want to use the zero-based budgeting method, don't pick a budgeting program that focuses on the envelope method. You also want to ensure the software doesn't share your private information with third parties.

REMEMBER

Don't forget to factor in any associated costs for using budgeting software. A lot of free budgeting software and apps are available, so you don't have to spend money to manage your money. But paid subscriptions to budgeting software and apps can unlock more features to help manage your finances and save money over time.

The budgeting software options in the following list all have downloadable apps from Google Play and the Apple App Store; however, the focus here is on budgeting programs that you can access online or download to your desktop.

>> **YNAB** (www.ynab.com): YNAB, short for *You Need a Budget,* is a great software for zero-based budgeting because it stresses that you give every dollar a job. You can see your money all at once by linking the program to all your financial accounts. This overall budget snapshot can help you see whether your money is going where it should be.

>> **Mint** (https://mint.intuit.com): Mint is an app but its software is great and has additional features you can use. Like YNAB, Mint has the capability to help you sync all your financial accounts. Mint automatically categorizes your expenses, so that's one less thing you need to do. It also tracks the bills you've paid and alerts you when you're going to be late with a custom setting you can put in place.

>> **Quicken** (www.quicken.com): Quicken is one of the oldest players in the budgeting software game. It scans your transactions and assigns them to the categories you set up. You can assess your spending to see whether you're hitting your financial goals. Quicken offers a few different tiers of software so you can figure out which one works best for you.

>> **Tiller** (www.tillerhq.com): If you love spreadsheets, Tiller is for you. The Tiller spreadsheets let you customize them in various ways to reflect your overall spending and daily account balances. You can access the spreadsheets through both Google Sheets and Microsoft Excel. Tiller is also great for couples. When you sign up for Tiller, you can link your and your partner's checking accounts to create shared spreadsheets. This setup allows you and your partner to stay in touch with each other's finances to work as a team.

>> **Goodbudget** (https://goodbudget.com): Goodbudget is based on the envelope budgeting method. It makes virtual envelopes for all your budget categories and can help you plan ahead and pay off your debt. If you're budgeting with a significant other, you can share and sync with your partner's categories and see each other's spending in real time, which means you're less likely to go over your budgeted amounts as a couple.

>> **PocketGuard** (https://pocketguard.com**):** Trying to figure out your finances for the first time can be challenging. That's why PocketGuard is great for college students. With this software, you can easily see how much money you have for whatever you need. PocketGuard negotiates your bills so you can save more money, which is an important life skill. It's also a way to budget with hashtags.

Looking at budgeting apps

If you don't have time for logging into software (see the preceding section), a budgeting app may be a great alternative. Every budgeting app is different, but they all have the same goal: to help you track your spending and save money. Budgeting apps are a convenient way for you to budget from anywhere. With real-time information, you can access your budget by tapping a few buttons on your phone.

Along with tracking your spending, each app has its own budgeting method. Different apps also allow you different ways to save money toward your financial goals. With some, you can set up automatic transfers into your checking account every time you make a purchase. Others find ways for you to cancel subscriptions and negotiate your bills. If you're finding it hard to remind yourself to transfer money into your savings account, these apps make it easy.

Apps can also pay your bills for you. Whether it's a push notification to pay your bills or being able to set up an automatic payment, an app can help you stay on track. This feature is great if you're new to budgeting or are forgetful. Paying your bills on time helps you avoid late fees or, even worse, service disconnection or disruption. (*Note:* You can link some apps to all your financial accounts, but others you can link to your checking account only.)

Another cool feature with budgeting apps is that they help you learn how to invest and give you opportunities to start investing. They're a great way for new investors to practice without spending much money. Investing is one of the key ways to grow your wealth, and the sooner you start, the better.

Here's a list of apps that are worth looking into. It isn't a complete list of available apps, but it's one to get you started. All these apps are available to download from Google Play and the Apple App Store.

>> **Simplifi by Quicken** (www.quicken.com/products/ simplifi): If you like the idea of Quicken but don't like sitting down at your computer, don't worry. Simplifi by Quicken is an app that allows you to customize your budget and track your spending just like you can with the Quicken software we discuss in the preceding section. The app also finds subscriptions you don't use and helps you cancel them. With features to also help you track your savings goals, it's an easy way to budget.

>> **Fudget** (www.fudget.com): For a basic way to track your finances, Fudget can't be beaten. You don't have to create categories or eagle-eye your expenses. This app allows you just to keep track of your income and expenses so you can monitor cash flow. Monitoring your cash flow can be important when you use pay-yourself-first budgeting. Fudget is also available from the Mac App Store and the Windows Store.

The following budgeting apps are great for couples:

>> **Honeydue** (www.honeydue.com): Are you managing money for the first time as a couple? If you and your partner are just starting your money journey together, Honeydue may be for you. You can sync your checking accounts to review purchases with ease and also coordinate bills with your partner. And it's free!

>> **Zeta** (www.askzeta.com): If you and your partner are busy people, Zeta is probably the budgeting app to use. Zeta is a bank that allows you and your partner to open a joint checking account. You can set up a budget and do a spending analysis to ensure you're both on the right track. Zeta can also automatically pay your bills for you and prevent overdraft fees by reminding you to transfer funds when your money runs low.

College students should try the following budgeting apps:

- » **Qapital** (www.qapital.com): Qapital has two features to help you save money. One is *microsaving,* where the app rounds up your purchases and transfers the difference into a savings account. The second is an automatic transfer function that works whenever you spend. For example, if you grab a coffee to go, the app automatically transfers a dollar to your savings account.

- » **Albert** (https://albert.com): Albert is technically a banking app, but the creators say it's more, and we can't disagree. This app allows you to ask a financial expert for advice directly at no additional cost. You also get cash back when you use the app for your daily spending. And if you're new to investing, Albert helps you start. You just need one dollar.

REMEMBER

Budgeting apps aren't magic. When your app notifies you of a spending trend, you still have to put in the work to reevaluate your allocations or dive deeper into your spending habits. But using an app as a tool can make navigating your finances easier than doing it on your own.

Picking the right app for you

Just because budgeting apps are an easy way to stay accountable doesn't mean you don't have to put some thought and effort into choosing one. You still have to do research to figure out the right budgeting tool for you, and note that you may use different apps at different stages in your life. When selecting your app, here are a few things to consider:

- » **Your needs and goals:** Different budgeting apps provide different things, so clarifying why you're using one in the first place is important. Is it to help you remember to pay your bills? Do you need push notifications telling you you're out of money? Figuring out this motivation can keep you from downloading multiple apps that lack the features you need.

- **Style of budgeting:** You can find apps for every budgeting method, so don't feel you have to conform to zero-based budgeting if you're more interested in the pay-yourself-first method.

- **Ease of use:** The app must be relatively easy to use, whatever that means to you. Some apps are more difficult and time-consuming than others. Some won't have enough involvement for your liking. The bottom line is that you're most likely to stick to something if it's easy to use, so keep it simple.

- **Features and benefits:** Every app offers different features and benefits, like paying your bills or providing cash back. Decide which options are most important to you and your lifestyle. For example, if you're not using credit cards to reap rewards because you're using cash envelopes, consider apps that give rewards.

- **New checking or savings accounts:** Although most budgeting apps allow you to sync to your existing checking account, some take it a step further by providing an opportunity to open a new account with them. Some of these accounts offer great perks, such as paying you interest like traditional high-yield savings accounts (HYSAs). Others allow you to open accounts with another person while using the app. Consider what ATMs these apps allow you to access for free or at least waive the fee for.

WARNING

If you open a new checking or savings account through an app, do your due diligence. Ensure the accounts are backed by the Federal Deposit Insurance Corporation (FDIC). Savings and checking accounts backed by the FDIC are insured up to at least $250,000 if something happens to the financial institution that the app is using. If an app's accounts aren't insured, proceed with caution.

- **Pricing:** Many, but not all, apps are free. Some budgeting apps charge a monthly fee, while others waive a fee if you open a checking or savings account with them. If the benefits of a paid app outweigh those of a free one, consider it money well spent.

Taking the DIY approach

If software and apps aren't for you, you may want to try a more do-it-yourself approach to your budgeting. By being as involved with your money as possible, you're more likely to take care of it.

One of the ways you can become more hands-on with your money is by writing your budget out in a notebook. You can list your income and then keep track of your expenses. Adding a category to each expense can help you keep an eye on your spending to ensure you stay under budget. Keeping a running ledger like a checkbook may work best for you; you can see an example in Figure 4-1.

October — Wells Fargo Account		
Date	Expense/Income with Amount Spent	Account Total (starting balance $537.80)
10/1	Netflix (–$14.99)	522.81
10/2	Spotify (–$17)	501.81
10/2	Paycheck (+$1,500)	2005.81
10/7	Starbucks (–$6.49)	1999.32
10/8	Target (–$75.67)	1923.65
10/8	Rent (–$975)	948.65
10/10	Venmo friend for takeout (–$20)	928.65
10/14	Sephora online order (–$36.45)	892.20
10/15	Uber (–$14.99)	877.21
10/15	Safeway (–$122.99)	754.22
10/16	Paycheck (+$1,500)	2254.22
10/20	Student loans (–$400)	1854.22
10/21	Electric company (–$79.55)	1774.67
10/22	Freelance payment (+$350)	2124.67
10/22	Starbucks (–$6.49)	2118.18
10/25	Internet (–$75)	2043.18
10/27	Amazon (Halloween costume) (–$59.33)	1983.85
10/28	Freelance payment (+$500)	2483.85
10/30	Hallow party supplies (–$43.67)	2440.18
10/30	Uber (–$35.66)	2404.52
10/31	Halloween candy (–$14.21)	2390.31
10/31	iTunes movie rental (–$5.99)	2384.32

FIGURE 4-1: A sample page from a budgeting notebook.

© John Wiley & Sons, Inc.

If you want to be more creative, you can make a budget binder. You can find free printable PDF worksheets online for your spending, income, saving goals, financial account login information, and anything else you want to keep track of. Consider the idea of being extra colorful by using various pens and highlighters. A lot of people find success when they use this creative approach.

Paper can come with a lot to keep track of, including clutter. If you still want DIY budget tracking but don't want a bunch of paper floating around, consider making a digital spreadsheet. You can download a budgeting spreadsheet from Google Sheets or Microsoft Excel (see Figure 4-2). Each spreadsheet has embedded math formulas that calculate how much money you have left to spend in each budget category. Spreadsheets can also keep your finances organized with hyperlinks to different financial accounts.

TIP

If you aren't a spreadsheet pro, don't worry! You can still use spreadsheets without knowing fancy formulas. Pop "free budget spreadsheet templates" into your favorite search engine, and thousands of options pop up. Some require you to sign up for a website's newsletter, but you can always unsubscribe after you get your spreadsheet. You can personalize the income sources and categories for easier use to make your money work for you.

Taking advantage of your accounts' resources

Many banks and credit cards offer a spender analysis tool already built into your account. This free resource can be the most accurate way to scrutinize your spending, particularly with specific merchants. It's also an easy way to flag billing errors or fraud in real time.

Simply log into your banking or credit account to see what's available in your account's dashboard. If you can't find anything online, reach out to customer service to see whether the company provides some sort of tool or, if not, what outside option it recommends.

	A	B	C	D	E
1	**Net Income**	**$3,000**			
2					
3		**Budgeted Amount**			**Actual**
4		Dollars:	% of Income:	Dollars:	% of Income:
5	Rent	1200.00	40%	0.00	0%
6	Car loan	300.00	10%	0.00	0%
7	Utilities	250.00	8%	0.00	0%
8	Cellphone	90.00	3%	0.00	0%
9	Student loans	200.00	7%	0.00	0%
10	Transportation	100.00	3%	0.00	0%
11	Car Insurance	110.00	3%	0.00	0%
12	Groceries/Dining out	300.00	10%	0.00	0%
13	Entertainment	200.00	6%	0.00	0%
14	Personal spending	150.00	5%	0.00	0%
15	Miscellaneous	100.00	5%	0.00	0%
16	**Total**	**3000.00**	**100%**	**0**	**0%**
17				3000	100%

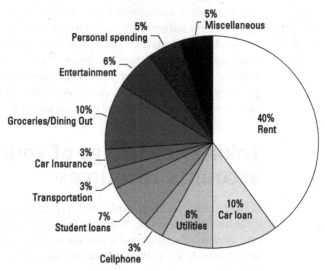

Recommended Budget

FIGURE 4-2: A Microsoft Excel budget spreadsheet.

© John Wiley & Sons, Inc.

Wells Fargo has a great example of such a tool. You can monitor not only your spending but also your cash flow and other items of your budget. This tool is great for visual learners because it formats your budget how you need to see it. Figure 4-3 shows you an example.

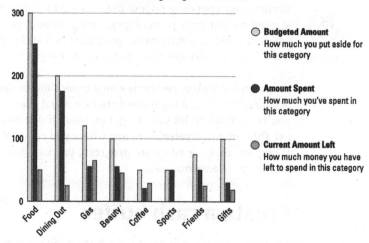

Bank of Budgeting For Dummies

○ **Budgeted Amount**
How much you put aside for this category

● **Amount Spent**
How much you've spent in this category

○ **Current Amount Left**
How much money you have left to spend in this category

FIGURE 4-3:
The result from a bank's spending analysis tool.

© *John Wiley & Sons, Inc.*

Practicing Makes Perfect

Think about budgeting like you would any new skill. It may be difficult at first, but over time it becomes easier to do. Practice makes perfect.

Learning how to budget and then sticking with it may be one of the hardest things you do when dealing with your finances. Even if it comes easily to you, you still need self-discipline. But after you put in the blood, sweat, and tears (well, hopefully not blood), the world can be your oyster. The following sections offer a few extra steps to help you ace your budgeting skills and feel liberated to take on your finances with confidence and less (or even no) stress.

Revisit your budget

No matter what budgeting method you choose to implement, regularly revisit it to see whether it's still working for you. Budgeting isn't a Goldilocks situation; the method that's just right for you today may not provide the structure you need down the road.

Review your spending no less than once a month, even if you're staying within your percentages. This schedule is a way to see whether a bill or subscription price changed and make sure you don't have any erroneous or fraudulent charges.

Your regular budget review is also a great time to see how much progress you're making toward your financial goals. See whether you're on track to hit your target on time. If you're not, you can use this time to strategize to see where you can make a change. If you are making adequate progress, you can use this time to bask in your awesomeness.

Create a cash buffer

Another way you can keep your budget intact is by practicing maintaining a *cash buffer,* an amount of money set aside to cover any bills or purchases that weren't in the budget. Keeping a buffer in your everyday checking account can also help you cover expenses you didn't plan for during a budget cycle and prevent stresses to your budget. For example, if you overspend on your groceries by $50 or your kid forgets to tell you about a field trip, your buffer can soften the blow.

You may say, "Isn't that what my emergency fund is for?" Well, no, not quite. Your emergency fund is strictly for emergencies — events you couldn't have planned for. You got a hole in a tire on the way home? Emergency. Is the dog sick and needs to go to the vet? Emergency. You want to go to a last-minute birthday dinner for a friend? Not an emergency, even though you really want to go. This expense comes out of your cash buffer.

WARNING

You should keep your cash buffer and emergency fund in separate savings or checking accounts from each other. Having your emergency fund in the account you use for everyday spending makes tapping into it way too easy, especially for overspenders.

How much your cash buffer should be depends on your everyday spending. You want it to be sufficient to cover those random expenses without leaving you strapped for cash. If you live below your means, you may be able to get away with having $100 to $200. If you have a family or spend more in general, consider saving at least $500. As you get a feel for your budget and spending, you can adjust the amount as necessary.

You can also practice goal setting by making creating a buffer one of your first financial goals. Whether you designate an amount or a percentage of your income, having a guideline in place can motivate you to get that cash buffer setup taken care of. And because it's a smaller goal, accomplishing it first can build momentum for other goals you have lined up in the queue.

If you need to, start small. Dedicate $10 or $20 per paycheck toward creating a cash buffer. Even a small amount can be enough to keep you from incurring an insufficient funds fee or dipping into your emergency fund.

TIP

Look for ways to make your system easier to follow

The best expert on you is you. You know what makes you feel frustrated or overwhelmed, and you also know when a system feels manageable and satisfying.

One of the ways to make your budgeting system easy is to approach it like you would a work project. Being realistic with how you see things can help you find a budgeting method you can easily follow. If an overall picture is easier to visualize than a bunch of tiny steps, use the pay-yourself-first method. If you need a lot of structure in life, try the zero-based budgeting method.

Another way to make your budgeting system easy is to allow for fun money. When you have money to do whatever you want, sticking to saving the rest is easier. Even if you can't think of anything fun you want to do or buy, still allocate for fun in your budget. The time will come when you want to use it, and having it ready to go will make your heart happy.

TIP

Chapter **5**

Spending Less and Saving More

How and where you spend your money is a matter of personal choice and priorities, but those choices can affect the amount of money you have left to save. Savings is essential to accomplishing many personal and financial goals. Having more can increase your options and freedom. This chapter presents ideas on how to get the most from spending and how to spend less.

REMEMBER

Some of the best savers get hooked on the accumulation of money and sometimes have a hard time using their savings and investments in the future for their originally intended purpose. Consider this a reminder that saving more isn't always better. There's something to be said for living for today and striking a balance since we can't know exactly what the future will be. That said, plenty of folks could save more and reduce unproductive and unfulfilling spending.

Containing Housing Costs

Housing and its associated costs such as insurance, utilities, furniture, maintenance, and repairs (for homeowners) are the largest or second-largest expenditure for most people. If you're like many other people nowadays, you may be renting. Keeping these costs (and taxes) under control, which the following sections explain how to do, goes a long way toward being able to save some money.

Reducing rental costs

The following sections point out what you can do to minimize your rent expense and associated costs.

Share a rental with roommates

Living solo is a pricey luxury some people can't afford. Doing so definitely has its benefits — you have more privacy and control over your home environment. Renting may sacrifice some of these advantages to living alone, but having roomies also has its pros. If you share a rental with roommates, the per-person costs should be substantially less than if you live solo.

You must be in a sharing mood, though, to live harmoniously with roommates. They may help themselves to your food or shampoo, stay up late when you need to get up early the next day, or invite over inconsiderate friends. Roommates aren't all bad, though, as they may brighten your social life.

WARNING

Before you choose to share an apartment or other dwelling with someone or multiple other people, make sure (as best you can) that you can live with those people for the length of the rental agreement. If you break the lease, you may owe a hefty amount of money, which defeats the purpose of saving money with a roommate.

TIP

Be sure to have a rental agreement in place with your landlord and to have all renters listed in the agreement. Don't allow others who aren't listed in the agreement to live in the rental, because you and the other renters could be on the hook for damage they cause and rent (and utilities) they don't pay.

Move to a lower-cost rental

You may realize that you're currently living beyond your means and you need to make some adjustments. You may have allowed your champagne tastes to exceed your beer budget when you went shopping for a home rental. So long as you're completing your current lease, there's no reason you can't move to a lower-cost rental. The less you spend renting, the more you can save toward buying your own place. Just be sure to factor in all the costs of moving to and living in a new rental.

REMEMBER

Of course, a lower-cost rental may be lower quality and not up to your standards. Don't accept living in a high-crime neighborhood, a poorly maintained building, or a location that causes you to burn much of your free time commuting to work.

Negotiate your rental increases

Every year, some landlords increase their tenants' rent no matter how good the tenant has been and regardless of the state of the economy. If your local economy is weak and the rental market is soft or your living quarters are deteriorating, negotiate with your landlord. You have more leverage and power than you probably realize. A smart landlord doesn't want to lose good tenants who pay rent on time. Filling vacancies takes time and money.

TIP

State your case to your landlord through a well-crafted and polite email/note and/or personal call or visit. Explain how you have been a responsible tenant, always paid your rent on time, and cared for your unit, and convey that your research shows comparable rentals going for less. Briefly explaining any challenging financial circumstances (such as reduced pay from your job) may help your case as well. If you can't stave off the rent increase, perhaps you can negotiate some improvements you value.

Live with relatives

Yes, living with relatives won't work for some families. However, if your relatives have the space and temperament to let you live under their roof, it can be a constructive way to keep your rental costs to a minimum. Just be sure to have some lengthy discussions first to set expectations and ground rules, raise concerns, and establish terms, including costs and rental agreements.

If your relative won't accept money from you, how about helping with some chores and other responsibilities around the house? That could start with your own things like doing your own laundry and helping with cleaning, especially and always of the space you live in and regularly use, like the kitchen and bathroom.

Get on the path to purchasing your own home

Purchasing a home always seems costly. However, over the long term, owning is usually less costly than renting a similar property. And as a homeowner, you build *equity* (the difference between the home's value and what you owe on it) in your property as you make mortgage payments and as the home's value increases over the long term.

If you purchase a property with a 30-year fixed-rate mortgage, the biggest expense of ownership — your monthly mortgage payment — is locked in and remains level. By contrast, as a renter, unless you live in a *rent-controlled unit* (which means that local government dictates and limits the percentage by which the rent may rise annually), your entire monthly housing cost is fully exposed to inflation.

REMEMBER

During periods like 2006–11, the decline in home prices in most parts of the United States coupled with low interest rates made housing the most affordable it had been in decades. At the time, that was great news for renters looking to become future homeowners as well as those who simply wanted to rent a nicer dwelling. While home prices generally rise over the long term, buying during a home price decline can be a great way to get into the housing market when it's having a "sale."

Of course, each local market is unique, and if you happen to live in an area with a strong, diverse economy and little developable land or excess housing, your local housing market may be stronger and more expensive than others.

Slicing homeowner expenses

If you own a home or are about to buy one, you can take many steps to keep your ownership costs down and under control without neglecting your property or living like a pauper. The following sections are full of tips.

Buy a home that fits your budget

Purchase a home that you can afford. During the booming real-estate market up until 2005, getting overextended with debt was pretty easy. You didn't need a decent-size down payment or even have to have your income verified to buy a home if you made a larger down payment. Furthermore, interest-only loans allowed borrowers to shrink their mortgage payments by delaying repayment of any of their principal.

However, the best way to buy a home is to examine your budget and financial resources before shopping for a home. As the real-estate market declined between 2006–11 in most parts of the United States, some of those people who bought homes that stretched their budgets lost their homes to foreclosure because they got in over their head, fell on hard times, and couldn't afford their monthly mortgage payments.

WARNING

Even if you can afford the monthly mortgage payment on a house you're looking to buy, if you have too little money left over for your other needs and wants — such as taking trips, eating out, going out with friends, enjoying hobbies, or saving for retirement — your dream home may become a financial prison. See Chapters 11 and 15 for help in figuring out what to do if you find yourself in a mortgage meltdown.

Get a roommate (and some rental income)

Owning a home may be more affordable if you have some monthly rental coming in. Consider renting a bedroom (or separate/in-law unit if you're lucky enough to have one) to someone who can pay monthly rent as well as possibly help with utilities. Through services like Airbnb (www.airbnb.com), Vrbo (www.vrbo.com), Tripadvisor (www.tripadvisor.com), Tripping (www.tripping.com), and so on, you can get an idea about what you may be able to charge in rent and find possible renters. You should also inquire with real-estate agents who are active and experienced in your local rental market and consider websites like Trulia (www.trulia.com) and Realtor.com (www.realtor.com) for listing your rental.

If you decide to take on a renter(s), make sure you check the renter(s) thoroughly through references and a credit report, and be sure to discuss ground rules and expectations before renting to someone sharing your space. Vet prospective renters before agreeing to meet them or show them the rental. You don't want to waste your time showing rentals to someone who can't afford it, isn't a good fit for your situation, or has a shady background! Also, ask your insurance company to see whether your home-owner's policy needs adjustments to cover potential liability from renting.

Contain your utility costs

You can take steps to keep your utility costs down whether you own or rent a home. First, don't waste energy, even if you don't pay for it out-of-pocket as a renter. Landlords absolutely factor your energy consumption into future rental-hike decisions. Paying for your own utilities should get you to consider wearing layers in the winter (you shouldn't be walking around then in shorts) and not expecting your home to feel like a meat locker in the heat of summer.

Adjust your thermostat to save energy — allow it to be cooler than normal in winter and warmer than normal in summer — when you're not going to be home for a while (for example, while you're at work or away for a weekend). Smart thermostats can help with this process but aren't required.

Especially if you have to pay for garbage service, recycle as much as possible. Seek the replacement of old, energy-guzzling appli-ances and, where possible, beef up your property's insulation. Obviously, if you're a renter, you have no control over these things, but you should certainly ask about utility costs and whether any appliances and insulation could be upgraded as necessary.

Cutting Your Taxes

Alongside the costs of owning or renting a home, taxes are the other large personal expenditure for most folks. Everyone gets socked with federal income taxes (and for most people state income taxes) when earning income and when investing and spending money. That's the bad news — the good news is that you can reduce the amount of taxes you pay by using some relatively simple yet powerful strategies.

The following two tax trimmers can help:

>> **Use retirement savings plans.** To take advantage of such plans, you must spend less than you earn. Only then can you afford to contribute to these plans. Many of these plans immediately reduce your federal and state income taxes, and once money is inside such an account, the investment returns are sheltered from taxation.

>> **Reduce the amount of sales tax you pay.** To do so, you must spend less and save more. When you buy most consumer products, you pay sales tax. Therefore, if you spend less money, you reduce your sales taxes.

Managing Food and Restaurant Spending

The following culinary strategies can keep you on your feet — perhaps even improve your health — and help you save money.

>> **Discover how to cook.** Take a course and read some good books on cooking. Learn from those around you — parents, other relatives, and friends come to mind — who can teach you a thing or two! Consider that most people eat three meals a day, 365 days a year. That's more than 1,000 meals yearly — a lot of eating! If you don't know how to cook for yourself and how to do so healthfully, you may end up spending a lot more money on food and eating out — and have poor health to boot.

Cooking meals for yourself doesn't mean having to make something for each and every meal. You can cook in larger quantities than you need for one meal and put what you don't eat in the refrigerator or freezer to eat at a later meal on another day. Making your own food can save you money, improve your health, allow you to enjoy your food more, and potentially make you more attractive to a mate!

>> **Find out about nutrition and prepared foods.** No, this point isn't contradictory with the first one about learning to cook. Everyone is busy, and buying prepared meals (including some frozen foods) that are easy to heat or ready to eat can make sense for some of your meals. But you want to be sure to buy healthy, nutritious affordable food.

TIP

Shop at stores like Trader Joe's — to find one near you, visit www.traderjoes.com/home/store-search. You can also try nutrition websites like Eat This, Not That! (www.eatthis.com), also the name of their popular book series; Healthline (www.healthline.com); and LiveStrong.com (www.livestrong.com).

>> **Consider store brands.** Name-brand companies spend a lot of money on advertising and marketing, which you, the consumer, end up paying for through higher prices. You can save a considerable amount of money by buying the store brand (for example, Walmart's Great Value, Target's Good and Gather, Aldi, Trader Joe's, or Whole Foods 365 Everyday Value), which is usually the same quality (and sometimes the same product) as the name brand but priced lower.

>> **Buy in bulk.** You can save substantially by shopping at stores that are able to sell groceries for less because of their operating efficiencies. Topping that list are wholesale superstores such as Costco and Sam's Club. The catch is that you must buy most items in bulk or in larger sizes. An additional advantage to buying in bulk: It requires fewer shopping trips (hence less gasoline) and results in fewer instances of running out of things.

You may be able to buy some of the foods you find you like in bulk online. Just be sure to order from a reputable online retailer that stands behind what it sells.

TIP

If you decide to buy in bulk, be careful with items that can spoil. Make sure that you buy what you can reasonably use (or freeze when necessary). If you're single, consider shopping with a friend and splitting the order. If you're looking for a store that sells more organic and natural products at a reasonable price and in smaller sizes, check out Trader Joe's.

» **Kick the bottled water habit.** Although tap water often does leave something to be desired, lab analysis of bottled water shows it has its own problems. You can save hundreds of dollars annually and drink cleaner water by installing a water filtration system at home and improving your tap (or well) water. Also consider pitcher-based water filtration systems like Zero Water and Brita.

» **Pack your lunch sometimes.** Eating out daily can rack up a lot of expense. Brown bag it sometimes.

» **Spend carefully when dining out.** Eating out can be fun and a way to socialize with family and friends, but keep in mind that you're essentially hiring someone to shop, cook, and clean up for you! You can save some money when eating out by remembering these points:

- **Eat out for breakfast or lunch rather than dinner.** You can generally get the most bang for your buck then. And this may be better for your health; studies show that the meals you eat earlier in the day should be the more substantial ones — not dinner!

- **Go easy on the beverages.** Alcohol is especially expensive when dining out (and at bars), and beverages in general are usually the biggest profit-margin items at restaurants.

Trimming Transportation Expenses

When you're considering the cost of living in different areas, don't forget to factor in commuting costs and wear and tear — not just on your car, but on you! Getting to and fro on a daily basis can get expensive if you don't keep an eye on your expenses. Many people rely on cars for their transportation. Buying and operating a car can be a tremendous financial burden, especially if you borrow to buy or lease the car.

You can control your transportation costs by following these suggestions:

>> **Opt for public transportation.** Choose to live in an area that offers reliable public transportation, such as a subway or bus system. You can often purchase monthly passes at a reasonable rate. If you live close to work, or at least close to a public transit system, you may be able to make do with fewer cars (or no car at all) in your household.

>> **Ride your bike.** During warmer months, consider jumping on your bike to get around. You can save money and get some exercise. Just be sure to be safe! Wear reflective gear and be sure your bike is easily visible. Stay off high-traffic, narrow roads and be on guard for bad and under-the-influence drivers!

>> **If you must have a car, look at cheaper options than financing or leasing one.** We can tell you from direct observation that spending on cars is one of the leading causes of overspending and under-saving. We understand that in some parts of the United States and Canada, going without a car is nearly impossible, and we also understand that driving a car is a wonderful convenience.

But if you can avoid having your own car, by all means do so. You can also consider renting a car when needed if you don't find yourself wanting to use one frequently. Or take an occasional taxi or use a Lyft- or Uber-type service.

The main reason people end up spending more than they can afford on a car is that they finance the purchase. When buying a car, you should buy one you can afford with cash, which for many people means buying a good-quality used car.

TIP

When shopping for a car, don't make the mistake of simply comparing sticker prices. Consider the total long-term costs of car ownership, which include gas, insurance, registration fees, maintenance, repairs, and taxes (sales and personal property). And be sure to consider the safety of any car you buy, as driving is surely the most dangerous thing you do. See the National Highway Traffic Safety Administration's website (www.safercar.gov), which has lots of crash-test data as well as information on other car-safety issues. Buy and drive cars that have the highest crash-test safety ratings (five stars).

Finessing Fashion Finances

The good news for you as a consumer is that in the fashion industry, global competition has driven down prices for consumers. Here's what you can do to look like a million bucks (on and off the job) while spending fewer of your bucks:

>> **Don't chase the latest fashions.** Ignore ads that splash celebrities wearing the latest looks. You can enjoy pictures on social media like Instagram, but recognize some of those photos are nothing more than veiled ads to promote particular lines of clothing and brands. (Also keep in mind that the person wearing the clothing and the setting for the photo greatly influence how the clothing appears and appeals to you.) You don't need to buy lots of new clothes every year. If your clothes aren't lasting at least ten years, you're probably tossing them before their time or buying clothing that isn't very durable. Of course, when you enter an office job for the first time, you're probably going to have to buy some new clothing.

True fashion, as defined by what people wear, changes quite slowly. In fact, the classics never go out of style. If you want the effect of a new wardrobe every year, store last year's purchases away next year and then bring them out the year after. Or rotate your clothing inventory every third year. Set your own fashion standards.

>> **Shun dry cleaning–required clothing.** Stick with cottons and machine-washable synthetics rather than wools or silks that require costly dry cleaning.

>> **Consider buying gently used fashion at consignment shops, vintage shops, or online.** You can find great bargains at these places that others may have worn only once or twice.

>> **Look for discounts.** Some stores have occasional big sales with major price reductions. Even premium retailers have sales, so be patient and sign up for email lists to be notified. And if you can wait until you're well into a particular season, you can get items on clearance when there's still time left to use them. For example, when stores are ready to put out fall/winter coats in August, they put

their swimwear on clearance. Depending on where you live, you may be able to wear that new (discounted!) suit for several weeks and of course in future years.

>> **Minimize accessories.** Shoes, jewelry, handbags, and the like can gobble large amounts of money. Again, how many of these accessory items do you really need? The answer is probably very few, because each one should last many years. Don't purchase accessories and then not use them.

Relaxing on a Budget

Having fun and taking time out for recreation can be money well spent. However, you can easily engage in financial extravagance, which can wreak havoc with an otherwise good budget. Here are some tips for getting the most from your recreation spending:

>> **Don't equate spending (more) money with having (more) fun.** Some entertainment venues offer discount prices on certain days and times. Cultivate some interests and hobbies that are free or low cost. Visiting with friends, hiking, reading, and playing sports can be good for your finances as well as your health.

>> **Hang out with people who share your values and aren't materialistic.** It's especially important that you find a partner who isn't a spendthrift and isn't overly impressed with material things.

>> **Take vacations you can afford.** Don't borrow on credit cards to finance your travels. Try taking shorter vacations that are closer to home. For example, have you been to a state or national park recently? Take a vacation at home, visiting the sites in your local area. For longer-distance travel, go during the off-season and off-peak times and days for the best deals on airfares and hotels.

TIP

If you've been disciplined about paying your credit-card bill in full each month, check out some of the better reward credit cards that offer benefits like free hotel stays and airline tickets.

Taming Technology Spending

It seems there's no end of ways to stay in touch and be entertained, as well as a never-ending stream of new gadgets. The cost for all these services and gadgets adds up, leading to a continued enslavement to your working full-time and earning more money.

Err on the side of keeping your life simple. Doing so costs less, reduces stress, and allows more time for the things that really do matter in life.

Keep the following in mind before you spend money on technology:

>> **Especially when it comes to new technology and gadgets, wait.** You don't have to be the first person to get something new. When something new first hits the market, prices are relatively high and the gadget inevitably has bugs. Wait at least a couple of years and your patience will be rewarded with much lower prices and more reliable products. If you're considering buying a new cell phone, ask about buying the previous model, which is likely far less than the new model and generally quite similar.

Also, do your homework before going shopping. *Consumer Reports* (www.consumerreports.org) and CNET (www.cnet.com) are useful resources.

>> **Be aware of how much you spend on your cell phone.** Cell phones are a particular device that can encourage the wasting of money. In addition to downloads, text messaging, web surfing, and other services, you can find all sorts of entertaining ways to run up cell-phone bills each month. Apps are especially problematic in this regard. Sure, the company behind most apps claims the app is free, but of course, you'll face numerous tempting ways to make in-app purchases. Ask yourself whether you really need all these costly bells and whistles.

Be safe with your cell phone, especially when driving, and don't hold a cell phone to your ear when talking because of long-term health concerns about the radiation emitted from these phones. Use the speakerphone or get an ear bud/headset for your phone.

TIP

Keeping Down Insurance Costs

Insurance is a big deal. The following tips help you minimize your insurance spending while making the most of your insurance, whether health, home, renter's, auto, or life insurance:

>> **Use high deductibles.** Each insurance policy has a *deductible,* which is the amount of a loss that must come out of your pocket before coverage kicks in. Higher deductibles can help to greatly lower your premiums. However, if you have a lot of claims, you won't come out ahead by instead choosing a low deductible, because your insurance premiums will escalate.

>> **Obtain broad coverage.** Don't buy insurance for anything that won't be a financial catastrophe if you have to pay for it out of your own pocket. For example, buying simple dental or home warranty plans, which cover relatively small potential expenditures, doesn't make financial sense. And if no one's dependent on your income, you don't need life insurance, either.

>> **Always shop around.** Rates vary tremendously among insurers.

>> **Take care of your health.** Exercise at least a few times per week and eat healthfully. Lose and keep off that extra weight if you're now overweight. You only get one body and one life, so take care of it.

Getting Affordable and Quality Professional Advice

Although your life may be relatively simple, sometimes you may have to deal with new challenges, and you may benefit from a seasoned pro at your side. Tax, legal, business, and financial advisors can be worth more than their expense if they know what they're doing and you pay a reasonable fee. Here's how to get the most out of your spending when you hire advisors:

- **>> Get educated first.** How can you possibly evaluate an expert on a certain topic if you don't know much about the topic yourself? Published and software-based resources can be useful, low-cost alternatives and supplements to hiring professionals.

- **>> Use professionals only when needed — not constantly.** Most people most of the time should hire a professional only on an as-needed basis. But be wary of professionals who create or perpetuate work and have conflicts of interest with their recommendations.

- **>> Scrutinize and interview thoroughly before hiring.** Do background research to evaluate each prospective advisor's strengths and biases. Be sure to check references and conduct an internet search to see what you can find out about the person. Check regulatory associations in your state for any citations or actions taken against an advisor. The U.S. Securities and Exchange Commission provides an advisory check service at https://adviserinfo.sec.gov.

Handling Healthcare Expenses

When you're in good health, you usually don't give much thought to healthcare expenses and health insurance. But you have health insurance for a reason, and unfortunately, the cost of healthcare continues to rise faster than the overall rate of inflation. Use these tips to protect yourself:

- **>> Shop around for health insurance and healthcare.** Many different plan designs are available with a wide variation in costs. Also, like any other profession, medical providers have a profit motive, so they may recommend something that isn't your best option, including extra testing that you may not need or benefit from.

REMEMBER

Don't take any one physician's advice as gospel. Always get a second opinion for any proposed surgery.

>> **Examine your employer's benefit plans.** Take advantage of being able to put away a portion of your income before taxes to pay for out-of-pocket healthcare expenses, especially in health savings accounts.

>> **Investigate alternative medicine and tread carefully.** Alternative medicine's focus on preventive care and treatment of the whole body or person are pluses.

WARNING

Just keep your antenna up for pie-in-the-sky promises and charlatans out to empty your wallet. Check with your physician before trying any alternatives.

>> **Kick your addictions.** Smoking, alcohol, drugs, and gambling can cost you financially and emotionally. Be honest with yourself about the damage that excesses in these areas are causing in your life and take action now to get on a healthier path. Seek support groups and 12-step programs in your area for sustained recovery.

If you find yourself in medical debt, head to Chapter 11 for help.

2

Making Sense of Credit Reporting and Scoring

Uncover the differences between FICO and VantageScore.

Order free copies of your credit reports from the big-three credit bureaus.

Understand whether credit monitoring is worth your hard-earned money.

Chapter **6**

Discovering How Credit Reporting Works

ave you ever looked at your credit report? We ask that question often. Once in a while we're surprised when a person tells us they have. Occasionally, we get a blank stare because it's something that never occurred to them. Most of the time, though, they shake their head and either say they don't want to look because they're afraid, or they just don't care because they don't use credit. That's a huge financial mistake. There are a lot of reasons to care about what's in your credit report and no reason at all to be afraid to check it.

Your credit history doesn't just come into play when you want to borrow money. Landlords, insurers, and even employers review credit reports. They use the information from your credit report to make decisions about whether you get a loan, an apartment, a car, and maybe even a job. A poor credit history can cost you thousands of dollars and cause you to miss opportunities you never even knew you had.

Credit reports sound mysterious and confusing, but they really aren't. Your credit report can be a powerful financial tool. You can know exactly what lenders, landlords, utility companies, and even your cellphone provider will see before you ever apply. Anytime lenders and others use your report to determine your credit risk — and especially in a tight credit market — knowing what they'll see is important. Your credit report and credit scores, calculated using the information from the report, can make a big difference in whether you qualify for a loan and how much you pay in interest or other terms of the loan. They can also make a difference in how much you pay for your auto and homeowner's/renter's insurance.

This chapter helps you understand why you need to take ownership of your credit reports and scores, what they really are, and where they come from.

TIP

After you're up to speed on credit reports and scores, challenge your friends to the credit score quiz found at www. creditscorequiz.org. *Hint:* This quiz was co-authored by VantageScore and the Consumer Federation of America.

Grasping the Importance of Your Credit Report

Wondering where all the data in your credit history comes from? Despite what you may have heard, there's nothing nefarious afoot. It may be a shock, but you're the first source of information that goes into your credit report. When you fill out an application with a bank, credit card provider, cellphone company, or landlord, the identifying information you provide is the first thing that goes in your credit report. After that, the lenders and other businesses you have accounts with will report your payments — or lack thereof — to the credit reporting companies. Chances are, they're reporting your financial transactions to all three major credit bureaus (Equifax, Experian, and TransUnion) and potentially other specialty bureaus that store information.

When you pay your car payment, mortgage payment, and credit card bill each month, your creditors report your payment history to the credit bureaus. If you miss a payment, your creditor reports that as well. Creditors review the information in your credit report or other specialty reports to determine the terms they may offer you for a credit card, loan, apartment, or insurance policy. So do utility companies and cellphone providers. A good credit history may result in lower security deposits to the utility company, and it will definitely help you get the coolest new mobile device.

Clearly, what you don't know *can* hurt you. You can't report your own credit history to the bureaus (although that may be changing a bit — see the later section "Revealing the facts about your financial transactions"), but you *can* be knowledgeable about what your credit report says and anticipate how it may influence others as you try to negotiate your way through the financial universe. You *can* head off situations that could cost you thousands of dollars or deny you opportunities. And you *can* catch inaccuracies on your report (a fairly common situation) and correct them.

TIP

You have no excuse for not knowing what's in your credit report because you can get a free copy of your report annually from each of the three credit bureaus. Getting the information is fast and easy. Simply visit www.annualcreditreport.com or call 877-322-8228 to order your reports.

What Is a Credit Report, Exactly?

REMEMBER

In its most basic sense, your credit report is your financial life history — as far as debts are concerned. Credit reporting companies collect information about your debts and compile it into a file that they then share (as allowed by the law — see Chapter 7) with your lenders or other businesses. Lenders and other businesses use the information as one part of making a decision about your application. There are three national credit reporting companies:

>> **Equifax:** www.equifax.com; 800-685-1111

>> **Experian:** www.experian.com; 866-200-6020

>> **TransUnion:** www.transunion.com; 800-888-4213

The name of the law that governs them — the Fair Credit Reporting Act (FCRA) — is a bit misleading. In fact, it regulates all consumer reporting agencies in addition to the credit bureaus. In addition to the three national credit bureaus, there are also 20 or more specialty consumer reporting agencies, which collect other kinds of information, like whether you've bounced a check or made insurance claims (see Chapter 7).

You can rest assured that your rights are protected in the reporting process because of the FCRA and the Fair and Accurate Credit Transactions Act (the FACT Act or FACTA) that amended it.

TIP

You can find more details on the FCRA and the FACT Act in Chapter 3. To read the FCRA, go to www.ftc.gov/system/files/documents/statutes/fair-credit-reporting-act/545a_fair-credit-reporting-act-0918.pdf; to read the FACT Act, go to www.congress.gov/108/plaws/publ159/PLAW-108publ159.pdf.

The following sections explain what your credit report reveals about your financial relationships — specifically your debts.

Revealing the facts about your financial transactions

Credit reporting has actually been around since the late 1800s. Back then, a person went from business to business in the town and asked merchants about how their customers managed their credit. It was literally the Wild West. Observations and opinions like, "He won't pay, but his father will," and "I won't give him store credit because he drinks too much," could be in the notes. That's in the far, far distant past.

Today, the information in your credit report is specific, factual, and limited to your financial transactions. Either the bill was paid on time, or it wasn't. That objectivity can empower you if you manage your finances well. Keep making your payments on time and don't take on too much debt, and lenders will flock to you asking for your business. On the other hand, they'll also see any signs of trouble very quickly. If you miss even a single payment, it can feel like they disappeared like a drop of water on the hottest day in August in Death Valley. Poof, they're gone.

In truth, credit reports are really pretty simple. All you have to know is that everything in your credit report is debt related. The following sections cover what you'll see when you get your credit report.

TIP

Credit reports are easy to read and are constantly being improved. Each of the three major credit-reporting agencies reports your information in its own unique format. The credit-reporting agencies compete with one another for business, so they have to differentiate their products. (Chapter 7 highlights the differences in each agency's presentation.) You can view sample credit reports from each of the three major credit-reporting bureaus at www.dummies.com/go/creditrepairkitfd5e (click Downloads, click the Download link, double-click the file downloaded to your computer, and look in the Chapter 13 folder).

Personal identification information

This info includes your name, Social Security number, date of birth, addresses (present and past), and a list of employers. There are a couple of things to understand about identification information:

>> Any variations of your name, Social Security number, and address reported to the bureaus will also be shown. Those aren't mistakes. They're listed so you have a complete record of what lenders are telling them is in their records. For example, if your name is Robert Smith and you also apply as Bob, you'll see both listed.

TIP

Be sure to check any variations closely. They could indicate you're a fraud victim and help you take action quickly.

>> The list of employers is not an employment history. The bureaus list the names of employers included in your credit applications. If you don't apply for new credit for a long time and change jobs several times, you may not see all your employers in the list. That's okay. The list is used as an additional identifier and doesn't affect scores or lending decisions in any way.

Be consistent with your personal information, especially how you spell your name and address. The credit bureaus maintain credit reports on more than 220 million people, and you aren't the only person with your name. Being consistent is a huge help in ensuring your credit information is matched correctly to you and not someone else. Contrary to common myth, the credit bureaus don't just match your information to your Social Security number. They use all the information reported to them to match your credit report details. Another common myth is that you have to have a Social Security number to have a credit report. In fact, you don't. If a lender opens an account without requiring a Social Security number and reports it, you'll have a credit report the bureaus would match to all the other information the lender provided.

Because the bureaus match to all the identifying information, changing your name won't cause a new report to be created. For example, if you're a woman and you take your husband's name when you get married, your files should be automatically updated when you get a reissued credit card or a loan in your new name.

Public record information

Here's a bit of good news. All public records, with the exception of bankruptcy, have been removed from credit reports. Civil judgments, tax liens, and other fines have been removed. That doesn't mean they won't be part of other specialty consumer reports (see Chapter 7), but they won't be in your credit report.

Collection activity

If you've had accounts sent to collection agencies for handling, your credit report contains that info.

Information about each credit account (or trade line), whether open or closed

Your credit report includes details on all your credit accounts, including

>> Type of account (such as a mortgage, installment, or revolving account). *Revolving* is a fancy word for credit card. You can carry the balance, or revolve it, from one month to the next.

>> Your account association. Whether the account is *individual* (just in your name) or *joint* (shared equally with another person), as well as whether you're a cosigner or authorized user. How you're associated with the account is very important because it's directly related to your responsibility for the debt. If you're an individual, joint account holder, or a cosigner, you're responsible for paying the whole debt, even if the other person doesn't pay his share. Authorized users have permission to use an account, but they aren't responsible for paying any of the debt.

>> The principle amount. How much the loan was at first. This applies to installment loans.

>> Your credit limit. The maximum amount you can charge on a credit card.

>> The remaining balance (for installment loans) or current balance (for credit cards) on the account.

>> Your monthly payment. This may be estimated, so it may not match exactly but should be close.

>> The account status. This indicates things like the account is open and active, paid in full, settled, or charged off as a loss.

>> Who you owe. The account entry will show the name of the creditor or collection agency.

>> Your payment history (whether you've paid on time or been late). This is by far the most important information in your credit report.

A list of companies that have requested your credit file for the purpose of granting credit

When your credit report is requested, a record of that request, called an *inquiry*, is added. There are two types of inquiries:

» *Soft inquiries* are made for promotional purposes (for instance, when a credit card issuer wants to send you an offer). They also include getting your own report, reviews by your existing lenders, and reports requested for employment or insurance purposes. These inquiries don't appear on the version of your credit report that lenders see, but they do appear on the copy that you get. Because only you see them, they don't affect credit scores or lending decisions.

» *Hard inquiries* are added in response to your applications for new credit. These inquiries *do* appear on the lender's copy of your credit report. They indicate you may have a new debt that doesn't show on your report yet, so they represent a bit of risk at first. New accounts are added at the end of the first billing cycle (about 30 days after it's opened). At that point, the inquiry will no longer have any meaningful impact on your credit scores.

An optional message or ten from you

You can add a message that explains any extenuating circumstances for your report overall or for any specific account in your report. One message may be enough, but if you have different explanations for more than one account, you can add individual messages to specific trade lines.

Maybe your utility, telecom, and rent payments

A relatively new development in credit reporting is the ability to have your positive cellphone, utility (natural gas, water, electricity), and rent payments added to your report. Services are emerging that enable you to give permission for credit bureaus to check your bank account or credit card statement monthly for your payment and add it to your credit report. For a number of years, landlords have been able to report your positive rent payments to credit bureaus if the landlord agrees to do so on your behalf, but you have to ask first.

TIP

Services like Experian Boost (www.experian.com/boost) are free, but they require you to enroll in a service and give permission to access your accounts. Many people report that their scores get better after enrolling in these programs, so they may help give your scores a step up, or they may not. They also require you to share information. Be sure you're comfortable doing so. If not, or if they don't help your scores, you may not want to use them. It's your choice.

Knowing what's not in a credit report

TIP

This may come as a shock, but credit scores are not part of a credit report. You can purchase a credit score and an explanation of it when you request your free annual report. You can also get free credit scores from a number of sources. Here are a few things to know when you request your score:

>> **The number won't match the one your lender has, but that's okay.** The score will be different depending on which one is used to calculate the number, the scale of the scoring system (we once saw a score with a scale from 75 to 108, but most are 300 to 850 today), the credit bureau information that was used, and when the score was calculated. Information from each bureau can be a bit different, and if something has changed between the time you got your score and the lender got theirs, the number could change, too. Even if the numbers are very different, they almost certainly mean the same thing in terms of risk, and that's what counts.

>> **Make sure you get a list of the risk factors that affected your score.** Although the numbers can be very different, the risk factors tend to be very consistent. They tell you what information from your personal credit report most affected the calculation. By comparing the factors to your report, you can begin to address the biggest issues that are dragging the number down.

>> **Work on the risk factors, and all your scores will get better.** The number gives you a sense of where you stand. The risk factors give you the information you need to change the number. Work on those factors and all your scores will get better.

Among the list of items also *not* included in your credit report are your lifestyle choices, religion, national origin, political affiliation, sexual preferences, medical history, friends, and relatives. In addition, the three major credit-reporting agencies don't collect or transmit data about your assets, including your income, checking or savings accounts, or brokerage accounts. How much money you have in the bank doesn't mean you'll use it to pay your debts. Credit reports and scores look at whether you pay your debts regardless of the assets you have. Believe it or not, there are many rich deadbeats out there.

Your reports also do not include business accounts (unless you're on record as being personally liable for the debt), bankruptcies that are more than ten years old, charge-offs or debts placed for collection that are more than seven years old, or your credit score. It's worth repeating that although your credit score is generated based on information in your credit report, it's not part of the report itself. (Find out more about credit scores later in this chapter.)

Providing insight into your character

Many entities use your credit report to predict your potential behavior in other areas of your life. Whether we like it or not, people are creatures of habit. The decisions you make and actions you take in one part of your life give insight into how you'll act in other parts of your life. It's why the fact that having a history of making credit card payments late suggests to a prospective landlord that you may be late with your rent, too. A home foreclosure in your file may indicate that you take on more than you can handle or that you're just one unlucky duck.

This financial snapshot, which brings into focus the details of your spending and borrowing, also paints a *bigger* picture of two important factors that are critical to employers, landlords, lenders, and others:

>> **Whether you keep your financial promises:** Your credit history is an indicator of whether you follow through with your financial commitments, a characteristic that's important to most people, whether they're looking for a reliable worker, a responsible nanny, a dependable renter, or even a faithful mate ("What's your score?" may be replacing "What's your sign?" as a pickup line!). Needless to say, a person or company that's considering extending you a loan, apartment lease, insurance policy, or job (although employers don't get scores) wants to know the same.

>> **Whether you fulfill your obligations in a timely manner:** Following through with your obligations in a timely manner is the other half of the credit-reporting equation. Tight lending standards make a history of past failures to pay on time harder to accept for lenders who can't afford any more defaults.

WARNING

In the lending business, the more overdue the payment, the more likely it won't be paid in full — or paid at all. That's why, as you get further behind in your payments, lenders become more anxious about collecting the amount you owe. In fact, if you're sufficiently delinquent, the lender may want you to pay back the entire amount at once rather than as originally scheduled. So the longer you take to do what you promised, the more it costs you and the more damage you do to your credit history and credit score.

The Negatives and Positives of Credit Reporting

Whether you're new to the world of credit or you're an experienced borrower, you may be mesmerized by the amount of information on your credit report. In simplest terms, it all falls into one of two categories: negative (information that indicates you may be a financial risk) and positive (information that makes lenders want to throw money at you, or at least not turn you down for a loan). The following sections zero in on the differences between the two so that you can focus on what matters and let go of what doesn't.

The negatives

This may come as a surprise, but you aren't perfect. And neither is your credit report. The good news is that you don't need a flawless credit report to qualify for financial products and services at competitive rates and terms. Perfection is always a good aspiration, but it's never a goal. When it comes to credit, it just needs to be good enough. Here are the answers to some common questions about the negative data found on the vast majority of Americans' credit reports:

>> **How long do bad marks stick around?** The rule of thumb is seven years, although there are a few exceptions, and when that clock starts depends on the information you're looking at. Late payments remain for seven years from the date of the missed payment. If you never catch up after missing the first payment, the charged-off account and any subsequent collections are deleted seven years from that first payment. It's called the *original delinquency date,* and it's the most important date most people have in their credit report.

Chapter 13 bankruptcy public records also remain for seven years, but from the filing date of the bankruptcy. You get a bit of a break because you pay off part of the debt. Chapter 7 bankruptcy stays ten years from the filing date because you don't repay any of the debt. Even though the negative information is out there for a long time, as the months and years roll by, the information becomes less important to your credit profile. For example, most creditors aren't concerned by the fact that you were late in paying a credit card bill one time three years ago, if everything else has gone well since.

>> **Just how much does one mistake cost you when it comes to your credit report?** That depends on the mistake and on the rest of the items on your report that make up your credit history. One late payment in a long, otherwise clean history will have less impact than one that

is among many late accounts. A default on a credit card is less serious than a mortgage default, although both are huge problems.

Lenders use credit scores to analyze the information in your credit report and evaluate the risk of lending to you. A *credit score* is a number that's calculated using the information from your credit report. Credit score formulas are developed by studying the information from millions of past credit reports and identifying patterns that indicate repayment risk. The number is simply a way to objectively indicate to the lender the likelihood a person won't repay as agreed. (Check out the later section "Cracking credit score components" for more info on credit scores.)

>> **How do those who view your report interpret bad marks?** Think of it this way: Say you have a new neighbor who comes over and asks to borrow your lawnmower. Because you want to establish a good relationship, you say yes. A week goes by and your grass needs mowed, but he hasn't brought the lawnmower back. So, you call and ask for it. The new neighbor promises to get it back to you in a few days. Another week goes by and no mower, so you go knock on his door and demand it back. When you pull the mower out of his garage, it's broken and you're stuck buying a new one. The next day, your other neighbor calls and says the guy wants to borrow *her* mower now. She knows you lent the guy yours and asks what you think. So, you share your experience for her to consider in her decision.

That's essentially how lenders use credit reports and scores. In business, as in friendship, trust and keeping promises are keys to success. Basically, any delinquencies or charge-offs count against you in a big way when it comes to earning the lender's trust and getting approved. However, a creditor tends to look at your bill payments in the creditor's specific area as most important. A car lender, for example, scrutinizes your car payment history more closely than a credit card issuer does. Other, less important concerns include how much you've used (maxing out your credit cards is second only to missing payments) and how much credit you have available (too much isn't a huge factor, but it can ding you).

Some unscrupulous lenders may claim negative information from your distant past as a reason to put you into a higher-cost (and potentially more profitable for them) loan, even though you may qualify for a less-expensive one. The scenario can go something like this: You're looking for a loan for a car or some similar big-ticket item. The lender you contact says they reviewed your credit report and offers you a loan at terms that are "a great deal considering your credit history." Translated, this means that the lender is charging you a higher-than-market rate because of your imperfect credit report, assuming you haven't checked them. Knowing your credit history and score can empower you to call their bluff and save you money.

This scenario is less likely today because the law requires the lender to tell you if you don't get the best rates or terms. If a lender offers you a loan at less than the best terms or denies you a loan, the lender must provide you with and *adverse action notice*, which must include an explanation of why you were denied or didn't get the best terms. It also must include the credit score the lender used and an explanation of that score, along with how your score compares to other U.S. consumers. You're also entitled to a free copy of your credit report from the credit reporting company that was used to obtain that report.

The positives

Positive information — the good stuff that everyone likes to see — stays on your report for quite a while. In fact, some positive data may remain on your report for 10, 20, or 30 years, maybe even longer depending on each bureau's policy and whether you keep your account open.

The more positive information you have in your credit files, the less effect a single negative item has on your ability to get the credit you need. So, if you're an experienced credit user with a long credit history, one missed payment will cause your score to drop, but you'll probably still be able to qualify if you apply. If, however, you're a young person or a new immigrant with only a few trade lines and a few months of credit history, a situation that's sometimes called a *thin file*, a negative item has a much larger effect because you have fewer positive items to balance things out. For pointers on beefing up (or just plain starting) your credit history, flip to Chapter 12.

Your Credit Report's Numerical Offspring: The Credit Score

Your credit score is typically a three-digit number that plays a vital role in a good portion of your financial life, for better or for worse. But where did this all-important number come from?

Starting back in the 1950s, some companies, including FICO (formerly known as Fair Isaac Corporation) and more recently VantageScore, began to model credit data in hopes of predicting payment behavior. A *model* is a series of formulas based on some basic assumptions to make predictions about future behavior. A weatherperson uses models to predict the weather. Credit scoring companies use models to predict whether a person will pay as agreed. The credit folks are much more accurate because people are naturally far more predictable.

If you have a spouse or partner, he probably knows what you're thinking before you start to think it. He's not reading your mind. He's just learned your habits and behaviors over the years. Credit scores predict the likelihood that someone will not meet their obligations in much the same way. They study behavior and identify predictable patterns.

You only have three credit reports, but there are hundreds of different credit scores. Lenders decide which scores they're going to use to evaluate your credit history. They do that in several ways:

>> They may get your credit report and then calculate a score.

>> They may have a third party get your credit reports, combine it with other information, calculate scores, and then send the results to them.

>> In many cases, many cases, the lender has the credit bureaus route your report through a score they pick as the report is being sent to them. They get the report and score at the same time, which makes it look like the score is part of the report, even though it isn't. In reality, the credit report is provided by the credit bureau. The score is proprietary to the company that developed it.

Today, there are two predominant credit scoring companies, FICO and VantageScore. The following sections take a closer look at what goes into the scores from those two companies to help you understand their components and ensure that your credit score is the best it can be.

REMEMBER

Here's the secret: There isn't one. You only have to do two things to have great credit scores: Pay your bills on time every time and keep your balances on your credit cards as low as possible. Everything else builds on those two things no matter what score is use.

Cracking credit score components

In order to have a credit score, you need to have at least one account open and reporting. FICO requires at least one account to be open for at least six months and for the account to have been updated in the last six months. In some cases, VantageScore can calculate a score after just one month of activity (they don't say it will be a good score), but it usually requires the account to be open for at least three months. For those who have been out of the credit market for a while, VantageScore can generate a score using data that is up to 24 months old. Most scoring systems are now evolving to include rent, utility, and cellphone history in the calculation, although not all do, yet. You can find out more about both main types of scores in the next sections.

REMEMBER

Although having no credit history makes it difficult to get credit initially, building credit for the first time is a lot easier than repairing a bad credit history.

What makes up a FICO score?

FICO scores are the most widely recognized scores. The brand is a bit like saying Kleenex instead of tissue. Its best-known scores have a scale from 300 to 850, but not all of them do. If you're buying a car, for example, the scale for FICO Auto Scores goes to 900. The higher the number, the better the credit rating and the better the terms you get when looking for your next loan or credit card. Your FICO score, and other scores, represent your credit history at the moment it is calculated. A new score is calculated each time your credit report is requested. The scores change over time, reflecting changes in your credit history.

Credit scores, including those from FICO, can take into account hundreds of factors when building your score. The importance of each factor is dependent on the other factors, the volume of data, and the length of your history. Your FICO score is made up of five components:

REMEMBER

>> **Payment history (35 percent):** Payment history is the most significant factor when determining whether you're a good credit risk. This category includes the number and severity of any late payments (30 days, 60 days, 90 days late or more), the amount past due, and whether you eventually repaid the accounts as agreed. The more late payments and the further past due they become, the lower your score.

>> **Amounts owed (30 percent):** The amount you owe is the next most important factor in your credit score. This category focuses almost entirely on the balances of your credit cards compared to your credit limit, or your *balance-to-limit ratio*. In the credit industry, that's called the *utilization rate*. The lower your utilization rate, the better your scores will be.

Ideally, you should pay your balances in full each month. Leaving a balance doesn't help your scores. It just means you'll have to pay interest on what's left, which costs you money. To a much lesser degree, this category includes the total amount you owe on all your debts, the amount you owe by account type (such as revolving or installment, which for FICO includes mortgage debt), and the number of accounts on which you're carrying a balance.

>> **Length of credit history (15 percent):** The number of years you've been using credit and the type of accounts you have also influence your score. Accounts that have been open for at least two years help increase your score.

>> **Credit mix (10 percent):** The mix of credit accounts is a part of each of the other factors. Also, a lender is likely to give greater weight to your performance on its type of loan, meaning that a credit card issuer looks at your experience with other cards more closely and a mortgage lender pays closer attention to how you pay mortgages or secured loans. The credit scores they use are often industry specific and predict risk for a certain type of loan or type of lender. An ideal mix has a positive credit history with a variety of different types of credit, such as installment and revolving

credit lines. That mix will grow with time — you can't create it overnight.

>> **New credit (10 percent):** When you apply for new credit or ask for a raise in your credit line, the creditor makes an inquiry into your credit report. A high number of inquiries in a short time has a negative effect on your credit score. The reasoning is that if you apply for several accounts at the same time and get approved for them, you may not be able to afford your new debt load.

What makes up a VantageScore?

VantageScore has been around since 2006. It now uses the same score range as traditional FICO scores: 300 to 850. As with FICO scores, the higher the number, the better the score. Your VantageScore is made up of four components. VantageScore does not assign percentages to each component. The following categories are listed in order from most important to least:

>> **Payment history (extremely influential):** Paying on time (satisfactory), paying late (delinquent), or not paying at all (charge-off) shows up here. Paying your bills on time every time builds your credit mix and affects credit usage. Pay your bills on time in order to have good credit scores.

>> **Total credit usage, balance, and available credit (highly influential):** This category represents your total utilization rate. To calculate your total utilization rate, add up all your credit card balances and divide the total by the sum of your credit limits. The lower, the better. VantageScore recommends keeping revolving balances under 30 percent of credit limits.

>> **Credit mix and experience (highly influential):** A history with mixed types of credit (mortgage, car loan, credit cards, retail stores, and so on) is best. The mix of credit you use usually grows over time. People with higher scores generally have a longer history of open accounts with good payment history. The longer your credit history, the better it is for your credit scores. Establishing credit early in life is important.

>> **New accounts opened (moderately influential):** This category includes the number of recently opened credit accounts and all new inquiries. Be careful not to open too many new accounts in a short period of time.

If you're just beginning to build credit, be patient. It'll take time for your scores to improve. To figure out what you need to do to help make things go a bit faster, get your credit report, a score, and the risk factors that are most affecting it. You can use the factors to identify what steps you need to take to make all your scores better. As you can see in these categories, the two most important are paying your bills on time, every time, and keeping your credit card balances as low as possible.

Also, ask your lender if they have other tools they can use if you lack a sufficient traditional credit history. For example, some lenders can apply a FICO Expansion Score, which draws from other data sources to help verify that you're a good credit risk.

For examples of ways to start a credit history, including using a secured card or a passbook loan, check out Chapter 12.

There is more to a credit decision than score component weightings. Consider the weighting factors as directional indicators rather than a guarantee of great credit rates and terms.

The reasoning behind risk factors

When you see your credit score for the first time, you may say: "They must be wrong; my credit is better than that!" If so, you're not alone. As a result, the two scoring companies, FICO and VantageScore, have developed risk factors and brief statements that accompany them to help you know what went wrong with your credit that resulted in your particular credit score.

VantageScore set up an online resource, www.reasoncode.org, that goes into more depth than the simple risk factors and corresponding statements that you get with your score by providing details about what each risk factor means in plain English. Features of ReasonCode.org include

>> A primer on what reason codes are and how they are used

>> Searchable and interactive reason code definitions and explanations

>> A glossary of common reason code terms

See Chapter 7 for additional information about risk factor statements.

TECHNICAL STUFF

Credit scoring companies are constantly studying the economy, market, and consumer behaviors. They regularly introduce updates to their scores to reflect changes in consumer behavior, and to incorporate new information. From time to time, they introduce scores that incorporate new technology that can help lenders better predict risk and help people gain access to lower-cost credit. It can take many years for lenders to adopt new scores. Validating that the scores will work for them and incorporating them into their underwriting systems is a complex and expensive process. As a result, you may not see these new scores right away.

ALLOWING FOR ACTS OF GOD

Sometimes things happen to people that are so far beyond their control that even lenders don't want to hold them responsible. We put what we call acts of God in this category. Things like hurricanes, earthquakes, fires, and pandemics affect large portions of the population. When those kinds of things happen, lenders may indicate that an account belongs to a natural disaster victim when reporting account activity to the credit bureaus. Reporting an account with the natural disaster reporting code means that the account will not have a negative effect on your credit scores. In most cases, the lender will also work with you to arrange a special payment accommodation, such as forbearance or deferment. Doing so will let you temporarily stop making payments so you can deal with the aftermath of the disaster.

The disaster codes made available by the credit bureaus, along with the payment accommodation by the lender will both appear in your credit report. The credit scoring systems will then either ignore the accounts or treat them differently. No new negative information will be added to your reports while your accounts are in forbearance or deferment. But catching up on late payments, reducing your credit card balances, or making other positive changes will still be shown and can help your credit scores.

Chapter **7**

Understanding Credit Reports and Scores

nformation in your credit report plays an important role in a growing number of financial decisions. Everything from getting a loan or credit card to qualifying for the best insurance rates can involve a credit report. If you've had money problems, it can seem as if the system is being used against you. But at its most basic level, that's what credit reporting is helping lenders do: Identify when someone has a greater chance of not fulfilling his financial obligations and when there is a strong chance he will.

When you understand how credit reports work, you can control what lenders and others see in your report. And, in a way, that gives you control over the decisions they make.

Credit information collected about you is contained in your credit reports from the three major credit bureaus. Getting copies of those reports and reviewing the information in them is as easy as it is important, and doing so shows you exactly what most people or programs evaluating your credit see.

This chapter explains how to get your credit report. It walks you through the process of reviewing your credit report from each of the three major credit-reporting bureaus and explains how to make sense of what's in them. It also explains how you can dispute any information you find in your reports that you believe is inaccurate.

Credit scores are also a part of the credit-reporting picture, although they aren't part of credit reports. This chapter shares how to obtain and make sense of your scores. By the time you're done reading this chapter, you'll be armed with the information you need to discover exactly how potential employers, lenders, landlords, and insurance agents see you when viewing you through the lens of your credit history.

Getting Copies of Your Credit Reports

The three main collectors of credit information in the credit industry today are Equifax, Experian, and TransUnion. These major credit bureaus are basically huge databases of information. (Chapter 6 reveals where all that information comes from.)

Given the enormous amounts of data that flow into and out of the bureaus every month, it's important to know what's there, or isn't, and to be sure it's all correct. Getting copies of your credit reports from the three credit bureaus to make sure that the information in your files is a true representation of your credit use is essential. By reviewing your reports, you'll also know if someone has stolen your identity and used it in an effort to establish fraudulent credit accounts.

REMEMBER

Any incorrect information included in your credit report has the potential to be very costly to you. For example, erroneous info could mean that you don't get the loans or terms you want or that you have to pay a much higher interest rate than you should have to pay. Lenders are not required to report to all three of the credit bureaus, so checking your credit report from just one bureau isn't good enough. The information that Equifax has may be slightly different from the information that Experian has, and the information that Experian has may be slightly different from the information that TransUnion has. Also, you can have a perfectly clean report with one bureau while another report contains some negative items in error.

The good news is that you don't have to do much heavy lifting to get your hands on all your credit reports thanks to the Fair and Accurate Credit Transactions Act (commonly referred to as the FACT Act or FACTA). This act entitles every American to at least one free credit report from each of the three bureaus every 12 months. You're also entitled to an additional free report from each of the bureaus if you

>> Were denied credit in the last 60 days from the credit bureau used by the lender.

>> Are unemployed and planning to seek employment in the next 60 days

>> Are on welfare

>> Are a victim of fraud or identity theft and request an initial security alert, also called a *fraud alert*, be added to your credit reports

If none of the above applies to you, you're still in luck! The three national credit reporting agencies — Equifax, Experian, and TransUnion — have permanently extended their program that lets you check your credit report at each of the agencies once a week for free.

REMEMBER

If you are a victim of fraud or identity theft, report it to the police and add a victim statement to your credit report. If you do so, you'll qualify for additional free reports.

Several states also provide for additional free credit reports each year (or weekly). Check with your state's attorney general to find out whether you qualify.

Finally, from time to time, credit card issuers offer free peeks at your credit reports as do the bureaus themselves. During the COVID-19 pandemic, the bureaus allowed free credit reports weekly.

The following sections explain how to get your reports, what kind of information you need to provide, what to watch out for, and when you should check your reports.

Where to get your reports

To obtain your one free credit report from each of the three major credit bureaus each year, simply visit the website www. annualcreditreport.com. Or, if you prefer, you can request copies by phone or mail:

Annual Credit Report Request Service

P.O. Box 105281

Atlanta, GA 30348-5281

877-322-8228

TIP

You need to fill out a request form if you use the mail to get your free copies from the central source. The request credit file form is included in the downloads available at www.dummies.com/go/creditrepairkitfd5e.

WARNING

Many different websites with similar-sounding names have cropped up since the central source for free credit reports was established. These sites advertise free credit reports, but the fine print is that your free report costs you something because you must purchase another product or service to receive it. You shouldn't have to purchase anything to get your free copies. If the site requires you to provide payment information, you're on the wrong site.

Note that your credit score isn't provided with your free annual credit reports when you use www.annualcreditreport.com. You'll be "offered an opportunity" to purchase your score after you get your free report. Credit scores are available free from a number of sources as well.

To request a report directly from the credit bureaus, you can get things started with a phone call, a visit to the bureau's website, or through the mail. Here's the contact information for the three major credit-reporting bureaus:

» **Equifax,** P.O. Box 740241, Atlanta, GA 30374; 800-685-1111; www.equifax.com

» **Experian,** P.O. Box 2104, Allen, TX 75013-2104; 888-397-3742; www.experian.com

» **TransUnion,** 2 Baldwin Place, P.O. Box 1000, Chester, PA 19022; 800-888-4213; www.transunion.com

When you order your credit report, the bureaus will offer to sell you a credit score as well. See the later section "Ordering your score" for more information.

What you need to provide

Whether you contact a credit bureau directly to get a copy of your report or you go through the free central source to get all three at once (see the preceding section), you need to provide information that helps the bureaus verify you are who you claim to be. So be ready to give all the information you've always been told not to give to a stranger over the phone or internet. In this one case, it's okay. The goal is to protect you from fraud and ensure your credit information isn't sent to the wrong person.

REMEMBER

The information requested can vary a bit from one bureau to the next, but the following is a list of some information you're likely to be asked for:

» Your full name

» Your current and former addresses

» Your birth date

» Your Social Security number

You'll likely also be asked a series of questions to further verify your identity. These questions can include things like what lender your mortgage is with, if you've ever had a car loan with a given company, the name of a previous employer, and other things that only you should know. The questions are typically based on your credit history and other information sources. They're sometimes called "out of wallet" questions, because the answers are not something an identity thief would know by stealing your purse or wallet.

When to get copies of your credit reports

You're entitled to a free copy of your credit report from each of the big-three credit bureaus once a year, and you should review them at least that often.

TIP

If you don't have any issues with fraud or other reasons we discuss in this section, you can get a report from one of the three bureaus every four months, rotating through the bureaus so that you have three separate chances, at evenly spaced intervals, to see whether something unexpected has shown up. To make it easy to remember when to reorder each report, consider picking three times during the year that stand out and are roughly four months apart. Consider New Year's Day, Fourth of July, and Halloween, for example.

There are several exceptions to the rule, though. You should check your reports more often if

>> You believe that a problem may be lurking as a result of identity theft.

>> You believe there may be an error in one or more of your reports.

>> You're going to be submitting a major credit application in the next six months or so.

In these cases, get all three reports at once in addition to your normal free annual report rotation.

Get copies of your reports from all three bureaus at the same time when you're planning to

>> Buy or lease a car

>> Buy or rent a house or an apartment

>> Refinance a mortgage

>> Apply for a job

>> Be up for a promotion

>> Apply for a professional license (such as to sell securities or insurance)

>> Apply for a security clearance

>> Join the military

>> Get married or divorced

>> Switch insurance companies or buy new insurance

WARNING

Real estate closings can be delayed, mortgage rates can go up, and job opportunities can be lost if your credit report contains incorrect negative information. So, give yourself time to correct your reports before going forward with your plans. Consider getting your reports a minimum of three months and up to six months in advance of your plans so that you have time to dispute any errors or fraudulent account information. As you get within a month or two of applying for credit, insurance, or a job, consider getting copies of your reports again to be sure everything is in order.

WHO ELSE HAS ACCESS TO YOUR REPORT?

Anyone can get a copy of your credit report if the person has a *permissible purpose* as defined under federal law — in other words, a valid business reason to review your report. You don't have to give your permission for a report to be accessed if the business has a permissible purpose, although you almost always provide it when you apply for credit. The permission is often buried in the fine print of a credit card application. The one exception is for employment purposes: If an employer wants to check your credit report, they have to first get your written permission on a separate permission form from your application.

What counts as a permissible purpose under the law? Here are some examples:

● **Getting your own report:** It may go without saying, but we're going to say it anyway. You can get a copy of your own report as often as you like. Doing so will not hurt your credit scores or

(continued)

(continued)

affect your ability to get credit. Don't be afraid to look at your own credit report. You can't do anything to make it better until you know what's in it.

- **Apartment rental:** It only makes sense that a landlord would want to know whether you're likely to pay your rent on time before giving you the keys to a piece of real estate. For that reason, most rental applications ask for permission to access your credit report. It stands to reason that if you pay your other bills on time, you'll probably pay your rent on time, too. Your credit report is often included in a *tenant screening report* that also includes any tenant history information that may be available from sources other than the credit bureaus. A couple of examples include MyRental (www.myrental.com) and RentPrep (www.rentprep.com).

- **Credit approval:** When you apply for credit (whether you're filling out a credit card application or applying for a car loan, student loan, or mortgage), creditors and lenders have the right to get a copy of your credit report. They need to know whether you have a history of defaulting on loans or whether you're overextended on credit already and about to miss your next payment.

- **Court order or subpoena:** If a court orders you to appear before the court or subpoenas information about you, the court can also get access to your credit file.

- **Employment:** When you apply for a job, the prospective employer can get a copy of your credit report, if they first get your written permission. Why would they need your credit report? There are two primary reasons.

  First, you're applying for a position that involves managing or handling the company's money. If you're having difficulties with personal finances, you may have trouble with company money, too, or so the logic goes.

  The second reason is to verify that you are who you claim to be. Employers match the identifying information in your credit report to what you say in your job application. That can help them prevent job application fraud, and maybe even protect public safety. One example is chemical plants, which check applicants' credit reports because they don't want a dangerous person to have access to something that could harm other people.

It's also important to note that employers never get credit scores. Despite what you're likely to hear, credit scores do *not* prevent you from getting a job. This is one of the most common credit myths.

- **Insurance:** Depending on the type of insurance you apply for and the state in which you live, the insurer may get a copy of your credit report and use the information in it to help predict the likelihood of your filing a claim. Insurers and their actuaries have shown that a strong relationship exists between past credit performance and future claim experience. So when you apply for car, homeowners, renters, medical, or any other kind of insurance, in most states, your insurance company has the right to get a copy of your credit report.

- **IRS debts:** If you owe the tax man and don't pay on time, the IRS looks in your credit report to find out if you have assets to attach or sell, like real estate, cars, or bank accounts.

- **Professional license:** Licensing authorities take their responsibilities very seriously. Before allowing you to become licensed — in other words, approved to perform a specific job — they want to know all they can about your background and how you've conducted yourself. If you want a license to be a financial planner and deal with someone else's life savings, for instance, it makes sense to see how you handle your own money. Want a gambling license? Same thing applies.

- **Review or collection of an existing account:** If your account is overdue and sent to collections, the collector wants to know who else you owe money to and what kind of payer you are. If you move a lot, the collector uses the information in your credit report to find a current address or phone number. (The industry term for this practice is *skip tracing*.) However, even if you're current in your payments to your credit card issuers, mortgage company, or other creditors, your creditors may look at your account from time to time to determine whether your credit quality is deteriorating or, on the brighter side, whether they should increase your limits.

Perusing Your Credit Reports

You may be hesitant to get your credit reports because you've heard scary stories about trying to interpret the codes and abbreviations in them. Years ago, that may have been true, but the credit bureaus have done a lot to make your personal credit report much easier to read and understand. Still, getting your credit report for the first time can be a bit intimidating. Don't let that stop you. Perhaps the best way to get a handle on the information in your credit report is to take it apart and break it into its various sections.

Credit reports can include information in the following general categories. Yours may not include everything. For example, if you've never declared bankruptcy, you wouldn't see that section in your report.

>> Identifying information

>> Accounts summary

>> Bankruptcy public records

>> Account history

>> Credit inquiries

>> Your 100-word statement(s) (optional)

The following sections cover each of these parts of your report in detail. Bear in mind, though, that the three credit-reporting agencies may use slightly different descriptions for each of these sections.

TIP

For samples of Equifax, Experian, and TransUnion credit reports, go to www.dummies.com/go/creditrepairkitfd5e.

Identifying information: It's all about who you are

This section of your credit report may be labeled "Personal Profile" or "Personal Information," depending on which credit bureau issues the report. The credit bureaus maintain files on more than 220 million credit active consumers, so all your identifying information is critical to making sure your credit report is accurate and complete.

Appearing first in the order of credit report elements, your profile section contains the key components that help you verify that the report is actually about *you*: your name (and any of your previous names — for example, if you changed your name because of marriage or divorce, or if you use multiple spellings or nicknames like Steve instead of Stephen), Social Security number, address(es), and current and previous employers.

TIP

Be sure to check the personal profile section and verify that all the information is correct. You may see variations of your Social Security number or street address if they're reported to the credit bureaus. Variations are not errors. They're included so you have a complete record of what your lenders are reporting is in their records. Variations you don't recognize could indicate you're a fraud victim, so check your identifying information closely.

Accounts summary: An overview of your financial history

Each of the three bureau reports includes a summary of your credit or accounts that gives you a high-level overview of what's included in your credit report, and things you may want to look at more closely. It includes open and closed accounts, credit limits, total balances of all accounts, payment history, and number of credit inquiries. The summary may also point out information that may be viewed negatively by lenders based on the credit bureaus' experience. If you have a short attention span, the summary provides a one-page snapshot of your credit history. But don't worry: If you're hungry for painstaking detail, you can find it in the Account History section, which is described later in this chapter.

TIP

A quick review of the summary section lets you know whether you need to scrutinize something in more detail that appears to be inaccurate or isn't related to your account at all. For example, if you don't have a mortgage, finding a mortgage account listed in your summary is an immediate red flag.

Bankruptcy public records: The most serious element in a credit report

Bankruptcy public records may be the most harmful entry in a credit report. They indicate that your debts have gotten so unmanageable that you've gone through a legal process to have them dismissed. Lenders will take a dim view of your creditworthiness if you don't pay them as agreed, and if you've declared bankruptcy, you may not have paid them at all. Bankruptcy public records can be a part of your credit report for up to ten years, depending on the chapter you filed. They'll drag your scores down for the entire time, although less as they get older.

WARNING

Defaulting on child-support payments may also be included in this section, but it could also be listed as an account by the state agency. Unpaid child support is the only thing that may be worse for your credit than bankruptcy.

In the not-so-distant past, there were other public records in credit reports — things like civil judgments if you were sued and lost, tax liens, and even parking tickets or library fines. The good news is that those have all been removed from credit reports. However, they may be included in a specialty credit report.

Credit inquiries: Tracking who has been accessing your file

Want to know who has asked for your credit report? This section is where you should look. It includes everyone who has asked for your credit report in the last two years. People who are legally allowed to view your credit information and have requested copies of your report are listed here.

There are two types of inquiries:

>> **Hard inquiries:** Hard inquiries are the result of your application for credit or other services. They indicate you may have additional debt that doesn't yet show as an account in your credit report, so it represents a bit of risk to lenders. For that reason, they're shared with lenders and

can have a small impact on your credit scores until the new account is added. You may see these listed in your report as "Inquiries shared with others."

TIP

Although hard inquiries don't have a very large impact on the average credit report, they can have a more serious negative impact on a credit file with a short credit history or few entries. These files are also called *thin files*. They may not cause a greater score decrease in terms of points, but when you already have a limited history and a low score, a few points could affect a lender's decision more than it would for a person with a high score.

>> **Soft inquiries:** Soft inquiries are shown only to you (not anyone else, like a lender) on your personal credit report, and they don't affect credit scores or lending decisions. They include things like preapproved credit offers, your requests of your own credit report, requests by employers to whom you've given your permission, and insurance companies requesting your report. You may see them listed under a heading of "Inquiries shown only to you."

REMEMBER

Inquiries are simply a record that someone with a permissible purpose under the law has asked for your report, such as employers, insurance companies, and lenders, as well as yourself. (For more information on this topic, see the earlier sidebar "Who else has access to your report?")

This section also shows the date of each inquiry and how long the inquiry will remain on your report.

Account history: Think of it as a payment CSI

Your account history section, sometimes titled "Account Information," is the heart of your credit report. It shows all open and closed accounts with near forensic detail about payment history, balances, and account status. How long the information remains on your report depends on the type of information. If you see negative items that you don't recognize or that have exceeded the allowed time frame, dispute them using the instructions included with your report and they'll be removed.

Each credit bureau displays these account details in its own unique way, as outlined in the following sections.

Equifax's version

Equifax reports account history by type of account, such as mortgages, installment accounts, and revolving accounts. Under each account type, open accounts are listed first, followed by closed accounts. A short summary at the beginning of each account includes your account status, which indicates whether you have paid as agreed or are late (and if so, how late).

Here's a list of all the information Equifax reports for each account in its Account History section:

>> **Account name:** A brief description of the account type and creditor. For example, 123 Mortgage Co., Address, Phone Number.

>> **Account number:** That long, alphanumeric string that's unique to your card or loan. Note, though, that account numbers are shortened for the protection of your account information.

>> **Account owner:** Indicates whether the account is an individual or joint account.

>> **Type:** Here are the account types you may find:

- **Mortgage account:** First mortgage loans, home equity loans, and any other loan secured by real estate.

- **Installment account:** Loans that are for a set amount of money and often for a set period. A car loan is an example of a common installment loan.

- **Revolving account:** An account that has a credit limit and a minimum payment and doesn't have to be paid off in a set amount of time. Credit cards fall into this category.

- **Other account:** Includes those accounts that don't fit into the set categories, such as charge accounts that must be paid in full each month, like some American Express cards.

- **Collections account:** An account that has been sold or turned over to a collection agency, usually when the account is more than 180 days past due.

- **Negative account:** A past-due account that is less than 180 days late, or a debt that was written off because you couldn't pay it and is now a collections account.

>> **Term duration:** The total number of payments you're expected to make (for example, 60 payments for a five-year car loan).

>> **Date open:** The date on which you opened the account.

>> **Date reported:** The latest report from the lender, whether provided monthly, quarterly, or less frequently.

>> **Date of last payment:** The date listed here may be different from the date reported. If you're past due, your last payment may be from September 2023, and the last date reported may be December 2023. If you had no activity on a credit card account for six months, the last payment date may be June 2023, and the last reported date may be December 2023.

>> **Scheduled payment amount:** Information that applies only to installment accounts, in which a set amount of money is due at a set time every month.

>> **Creditor classification:** The type of creditor.

>> **Charge-off amount:** Debt or portion of debt that the creditor wrote off because of nonpayment and inability to get the money from you. For example, if you don't pay your credit card for 180 days, it will be listed as charged off. You want this amount to be *zero*. Any amount — no matter how small — is not a good thing to have on your record.

>> **Balloon-payment amount:** The big lump-sum payment at the end of some loans. Your loan may or may not have one.

>> **Date closed:** The date you or the lender terminated an active account.

>> **Date of first delinquency:** Any late payments recorded during the seven-year reporting period.

>> **Comments:** Additional information about the closed account. Some examples are "Account Transferred or Sold," "Paid," "Zero Balance," and "Account Closed at Consumer's Request."

>> **Current status:** Whether you've paid or are paying as you said you would. You may see terms such as "Pays," "Paid as Agreed," or "X Days Past Due."

>> **High credit:** The highest amount of credit you have used.

>> **Credit limit:** Your maximum limit for this account.

>> **Term's frequency:** How often your payment is due (weekly, monthly, and so on).

>> **Balance:** The amount owed to the creditor.

>> **Amount past due:** The amount you owe that should have been paid by now but hasn't been.

>> **Actual payment amount:** The amount of your last payment.

>> **Date of last activity:** The last time you used the account.

>> **Months reviewed:** How many months are in the payment history section (up to 81).

>> **Activity designator:** A description of account activity, such as "Paid" and "Closed."

>> **Deferred payment start date:** Some accounts have no payment for a year or other promotional terms.

>> **Balloon-payment date:** When that big lump-sum payment at the end of some loans is due. Your loan may or may not have one.

>> **Type of loan:** For example, auto or credit card.

>> **81-month payment history:** Equifax shows each month's status for the last seven years of payment history. Terms used in reporting the status include the following:

- Paid on time
- 30 (30 to 59 days past due)
- 60 (60 to 89 days past due)
- 90 (90 to 119 days past due)
- 120 (120 to 149 days past due)
- 150 (150 to 179 days past due)
- 180- (180 or more days past due)

- C (collection account)
- F (foreclosure)
- V (voluntary surrender)
- R (repossession)
- CO (charge-off)
- B (included in bankruptcy)
- TN (too new to rate)

Experian's version

On Experian's credit report, potentially negative items are listed first. The remainder of your accounts in the Account History section are listed as accounts in good standing. You of course want all your accounts to be listed as being in good standing.

Here's a list of the information that Experian reports for each account in its Account History section:

>> **Name of creditor**

>> **Account number**

>> **Account type:** Installment account, revolving account, and so on.

>> **Responsibility:** Individual, joint, authorized user, and so on.

>> **Date open:** The date you opened the account.

>> **Status:** Open or closed and paid, past due by X days, or settled for less than originally agreed.

>> **Balance:** The amount you owe. Sometimes balance information is on the report and sometimes it's not. This isn't because the credit bureau wants to save trees but because some creditors don't want their competition to know what a big spender and great customer you are.

>> **Monthly payment:** The last reported minimum payment you owe(d). This typically applies for installment loans such as auto loans and mortgages, if reported at all.

>> **Credit limit:** The highest credit limit you've ever been approved for.

>> **High balance:** The most you've ever owed on the account.

>> **Terms:** The total number of payments you're expected to make (a 30-year mortgage would be 360 payments, for example).

>> **Recent payment:** Your most recent payment amount.

>> **Account history:** Whether you've paid late, and if so, how often.

>> **Your statement:** This is where you tell your side of the story. For example, you may contest an account that shows you haven't paid as agreed if you contend that you didn't receive the services for which you were charged.

>> **Account history for collection accounts:** Comments that the creditor may have sent to the bureau, such as when the account was placed for collection.

>> **Creditor contact information:** The creditor's mailing address.

TransUnion's version

TransUnion reports public records and collection accounts first. The Account History section for all other accounts is listed under Trades.

Here's a list of the information that TransUnion reports for each account in its Account History section:

>> **Account name:** Name and address of the creditor.

>> **Account number:** Only a partial account number is included.

>> **Account type:** Automobile, credit card, and so on.

>> **Credit limit:** The maximum amount of credit approved by the creditor. The creditor doesn't always report this information if your limit isn't firm (such as with American Express) or if you're allowed to exceed your limit under the terms of your agreement (such as with Visa Signature accounts).

>> **Balance:** The balance owed as of the date of verification or when closed.

- >> **Date opened:** The date the account was opened.

- >> **Responsibility:** Individual, joint, authorized user, and so on.

- >> **High credit:** The highest amount ever owed on the account.

- >> **Past due:** Amount past due as of date verified or closed.

- >> **Terms:** Minimum payment amount.

- >> **Pay status:** Whether you are paying as agreed or otherwise.

- >> **Account type:** Open or closed.

- >> **Date paid:** The date the account was last paid.

- >> **Remarks:** Explanation of dispute or account credit condition as reported by the creditor. Includes account closed by consumer.

- >> **Terms:** Number of payments, payment frequency, and dollar amount agreed upon.

- >> **Date closed:** If the account is closed, the date on which it was closed.

- >> **Date updated:** The date of the last update on the account.

- >> **Loan type:** The type of loan and/or the collateral used for an installment loan. Includes home equity loan, mortgage, and automobile.

- >> **Late payments:** A graphical representation of all paid months being reported as agreed or late.

- >> **Payment information:** Notations ranging from "current" to "120+ days late" or if the account is in "collections," "charged off," and so on.

TIP

Your revolving utilization rate is a key component of your credit scores. *Utilization* is the ratio of your credit card balances compared to your credit limits. It's the second most important factor in credit scores. If you have credit cards charged to the limit, or close to it, pay them down to see a quick increase in credit scores. For more on how your credit score is calculated, see the later section "Getting and Understanding Your Credit Scores."

Your optional dispute statements: Making sure your voice is heard

You have the right to add a statement to your credit report that can help explain any extenuating circumstances that may have led to negative information being included. You can add an overall statement that covers all your accounts, and you can add a statement for one or more trade lines with which you disagree. For example, a general statement describing a temporary job loss can explain why many of your accounts were 60 days late. A trade line or individual account statement can explain why a particular account is being reported negatively and why you disagree.

TIP

The length of the statement you're allowed to add to your credit report varies. You can add a 100-word statement to your Experian report, a 475-character statement to your Equifax report, and a 1,000-character statement to your TransUnion report.

If you disagree with the results of a dispute, you should add a statement explaining why. These *statements of dispute* ensure you have an opportunity to explain your side of the situation. Just be sure that it's a reason that lenders would understand and appreciate. If you forgot to mail your payment because you were on vacation, a statement to that effect probably won't help. A lender's response would just be, "I hope you had a great vacation. I still need my payment on time." On the other hand, a statement explaining that your lender misapplied your payment to the wrong account and still reported it as late, even though it was sent to them on time, could be very helpful.

The credit bureaus are required to include these statements whenever anyone accesses your credit report. Anyone who requests your report will be alerted that there is a statement on your credit file. On the flip side, lenders may not always pull a full credit report when ordering a score for screening, so keep in mind that your statement may not always be seen.

REMEMBER

Use the dispute statement privilege with care, and be sure to circle back to make sure it's deleted when the negative information is removed. In most cases today, that happens automatically, but it's good to be sure. If you don't request that it be removed, your comments could stay on the report and raise unwanted questions from a potential lender.

Correcting Any Errors You Find

Considering how many individual credit histories are maintained and the vast amount of information flowing into and out of the credit bureaus every day, credit reports are highly accurate. But they aren't perfect, and mistakes can happen. The good news is that if you find mistakes, they don't have to remain a part of your credit file.

REMEMBER

Credit-reporting agencies are required to investigate all disputed listings. They must verify the item in question with the creditor *at no cost to you*, the consumer. The law requires the creditor to respond to and verify disputed entries within 30 days, or the information must be removed from your credit report. In most cases, though, disputes are completed within 10 to 14 business days, and often much faster, today. The credit bureau must notify you of the outcome of your disputes. If information in the report is changed or deleted, you can get a *free* copy of the revised report. If a lender makes a change to one credit bureau as a result of your dispute, they must also notify every other consumer reporting agency to which they reported it to make the change, too. It's a good idea to check your other reports after a change just to be sure the update has been made with all three.

You have two options for fixing errors that you find on your credit reports: contact the credit bureau or contact the creditor who reported the incorrect information. The following sections walk you through both processes.

Contacting the credit bureau

If you notice incorrect information on your credit report, contact the credit bureau that reported the inaccurate information. Each of the three major bureaus allows you to dispute information in your credit report on its website, or you can call the bureau's toll-free number (find contact info for the big-three credit bureaus in the earlier section "Where to get your reports").

Having a current personal credit report, not one from a lender, when you dispute online makes the correction process simple. In most cases all you have to do is enter the report number and follow the instructions. Experian will even give you a free report if you don't already have one and need to dispute something.

If you opt to call the toll-free number, you're unlikely to get a live person on the other end, but you'll be told what information and documentation you need in order to submit a written request. Either way, after you properly notify the credit bureau, you can count on action.

Contacting the creditor

Another way, and sometimes a better way, to remove inaccurate information from your credit report is outlined under the FACT Act: Deal directly with the creditor who reported the negative information in the first place. Customer service contact information appears on your billing statements from that creditor, and the general address and phone number are on your credit report. After you dispute the information, the creditor must look into the matter and can't continue to report the negative information while it's investigating your dispute. This approach is more direct and eliminates the possibility of your dispute being miscommunicated or delayed as it's passed between you, the bureau, and the lender.

TIP

We recommend that you contact the creditor directly. A call or email may be sufficient. If your relationship is testy, consider submitting your issue in writing and through the mail, requesting a return receipt for every piece of correspondence you send.

For new delinquencies, the FACT Act requires the lender to notify you if negative information is reported to a credit bureau. Be sure you read the fine print carefully. Anyone who extends credit to you must send you a one-time notice either before or not later than 30 days after negative information — including late payments, missed payments, partial payments, or any other form of default — is furnished to a credit bureau. This includes collection agencies, as long as they report to a credit bureau. The notice (known as an *adverse action notice*) may look something like this:

>> **Before negative information is reported:** "We may report information about your account to credit bureaus. Late payments, missed payments, or other defaults on your account may be reflected in your credit report."

>> **After negative information is reported:** "We have told a credit bureau about a late payment, missed payment, or other default on your account. This information may be reflected in your credit report."

REMEMBER

Receiving notification about what a creditor has reported about you to the credit bureaus isn't a substitute for your own close monitoring of your credit reports, bank accounts, and credit card statements.

Getting and Understanding Your Credit Scores

Getting your hands on your credit reports is pretty straightforward. You only have three of them and you can request them all from the same website. Getting copies of your credit scores isn't as straightforward. Your credit score is a tool used in most credit reviews to objectively analyze the information from your credit report. When a lender orders your credit report, it often also orders a credit score, which helps predict the chances that you won't be able to pay a new loan as agreed.

The two best-known credit scoring companies are FICO and VantageScore. They developed the credit scores most commonly used by lenders today. FICO is the best known name in credit scores. VantageScore is its largest competitor, although less well known. Four of the top five financial institutions, all credit card issuers, and two of the top five auto lenders use VantageScores for lending decisions. The most common scores from both companies range from 300 to 850.

REMEMBER

Don't get hung up on a number. Be as good as you can be, but don't get excited and yell at the cat over a score of 820 instead of 850. The most important thing is to know what your *lenders* know about your credit score and what's in the credit report they look at. On this topic, you want to be on the same page.

The main points to keep in mind regarding credit scores are as follows:

>> Your score is different for each credit bureau report, if only because each bureau has slightly different data about you in its files.

>> Be sure you know which score you're getting: a FICO score, a VantageScore, or a proprietary score from the service providing it.

>> You can only improve your credit score by improving your credit history, not the other way around. Perhaps the most important thing we can share is that if you take care of your credit report, your credit scores will take care of themselves.

>> About 5 percent of credit reports have errors that would result in a score change of 25 points or more according to the Federal Trade Commission. A larger percentage have errors that don't make a scoring difference. If your report has errors, that can be enough to cause you to be declined or pay higher interest rates. That's why it's important to check your report regularly. Dispute errors and outdated items to ensure your credit score accurately reflects your creditworthiness.

With a grasp of the essentials about credit scores, you're ready to take the plunge and get your score. Of course, once you have it, you can count on this section to explain what it means for you and what you can do about it. Read on!

Ordering your score

The Fair Access to Credit Scores Act that was bundled into the massive Dodd–Frank Wall Street Reform and Consumer Protection Act allows you free access to your credit score if you've been denied credit or if some other "adverse action" (denial of insurance or utilities, for example) was taken as a result of your credit score. In fact, the law requires the lender or business that took adverse action to give you a score it used. You don't have to request your credit score if such an adverse action is taken based on that score; a copy of the score used to make the decision is automatically sent to you.

To get your current score, you need to order a credit report at the same time, because your score is calculated based on the information in your credit report at the time you order the score.

If you want your credit score, you can get it from a number of places today for free:

>> **Your lender:** Your lender may provide a FICO score to you through its online banking app or with your billing statement.

>> **Experian** (www.experian.com): You can get your FICO score for free when you enroll in its basic monitoring service or sign up with its mobile app. You'll get offers for credit cards or other services. Just be prepared to say no.

>> **Equifax** (800-685-1111; www.equifax.com): Enrollment in its service at the time of writing is $4.95 a month.

>> **myFICO.com** (800-319-4433; www.myfico.com): Enrollment in its basic service is $19.95 a month at the time of this writing.

>> **TransUnion:** You can get the VantageScore through its online service, which is $29.95 a month as of this writing.

The credit bureaus worked together in development of the VantageScore (a fierce competitor of FICO). Oh, and all three credit bureaus compete with one another every chance they get.

REMEMBER

The number you get will almost never match the one your lender gets exactly. That's okay. When you get your score, you should also get an explanation of what the number means in terms of risk. If the score you get says you're a good risk, your lender's score will as well. What's important is to know what the number you get means within its scale, not that it matches the score your lender has. You should also get a list of risk factors (also called *reason statements*) that explain what in your credit report most affected the number. Although the numbers may differ, the risk factors tend to be very consistent. Address them, and all your scores will improve. Find out more about risk factors and reason statements in detail later in this chapter.

WARNING

When you're ordering scores, most sites try to get you to sign up for a credit-monitoring service. Be sure you understand what you're agreeing to before you do. You should be able to get your one-time credit report and a score without signing up for a long-term service, but monitoring services may have advantages, too. Just be sure you read the fine print and know what's in it for you before you sign up. Chapter 8 discusses credit-monitoring services and their benefits and costs.

Telling a good score from a bad one

There are many scores with different ranges for different kinds of lenders and different kinds of lending. So, how do you know if your score is a good one, or not? The answer is that a good score is one that's good enough to get you what you want at a price you can afford. A really good score will get you the amount you want to borrow at the best interest rates and terms.

An important bit of good news is that if you have a good score on one scoring system, you'll have good scores on the others, too. For purposes of discussion, we're going to use examples from FICO, which produces the most widely used scores in the market.

REMEMBER

As you look at scores, note that they change to reflect the behavior of the "market," which just means all consumers as a group. When the economy crashed in 2008, average credit scores dropped like lead balloons. As a result, the definition of *good* shifted down the scale somewhat. As the economy recovered, average scores improved and what was defined as a "good" score moved back up the scale. That shift was fairly small. Generally, a "good" score starts somewhere around 700 on the FICO scale. A "really good" score is usually is 750 or higher.

FICO likes to give you a picture of where you stand in comparison to others using an eight-bar graph and an eight-column chart.

It may be hard to move your score, but it's not impossible. What's the best way to do so? With a plan and over time! Anyone who claims that he can turn your credit score around overnight is not telling the truth. But there are tools today that may help you make that jump a bit faster.

REMEMBER

The difference in loan terms between a score of 750 and a score of 800 (the top two groups) may be small, but those with a score of 650 or lower may not be eligible for credit at all. This tends to be true no matter what the economy is like at the moment. However, not all lenders view risk the same way. One lender may consider a credit score of 650 to be a high risk, while another lender may not consider such a score to be too risky to take a chance and may have a special program to give credit to lower-scoring consumers — just be aware that it may not be the kind of credit you really want. You'll likely be charged high fees and interest, and you could find yourself in a debt trap.

WARNING

A bad credit score and history can make you a target for unscrupulous lenders. If your credit is damaged, read the fine print on any credit agreement carefully and understand all fees, penalties, and interest rates before you act.

So, how high is high enough? In a time of relatively easy credit, the saying often is all you need is a pulse to get a loan. Although this may not be entirely true, getting a loan with a lower score in good times is certainly easier than it is when times are hard. Over time, the standard for lending tends to swing like a pendulum from easy to tight and back again. So keeping your credit as clean as you can is all the more important, because today's record will be there for at least the next seven years, while tomorrow's credit market will surely change.

Connecting pricing to your credit score

Most lending today is done using something called *risk-based pricing*. Risk-based pricing means that instead of saying "no" to a high-risk customer, a lender would say "yes" and still make money on the risky loan by charging a higher interest rate and fees. This model allows more people with lower scores to get more loans, albeit at a higher cost. That doesn't mean everyone can qualify for a loan. Lenders still have a threshold below which an account is too risky to accept. So, although your credit score may get you a higher or lower interest rate, if it's too weak for the lender's standards, you may get a "no, thank you" instead.

To get the best deals on credit, you need to have a good credit score, which means you have a good credit report. Having a perfect credit score (a FICO or VantageScore of 850) is extremely rare and not necessary. Lenders aren't looking for a perfect score. What they want to see is a good enough score to approve the credit for which you're applying. All that takes is common sense and good credit management. When you hit the number for the lender to give you the best rates, you're good to go. That number won't even be close to a "perfect" score.

For a given type of credit — such as revolving (credit cards) or installment (car loans and mortgages) — credit grantors divide customers into different score ranges or buckets and offer them different rates and terms based on where they fall. For example, the rate for a 30-year mortgage may be the same for people with scores between 760 and 850, all other underwriting criteria (such as income and job stability) being equal.

Maintaining the highest credit score possible can save you hundreds a month and tens of thousands in mortgage payments over the term of the loan. You can plug in your own mortgage amount and interest rates to see exactly what you'll pay using the calculator at www.myfico.com/credit-education/calculators/loan-savings-calculator.

Although the amount of money you save on smaller loans may not be as high as that associated with a mortgage loan, a high credit score saves you money in interest charges for any amount you plan to borrow. In addition, in a tight credit market, a low credit score may mean that you don't qualify for credit at any price.

Your goal is to get into the best bucket you can by the time you need the type of credit in question. How? By building a plan that gets you to your goal of "good enough" credit. Take some time and include everyone with whom you share your life. List your credit-oriented goals, and then check a resource like www. bankrate.com to find out what credit score will get you into the next-highest tier of borrowers. Unless you're in the top tier, come up with actions to take based on what you find in your credit report.

New tools like having your positive rent payments reported or adding your cellphone, utility, or video-streaming service payments can also help bump up your scores if you have a limited credit history. Talk with your landlord and consider services like Experian Boost (www.experian.com/boost). Be sure you understand what you're agreeing to before signing up. There is generally little or no fee for these kinds of services, but they'll likely ask for information so they can make other offers for you to purchase. If you can say no to credit card offers or other products, Experian Boost can work to your advantage.

FICO has also introduced a new score called UltraFICO that looks at the information from your bank accounts, like checking and savings. A history of maintaining good balances in your checking and savings accounts is a good sign you'll manage credit well, too, especially if you don't have a very extensive credit history. You have to opt in for your lender to use the UltraFICO score. Learn more at www.fico.com/ultrafico.

You can find details on how a credit score is built in Chapter 6.

Credit scores also are changing the way they look at some kinds of information in a credit report. For example, collection accounts used to do serious harm to your scores the entire time they were in your report. New scores from FICO and Vantage-Score, though, now exclude paid collections from the calculation or significantly reduce the impact. So, paying off a collection account could help your scores as soon as they show "paid" in your credit report.

You should also check your credit reports regularly and make sure there are no errors or out-of-date information. Disputing any you may find can pump up your scores. Because credit scores normally look back over several years of credit history to develop an accurate picture of your risk profile, overcoming any negative data that may be hurting your score takes time. Removing errors or out-of-date information, however, has an immediate effect on your score.

WARNING

Avoid companies that promise to improve your score by removing accurate negative information from your credit report. They can't do what they claim, and they may get you into even more trouble if, for example, you're approved for a loan based on fraudulently altered credit information.

Knowing the reason for reason statements

Along with your credit score, you get up to five reason statements, sometimes called *risk-factor statements*, on your credit-score report. A *reason statement* is a simple explanation of why your score is less than perfect. What's the reason for reason statements? Well, a lender can't make money turning down business, so if a poor score is keeping a lender from approving your application, knowing the reasons your credit scores aren't up to snuff can help identify how to dig out and get those fees and loans flowing again!

Creditors get what's called a *reason code* or *risk-factor code*, and you get the interpreted version of that, which is called a *reason statement*. For example, if a reason code reveals that your lower-than-it-could-have-been score is because your credit cards are maxed out and not because you never pay on time, you can focus on reducing balances and using less of each credit line to raise your score.

There are more than 100 possible reason codes for some scores that give you and your lender specific information about the most important things causing your credit to sag. Although the numbers from credit scores can be different, the reason statements tend to be very consistent. By addressing the reason statements you receive, you'll be able to improve all your credit scores.

Reason statements are generated every time a credit score is calculated. When you get a credit score, you should also get the reason statements along with it. If you get credit scores as a service along with your credit report, you'll typically find the reason statements listed immediately following the credit score. In some cases you may only see the things that are hurting your credit score, called the *negative reason factor* for obvious, well, reasons. Some may list both positive and negative reasons for your score, with tips to help increase your score muscle.

According to FICO, the most frequently used reason statement is "Proportion of balances to credit limits on bank/national revolving or other revolving accounts is too high." This tells you that you're using more of your limits than the scoring model thinks is safe. A high percentage of usage — say, 50 percent ($10,000 on a $20,000 credit line) — is inherently riskier than 25 percent (or $5,000). The lower the balances on your credit cards, the better for your credit scores.

Ironically, VantageScore's most frequent reason statement is "Available credit across all open, recently reported accounts is too low." That's just another way of saying the balances on your credit cards is too high, exactly like the FICO example. If you see this reason statement in your credit report or one like it, you need to reduce your credit card balances. It's time to slow your charging and increase your payments.

The bottom line is that you need to focus on the top reason statements you received and that are affecting your scores. They're different for everyone.

To help you decode your reason statements, VantageScore developed a microsite that explains them. See www.reasoncode.org for more info.

Chapter **8**

Monitoring Your Credit Reports and Scores

The next time you get a billing statement from a credit card company, bank, or insurance company, you may find that in addition to asking for your payment, they're offering to check your credit report and credit scores monthly, too. As a perk for customers, or an enticement to be a customer, they may offer a credit monitoring service at no cost, or to help with their profit margin they could ask you to pay for it. The question is, should you sign up?

As with almost all things related to credit, the answer is, it depends. Have you had issues with fraud in the past? Are you planning to make a big credit purchase in the near future? Are you just the kind of person who worries a lot about your credit? This chapter lays out what you should think about before signing up for a monitoring service, whether free or for a fee.

REMEMBER

Don't confuse credit monitoring with identity theft protection. Credit fraud can be the result of identity theft, but it can also lead to other kinds of crimes that don't affect your credit report. Credit monitoring won't stop someone from stealing your identity and using your Social Security number in a false job application or to file taxes in your name, but it may enable you to detect a potential problem early and take action to stop it.

This chapter discusses how credit monitoring works and what you get when you enroll so that you can decide if it's worth the effort or you should just handle checking your credit reports on your own.

Getting a Handle on How Credit Monitoring Really Works

Enlisting a company to monitor your credit means that you give the company access to your credit reports so that it can watch them and notify you of any suspicious additions or changes. Basic services are often free, but for more premium services you may have to pay a monthly or annual fee.

So, how does credit monitoring happen? It's pretty much exactly what it sounds like. Each service provider has a series of programs that it runs against databases to which it has access. Some, like Experian, have their own credit database but also have access to others and search social media and the dark web, looking for changes, updates, or patterns that indicate something may be amiss in your world.

WARNING

The *dark web* consists of web pages on the World Wide Web that are not indexed by search engines and are not viewable in a standard web browser like Chrome, Firefox, or Safari. The dark web is where lots of nefarious and illegal activities take place.

Some services monitor only one credit bureau, others monitor all three, and still others monitor some of the many national, specialty, consumer-reporting bureaus for activity or changes to your reports such as

- The opening of new accounts

- Larger-than-normal charges

- Unusual account activity, such as a change in the frequency, location, or type of charges appearing on your credit reports

- A surge in balances

- Other changes to your accounts, such as payments, late payment notices, credit inquiries, public records, employment, addresses, and fraud alerts

Some monitoring services also search the internet, the dark web, social media sites, and other public records for suspicious use of your identifying information. They may produce detailed reports about your credit score and even suggest ways to make it more attractive to lenders and improve your creditworthiness. Most also give you free credit reports and scores (they may be proprietary scores or a FICO or VantageScore; see Chapter 6 for the differences between score types).

Lastly, monitoring services check your data with differing frequency. Some check daily, others weekly, others monthly and others quarterly, depending on their service level. The more they do and the more often you can get updated reports, the more you'll likely have to pay.

Understanding the Types of Monitoring Services Available

A universe of services is available to help you monitor or safeguard your credit.

REMEMBER

Keep in mind you can handle most of the monitoring on your own *if you have the time and inclination*. For instance, you're entitled to a free credit report from each of the three major bureaus annually. You get additional free credit reports under certain circumstances, such as if you think you've been the victim of identity theft or if you don't receive the best rates available for a loan or insurance policy based on information in your credit report. In the case of a natural disaster, the credit bureaus may provide more frequent access to your credit reports. (The three major credit reporting agencies made permanent a COVID-related program to offer free credit reports once a week.) So, with at least one opportunity to get a free look at your reports every week, you can do a credible job of monitoring your credit at no cost, especially if you don't have anything causing you concern or giving you a reason to check more often. You just have to remember to order your report and then examine it to see what's changed. (For more on monitoring your credit yourself, see the later section "Monitoring on your own.")

If you're interested in having someone else do the monitoring for you, here's a look at each type of service in more detail:

>> **Credit report monitoring:** This service notifies you about changes to your credit report(s). It often provides frequent access to your credit report upon request. Some services monitor only one credit report, while others monitor reports from the three major credit-reporting agencies (Experian, Equifax, and TransUnion) as well as some of the national specialty-reporting bureaus. Credit report monitoring may provide limited help in giving you an early warning about identity theft, but because such services monitor only the data in your credit report, an identity theft that involves noncredit or unreported areas won't be addressed.

>> **Credit score monitoring:** This service may include all or some of the credit report monitoring services, but it also includes checking your credit score or credit scores. Which score or scores depends on your service provider. For example, Experian's free basic service includes a FICO 8 score. Its premium service will give you up to six more FICO scores, including industry-specific scores, like auto and bankcard scores.

>> **Identity theft monitoring:** This service may include additional monitoring areas beyond credit. It focuses mainly on financial databases and not on criminal or law enforcement data, medical billers that don't report to the credit bureaus, or government data.

>> **Credit freeze or lock products:** These products, offered by the credit bureaus, work by limiting access to your credit report. When your information is used to apply for new credit, you must first give express permission before your report can be accessed. Typically, a lender reviews your credit file before issuing a new loan or credit card. The inability to do so may prevent the issuance of new credit to criminals. For more info, see the later section "Setting Alarms, Alerts, and Freezes."

>> **ID theft recovery products:** By definition, recovering from identity theft requires a clearing of all fraudulent records and charges created by an identity thief. You can find companies to do all the research and restoration work for you.

>> **Data sweep services:** Data sweep companies monitor the internet for listings of your personal identifying information that may expose you to identity thieves or use of your information that indicates you're already a victim. They may also monitor specific websites known for questionable activities on the dark web. If your personal data is detected, these services alert you. They may also offer insurance if they fail to perform.

>> **Virtual account numbers:** Superman used Clark Kent, Batman had Bruce Wayne, and you have a virtual credit card number to protect your identity from being discovered and misused by evil forces! These onetime computer-generated surrogate numbers enable you to better limit what personal information of yours — such as billing address, account number, or email address — appears when you're online shopping, paying bills, or registering at websites. It does so by replacing your real information with anonymous data that has a very short life span and is useless after your transaction is completed. It works for almost any type of purchase except for items to be picked up later that may require you to match your credit card number to the receipt. Movie/game tickets fall into this category. If your number is stolen, you have to cancel only that number instead of your main account number.

A similar technology is being incorporated by credit card companies using your smartphone. Some credit cards that now reside in your "mobile wallet" generate a unique transaction code for every purchase, making it harder to steal your card number or identity.

>> **Identity theft insurance:** ID insurance may be a stand-alone policy or an add-on to one of your existing policies. It helps replace out-of-pocket expenses you may incur after your identity is stolen and misused. Note that ID insurance doesn't keep you safe from theft itself. Collecting legal costs used to defend yourself against a crime committed by an ID thief may require an acquittal or a dismissal of charges.

Making a Case for and against Third-Party Credit Monitoring

You really only need your credit score when you're applying for credit — when it has a reason or a purpose. Paying someone to monitor your credit or score without a specific purpose or reason is an equally empty exercise. Before paying for a monitoring service, ask yourself why you need it or want it. If you're trying to improve your credit or get to a certain credit score so that you can make a large purchase like a home or a car, laying out some dough for a professional monitoring service can make sense. Also, if you are a "credit worrier," checking your credit scores daily, and you can't sleep soundly without all the safeguards and early warning bells in place, then a monitoring service may be right for you.

REMEMBER

Your lender's score may well differ from the one you get because it may come from another company (FICO, VantageScore, a credit bureau, and so on), because the information in your report may have changed between the time you received a score and your lender did, or because the lender applies its own algorithms based on proprietary factors that it weights based on its specific business experience.

WARNING

No credit monitoring service can offer you complete protection. If a lender or vendor doesn't report to the credit bureaus, or if it does report but not to the bureau monitored by the service you've chosen, you won't know whether a fraudulent account has been opened in your name until a problem arises down the road and a collector or the authorities call. Furthermore, creditors typically update your account information once a month, so you're likely to experience a delay in catching fraud indicators in your credit report.

REMEMBER

You shouldn't rely on a credit monitoring service alone. Always check your billing statements and watch for other signs that fraud may be occurring, like getting collection notices for accounts that aren't yours.

Monitoring on your own

TIP

You can monitor your credit on your own by taking these simple actions:

>> Get a free copy of your credit report at least every 12 months or as often as weekly from each of the three major credit-reporting agencies (Experian, Equifax, and TransUnion) at www.annualcreditreport.com. Review them and dispute any inaccuracies.

>> Be sure to get a free credit report if you dispute an item on your report. You're entitled to a free report to make sure that the mistake has been removed.

>> Get extra free copies of your credit reports directly from the bureaus (not from www.annualcreditreport.com) if you live in Colorado, Georgia, Maine, Maryland, Massachusetts, New Jersey, or Vermont. These states require that you be allowed an additional free report annually — except you lucky Georgia residents, who get two more free reports a year from each bureau, for a total of three. Puerto Rico, not a state (yet), requires that residents be given free credit reports as well.

>> Get a free report if you're turned down for credit. Anytime you are turned down for credit, you're guaranteed a free report from the credit bureau the lender used.

>> Get a free report if you're unemployed and looking for a new job. Within the first six months of seeking employment, you can have a freebie.

>> If you apply for a mortgage, you're entitled to a copy of the credit report and score the lender uses.

>> Order your free national, specialty consumer reports annually. Doing so may give you many more free looks into your cyber files.

>> Need to add a fraud alert or an extended fraud alert to your credit report? You get one or two additional free reports, respectively, over the next 12 months from each bureau.

>> Every time your insurance renews, look at the disclosure language, which is usually in the front of your policy, to see whether your insurance company used a credit report to set your rates. If so (and it's very likely), follow the instructions and get another free credit report if you didn't get the best rates.

>> Monitor your bank and credit card accounts online weekly. If something funny is going on, you'll know about it sooner.

>> Set up free alerts on your accounts that tip you off when certain types of transactions are made or if a dollar limit is exceeded.

>> During natural or declared disasters, you may be able to get additional free reports, too. During the COVID-19 pandemic, the credit bureaus allowed everyone a free report once a week.

Knowing when to use paid monitoring

Depending on the depth of your wallet and your degree of credit anxiety, paid monitoring may be for you. Here are some circumstances when paid monitoring makes sense:

>> Your credit is damaged and you've been trying to improve it for some time. Rather than ordering your report frequently at a premium price, a service that gives you more frequent access for a low monthly or annual fee may make sense so that you can make a plan and track your progress.

>> You're planning on making a large purchase that requires your credit score to be in primo condition. You can take your scoring temperature often so you know when the time is right to see the man. Always start checking your

report at least three to six months before you plan to apply so you have time to address any issues and make improvements.

>> You've been the victim of identity theft and accounts are being opened in your name. After you add fraud alerts and maybe place a credit freeze, monitoring may help you sleep better at night.

>> You're slightly obsessive-compulsive about your identity or credit file. Monitoring may give you a sense of security.

REMEMBER

Credit report or score monitoring isn't done in real time. Information can be days, weeks, or months old. In addition to the fact that monitoring companies report at differing frequencies, not all credit issuers (small credit unions, medical providers, utilities, and so on) report to the credit bureaus. As you find out earlier in this chapter, credit monitoring doesn't prevent someone from stealing your identity. Credit monitoring alerts you only after you have a problem so you can take action.

TIP

If you decide to try a monitoring service, check to see whether it offers a free trial period. Most do, and many services today are entirely free, at least for their basic level. If you do take advantage of a trial period, don't forget to cancel before the trial period ends if you're not going to stay with the service.

TIP

Sadly, data breaches are all too common today. In response to a breach, companies often offer a free credit-monitoring subscription. Taking advantage of those offers can be a good idea. Just be sure you understand the terms. Like free trial periods, the no-cost service may expire and you could find yourself stuck with a credit card charge you didn't expect.

Recognizing the protection you have already

You and your credit card are already protected against fraud under federal law. Unless you fail to notify your credit card company about erroneous or questionable charges on your statements within 60 days, your total liability for fraud is limited to

$50 per card. That's not much, but if you have several cards that are affected, it could add up. On a positive note, most credit card companies will wave that liability today if you contact them in good faith, even after the 60 days. If you have homeowners insurance, the $50 charge is probably a covered peril for which you can get reimbursed. Debit card liability also begins at $50 but can escalate after two days have passed from the time you find out about the fraud. Where debit card fraud is concerned, act in haste or you may repent at leisure!

Many of the major creditors have adopted zero-consumer-liability policies to further limit your exposure and increase your confidence in being able to use your cards safely. They've also become much more sophisticated in identifying patterns of card use that could indicate fraud.

Many credit card companies and banks today can adjust the sensitivity of their systems to recognize you are the one making the purchases, even if you're traveling outside of the country.

Still, most lenders appreciate your help in letting them know when you're traveling away from home. Be sure to check on their policies by calling customer service and asking whether you need to notify them.

TIP

Check your lender's website to see what it offers in terms of optional alerts that you can set up. One major credit card company will notify you by email or on your mobile phone if

>> A cash withdrawal is made.

>> A purchase exceeds a limit that you set, is made outside the United States, or is made online or over the phone.

>> Someone tries to reset your password or billing address.

>> They see a questionable transaction.

These types of services are becoming increasingly common.

Getting Your Money's Worth from Monitoring Services

If you decide that monitoring is a good fit for you, you may need some help to cut through the huge volume of providers. We can't analyze each one, but we can provide tips to help you make your decision.

TIP

Asking the right questions before you buy a service is important. Here are some questions you should ask before you sign on the dotted line, or sign up online, to be sure you get the most out of the service, even if it's free:

>> **What are the total costs and fees?** Set a limit that you're willing to pay and stick to it. Weigh the possible $20 to $50 a month charge against your odds of suffering a credit card fraud that you'd be liable for. Any liability is likely to be low. Also, banks, insurers, and the big-three credit bureaus all offer products to detect fraud and give you a credit score. Shop around for the best price. You may get a better price from someone you already do other business with.

Free isn't always, free, either. You usually trade something for the service. In most cases, the currency is your information. In return for the free monitoring service, you agree to get offers for things you may want to buy or credit you would qualify for if you choose to apply. Be sure you're comfortable with that exchange. Information today is as valuable as cash. If you can say no, or want to take advantage of opportunities you thing you'll find useful, sharing your information can be a worthwhile price to pay.

>> **What is the monitoring company's reputation and track record?** Like nearly everything else today, you can get reviews of services online. Sites like www.cnet.com/personal-finance offer user ratings that you can compare.

>> **Exactly what will you get for your money or information?** Know how comprehensive you want the monitoring to be. Be sure that you're getting the type of score you want; some services offer proprietary or bureau scores that lenders don't use. These scores may be okay for reference but won't be as easy to compare if you're using

them to estimate the loan interest rates or deal terms you'll get. Here are some common safeguards you can expect:

- Frequent or unlimited access to your credit report

- Frequent or unlimited access to a credit score of some type

- Monitoring of one or more credit reports

- Alerts when critical changes are made, including address changes

- Alerts if your credit score deteriorates into a lower lending category

- Alerts if personal information like your Social Security number or your credit card number starts showing up on public websites

- Warnings if patterns of credit use change or multiple applications for credit occur within a short time span.

- A periodic statement summarizing your credit report changes, score, and alerts

- Assistance in restoring your identity if it's stolen

>> **What is the monitoring company's cancellation and renewal policy?** Avoid automatic renewals unless you're absolutely certain you'll continue to use the service. They require storing your credit card data, so you'll have to remember to end the contract in accordance with their terms of service or you'll face ongoing charges.

>> **Can you get help from a live customer service person when you want?** Be sure to check the hours the service reps are available. If you need help, you don't want to have to wait until Monday morning.

>> **What exactly will the company do to restore your identity if your identity is stolen and misused?** The service should pay for and perform all the tasks needed to restore your identity. The service shouldn't push this time-consuming, expensive, and difficult process off on you.

If a company makes unrealistic claims or offers unlimited guarantees, chances are it may not be able to deliver. Be sure to check user reviews and industry ratings.

Setting Alarms, Alerts, and Freezes

Everyone has seen the spy movies where they put a piece of tape across the door seam to know if there has been an intruder. Although you can't use a piece of tape to warn you of credit or identity intrusions, you do have access to an array of early warning tools that can warn you something is amiss.

Alarms

You can set an alarm to go off with your bank or credit card company by establishing certain parameters for notification. For example, if a charge for more than a certain amount hits your checking account, they can send an email. You can do the same and more for your credit card accounts easily and for free. Check out your card's website and look for options. You can use texts or smartphone messages if email is too slow — or use all three to make sure you get the alert.

Fraud alerts

You can place a fraud alert on your credit file if you think that someone may be trying to compromise your information. Say you're notified that your personal information was accessed in a data breach. You may or may not have anything to worry about, but a fraud alert requires anyone using your report for new accounts or limit changes in the next 12 months to exercise extra caution and make sure that you're actually the one doing the asking. You also get a free credit report from each bureau.

>> **Extended fraud alerts:** These longer-lasting alerts give you seven years for fraud alert protection and two additional free annual credit report reviews. You need to give the credit bureau a copy of the police fraud or identity theft report you filed.

>> **Active-duty alerts:** If you're an active-duty military person, there's an alert just for you. An active-duty alert lasts for one year on your credit report.

>> **Widget alerts:** Norton, the antivirus software company, has a free widget tool called the Norton Cybercrime Index that sits on your desktop or phone and warns you about real-time cybercrime so you can take preventative measures. The tool also provides in-depth information on cybercrime trends and patterns. Think of it as a traffic report that alerts you to trouble spots, areas and streets to avoid, and potential hazards on the road. Others are now providing similar services.

Credit freezes

A freeze on your credit report locks your report against applications for new credit in your name. In order to review your report, a lender or other party would need to ask you to unfreeze your account. This request tips you off that your identity is being used to apply for credit right away and prevents new accounts from being opened without your permission. There is no fee to freeze or unfreeze your credit report with the national credit bureaus. Unlike fraud alerts that are shared among the bureaus, you must request a freeze separately from each of them. Before you apply for credit or other services, you also must remember to lift the freeze by providing a PIN or following the instructions for each separate bureau.

REMEMBER

A credit freeze will not prevent identity theft. If someone is using your information to apply for credit, you're already a victim. After placing a credit freeze, you must still be vigilant in protecting your identity and ensuring that it isn't being used in ways that are not credit related. Things like tax fraud, making purchases with your existing credit counts, buy-here-pay-here loans, payday loans, job application fraud, and other crimes could still happen using your stolen identity.

3

Taking Action on High Debt and Bad Credit

credit assistance

» **Taking care of some credit problems yourself**

» **Finding free mortgage help, credit counseling, and legal advice**

Chapter **9**

Getting the Best Help for Bad Credit for Free

The only legitimate way to get rid of bad credit is to get your spending and income in sync and then make all your debt payments on time, as agreed. Doing so can be easier said than done, so you may need some help. Getting help from someone with lots of experience is a smart thing to do. Getting it for free is even better. Yet many people avoid seeking help for money or credit problems. Why? Because getting the wrong help can just make matters worse. After all, haven't you been taught that when an offer is too good to be true, it usually is?

This chapter helps you sort through the conflicting and over-blown claims for help that you find in the media. You also find valuable insights to help you decide which problems you can handle on your own, when to turn to others for assistance, and where to get the help you need.

Knowing Whether You Need Help

If you're asking yourself whether you need to get some outside advice or help, you're no doubt feeling some pressure, even if it's only a squeeze. This is a very personal decision with one or two exceptions.

Gauging your need for outside assistance

TIP

To help decide whether outside assistance is right for you, ask yourself — and include your partner if you're not in this alone — a few simple questions:

>> **Are you stressed out?** You know you need to get some help when

- You screen your calls to avoid creditors (see Chapter 10).

- You argue with your partner about money or credit.

- Your sleep is interrupted because of financial worries, and you don't look forward to greeting the day in the morning.

>> **Are you (or you and your partner) being pulled in multiple directions regarding possible solutions?** You may be unsure about which approach to use:

- Increasing income to support your current bills and future goals.

- Decreasing expenses to bring your lifestyle in line with your present income (check out Chapter 13).

- Getting a loan to pay off debt or reduce payments.

- Filing for bankruptcy.

>> **Are you dealing with multiple creditors or multiple problems?** You probably can use outside help if

- More than two or three collectors or creditors have you on speed dial (check out Chapter 10).

- You have many problems (financial, employment, medical, and/or marital) creating stress in your life at the same time.

>> **Are you more than one month late on your mortgage payment?** No matter what else is going on, you need to see a counselor now! A delay or the runaround from your servicer can cost you

  - Thousands of dollars.
  - Your credit.
  - Your home (see Chapter 11 to avoid a foreclosure).

>> **Are you thinking that bankruptcy may not be so bad for your credit?** Get professional, nonprofit counseling before you decide; otherwise, you may not know

  - Whether bankruptcy will solve your problems or make them worse.
  - Whether other alternatives exist that may be less damaging to your credit.

>> **Are you new to credit or to the United States and can't seem to break into the financial mainstream, but don't know what to do next?** You'll benefit from help if

  - You don't understand how credit works.
  - You need to establish credit.
  - You want to get started on your own version of the American Dream as soon as possible (see Chapter 12 for more info).

Handling situations on your own

The following sections outline three credit situations that you can probably resolve without much help.

To solve any credit/debt problem, you need to

>> Identify the cause of the problem and resolve to fix it.

>> Know how much money you have to work with.

>> Act quickly.

Credit cards

If you can't make this month's credit card payment, or if you've missed a payment already, you need to take action. As long as you know what you can afford and you don't mind explaining your situation over the phone, you can get quick results.

Here's what to do: Call the toll-free customer service number and explain who you are, what happened, and how you'd like to handle the situation. If you need a break from making payments, say so. If you can make up the missed payments over the next month or two, make an offer. Just make sure that you can make good on your offer. Be sure to ask the customer service representative not to report your account as late to the bureaus. This decision is up to the credit card company; often, the company is willing to go along with the request as long as you keep your end of the bargain.

If you're polite and proactive and you contact the credit card company before the company contacts you, this approach establishes you as a good customer who needs and deserves special consideration — much better than a customer who is behind in payments, doesn't call, and may be a collection risk.

WARNING

Be careful about asking that a payment be stretched out for more than a month or two. If you need three months to catch up, you may get it — or even qualify for a longer hardship program — but the creditor may close your account, which hurts your credit. Also, don't be surprised if the company asks you to pay more than you think you can. The company doesn't know the details of your situation. Do *not* agree to anything you don't think you can deliver. Saying that something isn't possible and explaining why is much better than caving in but not being able to follow through. Ask to talk to a supervisor — he or she may have more authority to bend the rules.

Mortgages

If you're behind on your mortgage payment, but you're within the grace period allowed in your mortgage loan documents (typically 10 to 15 days from your contractual due date) and you have the money to make up the shortfall, send it in. If you're past the grace period, what you need to do to catch up depends on the state in which you live.

Say you haven't yet made your payment of $1,000 from last month. This month you can send in only $500 extra with your $1,000 payment. So you're short $500, right? Wrong. You may be behind the full $2,000 if the bank doesn't accept either payment because you didn't catch up in full. Or the bank may apply the extra $500 to this month's principal payment rather than to last month's deficit. The gist is, if you aren't far behind and you can catch up in one shot, do it. Otherwise, don't delay — see the later section "Considering credit counseling" and get help.

WARNING

Mortgage lenders count delinquency occurrences differently than credit card issuers. As soon as you're one day beyond the grace period, mortgage lenders consider you late, back to the original, contractual, non-grace due date. After you're 90 days late from the contractual due date (not the grace period), all the rules change, and you're in serious danger of a foreclosure! (Check out Chapter 11 to find out what a foreclosure can do to your credit and how to avoid it.) Also, be mindful that some banks have shorter grace periods for mortgage holders who don't have bank accounts with them.

Student loans

Getting some breathing room on a student loan isn't difficult if you have a qualifying reason for being unable to pay. Unemployment, a low-paying job, illness, a return to school — any of these reasons may qualify you for a short-term waiver, but only if you give the lender a call before you get into a default situation. Student loan people usually cooperate as long as they think you're playing it straight with them.

REMEMBER

If you don't think that you have enough money to catch up on your payments, you may have an alternative: The money may be hidden in your financial budget clutter. The first step in addressing a financial problem is to maximize your income and minimize your expenses. A spending plan (or budget) helps you with that. Only a real spending plan that accounts for at least 90 percent of your income and expenses will help; rough guesses don't yield the results you need. Turn to Chapter 16 for more on dealing with student loans.

Identifying Help You Can Get for Free

Despite the ads that seem to promise better credit and relief from debts, collectors, and even the IRS, only three sources provide truly helpful, truly free assistance for those with credit or debt problems:

» **HUD-certified mortgage counselors:** Mortgage counselors can obviously help you with mortgage issues. They're experts at helping people decide whether to stay in their homes and then making the decision work in the best way possible.

» **Nonprofit credit counseling agencies:** We're big fans of good credit counselors for a number of reasons: They're free, they take the time to tailor solutions to your situation, they're well trained, and their mission in life is to help, pure and simple. The main things they deal with are goal setting, identifying the sources of problems and solutions, and budgeting (the foundation of everything financial).

» **Pro bono lawyers:** Because credit and collections are governed by laws, and because life isn't always fair, the time may come when you need an attorney. But if you're broke or quickly getting there, paying for an attorney may not be possible. Pro bono lawyers work for little or nothing.

Getting help with your mortgage

TIP

Home mortgage debt is different from all other types of debt and can be very complicated. We strongly urge you to use a professional to make sure that you don't make costly and damaging credit mistakes. Here are a few places to look for professionals:

» **BALANCE:** Also known as Consumer Credit Counseling Service of San Francisco, BALANCE is a nonprofit credit counseling and financial education agency, serving families nationwide. Since its incorporation in 1969, BALANCE has helped hundreds of thousands of individuals and families overcome their financial challenges and reach their goals. BALANCE is a national HUD-certified housing counseling intermediary agency and accredited by the Council on Accreditation. Its mission is to provide comprehensive financial housing counseling and education programs aimed at helping consumers achieve financial independence through debt reduction, home ownership, and improved money management skills. For assistance, call 888-456-2227 or go to www.balancepro.org.

>> **995Hope:** This organization is an alliance among counselors, mortgage companies, investors, and other players. It helps distressed homeowners work out mortgage problems so that they can stay in their homes. The folks at 995Hope know the ropes, have access to decision makers, and can help you with the necessary paperwork for free. For help, call 888-995-4673 or go to www.995hope.org.

>> **State housing authorities:** Every state has a housing authority. These organizations offer help to first-time homebuyers and homeowners in crisis, referrals to counseling, and sometimes funds to cure a delinquency. You can find the housing authority in your state or community at www.ncsha.org/housing-help.

>> **Legal/document review:** One of your last resorts is to have an attorney review your loan documents. Some documents may have been drawn or executed incorrectly and may be challenged in court. A pro bono attorney may be able to help you for free. See the later section "Working with an attorney."

Considering credit counseling

A legitimate, certified credit counselor may offer just the help you need to get a handle on your financial problems. A nonprofit credit counseling agency serves as an objective party to help you see your financial situation without emotion and fear clouding your vision. In addition, a trained and certified counselor may be able to offer you some credit education, personalized budgeting advice, and a custom-tailored plan to get you out of debt — all for nothing or next to nothing.

Recognizing debts that credit counseling can help with

Although credit counseling can help in a variety of circumstances, it's essential in five situations. So if you find yourself dealing with any of the following scenarios, get some outside advice pronto, before matters get further out of hand.

>> **Mortgage default:** The rules are complex, the dates are often inflexible, and the servicers are often paper pushers who waste your time until a foreclosure is imminent. Many credit counselors, but not all, are certified mortgage counselors who can get to the right people faster than you and can lead you through a complex process based on a lot of experience and special access to decision makers.

>> **Multiple bill collectors:** You can handle one or two collectors, but when you get to five, ten, or even more, conflicting demands can be impossible to balance.

>> **Joint credit problems:** Credit problems are exacerbated when you share them with someone who doesn't see things the way you do. An outside, dispassionate point of view can make all the difference.

>> **Debts that are backed by assets:** Loans for cars, houses, and boats are all secured by assets. If you don't or can't pay, the lender can repossess and sell your car, home, or boat. If you don't pay your credit card bill, the lender doesn't have any collateral that it can take, because it has no security beyond your word and your willingness to pay as agreed. As a general rule, the more security lenders have, the less willing they are to work with you to solve what they see as your problem.

>> **Bankruptcy:** You must get credit counseling before you can file for bankruptcy. Be sure to pick a good agency that does a lot of this stuff. The agency should be fast, efficient, and cost-effective, or you may run into problems and delays later on.

In all these situations, you stand to benefit from talking to a professional who can help you with experience, resources, and a clear and unbiased outside view of your situation that you can't get when you're stuck in the middle.

Knowing what a credit counseling agency can offer you

Although no magic wand exists to make all your financial problems disappear, a good, certified credit counselor can offer thoughtful and useful solutions. Expect more than one option for resolving things, including some options you won't like. Your counselor can give you a balanced perspective of what you need to do, how long it will take, and what resources are available to help you along the way. Your counselor will probably discuss bankruptcy as well as other solutions.

>> **Goals for the future:** A good credit counselor offers solutions with your future goals in focus. A solution that works for you not only deals with current issues but also takes into account how you see your future. For example, if you're planning to buy a house, get a security clearance at work, or send your triplets to college in five years, that future goal affects which courses of action best fit your needs.

>> **Improved communication with your family:** For about 70 percent of the approximately 2 million people who bare their souls to credit counselors each year, advice and direction are all they need. One unexpected by-product of credit counseling is improved financial and other communication. For many couples and families, the credit counseling session is the first time they openly communicate about goals, spending priorities, and even secrets such as hidden debts.

>> **A plan that works for you:** Expect to have a customized action plan when you're finished with credit counseling. An action plan has to fit the way you live, or you won't follow it. A comfortable budget designed with your spending and saving style in mind is more likely to be effective.

An often overlooked aspect of using nonprofit credit counseling agencies is that they know a lot about other community resources that may be able to help. Doing due diligence before making referrals to community, legal, and other resources is part of a good agency's service.

The credit counseling process isn't something you can breeze through in 15 minutes, because the plan you walk away with is tailor-made for you and your financial situation. Many nonprofit credit counseling agencies have the ability to provide a full online or phone credit counseling experience. Be prepared to take the time to go through the details and make sure you follow up with any requests so that you get a comprehensive plan of action.

>> **Periodic checkups:** Expect some fine-tuning to adjust to changes down the road. Although your counselor anticipates bumps in the road as much as possible when developing your plan, the counselor can't foresee the future. Murphy's Law applies to financial and credit problems in spades. Not only can things go wrong, but with limited financial resources, every bump in the road feels much worse. Ongoing involvement with your credit counseling agency as you navigate this credit repair journey helps you stay the course.

Expect the agency to make it easier for you by giving you the names, email addresses, and phone numbers of people to contact beyond the agency for more help. You should be able to ask your counselor for additional suggestions and referrals as you go along, although most people, when they have a workable plan in hand, are often capable of handling the execution of the plan on their own.

Finding a great credit counseling agency

Here are some things to look for in a quality credit counseling organization:

>> 501(c)(3) tax-exempt status

>> Accreditation by a national independent third-party accrediting organization, especially the Council on Accreditation

>> A willingness to spend at least 45 to 60 minutes with you, and more if needed — and for free

>> A willingness to offer help the way you're most comfortable receiving it — in person, by phone, or via the internet

TIP

Here are a couple of organizations that can help you with your credit counseling needs:

>> **The National Foundation for Credit Counseling:** www.nfcc.org; 800-388-2227

>> **BALANCE:** www.balancepro.org; 888-777-7526

Deciding on debt management plans

For about 25 percent of those who turn to credit counselors, more than advice is prescribed. In these cases, in addition to an action plan, a debt management plan is recommended. A *debt management plan* (sometimes called a *debt repayment plan*) requires that the agency act as an intermediary, handling both communications and payments on your behalf for a small monthly fee. This plan includes revised payments that

>> Are acceptable to all your creditors

>> Leave you enough money to handle your living expenses

>> Generally get you out of debt in two to five years

Debt management plans are an alternative to bankruptcy and often go by other names, such as a *workout plan*, *debt consolidation*, or an *interest-rate-reduction plan*. A debt management plan offers all these benefits and perhaps a lot more. Here's how it works: When creditors realize that you can't meet the original terms of your credit card or other loan agreements, they also realize that they're better off working with you through your credit counselor. Under a debt management plan, your creditors are likely to be open to a number of solutions that are to your advantage, including

>> Stretching out your payments so that the combination of *principal* (the amount you originally borrowed) and interest pays off your balance in 60 months or less

>> Changing your monthly payment to an amount you can afford to pay

>> Reducing your interest rate and/or any fees associated with your loan

>> Refraining from hounding you day and night with collection calls

Why would creditors be willing to do these things for you? Because if they don't, and you really can't make the payments, they'll spend a lot more money on collections than they'd give you in concessions. Plus, if you file for bankruptcy, your creditors may *never* get their money.

REMEMBER

The critical point here is that the creditor has to believe you can't make the payments as agreed. But how does the creditor believe that without staking out your home? The creditor generally takes the word of the nonprofit credit counseling agency you go to for help. Still, being lenders, creditors check your credit report from time to time while you're on a debt management plan to make sure that you haven't opened new lines of credit.

WARNING

Sounds like a good deal: lower interest rates and smaller payments. Well, a debt management plan isn't a free lunch. The minuses may include

>> A potentially negative impact on your credit report, depending on how your creditors report your credit counseling account (although just being in a debt management plan doesn't affect your credit score)

>> Restricted access to credit during the term of the plan

>> Difficulty changing credit counseling agencies after you begin a debt management plan

REMEMBER

The bottom line is this: If you're in debt crisis or you're concerned that you may be getting close to it, a debt management plan from a good credit counseling agency may be a solution. If you're just shopping for an interest-rate reduction or a consolidation-loan alternative, a debt management plan may *not* be in your best interest.

Working with an attorney

You may be asking yourself if an attorney can possibly be free or low-cost. The answer is yes, if that's what you need. If you can't afford an attorney, free or very-low-cost services are available if you know where to find them, and that's what this section is all about.

TIP

Here are some suggestions for finding free legal help:

>> **Legal Services Corporation (LSC):** LSC is the largest provider of civil legal aid for those who can't afford it. LSC is a nonprofit corporation that supports 132 legal aid programs through more than 800 offices throughout the United States. It offers a variety of help, including cases involving family law, housing and foreclosure issues, and consumer issues such as protection from lenders, debt management, and bankruptcy. LSC serves consumers who are at or below 125 percent of the poverty level. Visit www. lsc.gov or call 202-295-1500.

>> **Local bar association:** Your local bar association can help you find the help you need for what you can afford to pay. The American Bar Association has a consumers' guide to legal help on its website to help you find such resources in your state; see www.americanbar.org/groups/legal_services/flh-home or go directly to www.abafree legalanswers.org to get your questions answered.

>> **LawHelp:** LawHelp (www.lawhelp.org) helps low- and moderate-income consumers find free legal aid programs in their communities and provides links to other social service agencies.

>> **American Bar Association:** All branches of military personnel, veterans, and their families can find access to ABA resources at www.americanbar.org/groups/legal_services/milvets.

REMEMBER

A qualified attorney can handle anything a mortgage counselor or credit counselor can. The big difference is that most attorneys don't deal with credit situations every day. As a result, they'll probably take longer to get to the same place than someone who deals with hundreds or thousands of these cases every month. So although you can make a versatile tool fit most situations, sometimes you're better off with one designed specifically for the job at hand — especially when it comes to mortgage issues.

Chapter **10**

Coping with Debt Collection

I f you're reading this chapter, you're probably feeling anxious about your debts. You may be behind on your bills and wondering what to do. You may be getting calls from collectors and wondering how you can possibly meet their demands for payment. If so, you've found the right place to relieve your anxiety, or at least reduce it. Relax, take a calming breath, and read on.

When it comes to coping with bad debt, you have an important ally in the Fair Debt Collection Practices Act (FDCPA). This federal law prohibits abusive practices by debt collectors. That's right, laws exist to protect you from overzealous collectors, who can be stopped and potentially prosecuted if they threaten you, harass you, or lie to you. Knowing that specific rules govern how far a collector may go and that you have rights — legally enforceable rights — should help you feel a little better right away! Knowing your rights under the FDCPA will give you some much-needed confidence when you must communicate with those who attempt to collect from you. This chapter covers your rights and protections in detail.

Handling Those Collection Phone Calls

You couldn't pay some bills, you put off dealing with them, and now you're getting calls from collectors. You may find yourself in the middle of a recurring nightmare of persistent callers who won't go away and who seem to become more determined when you can't give them what they want.

This scenario doesn't have to be the case. The FDCPA protects debtors from harassment by collectors, particularly harassment via telephone. Armed with your knowledge of the rules and a plan of action, as the following sections describe, you can take control of those calls before they control you.

Knowing what collectors can do

There are a few things a collector absolutely must do when they first contact you. If a collector contacts you about a debt by phone, the collector has five working days to send you a written notification. That notification has to

>> State the current amount of the debt you owe along with an itemization of the current amount of the debt reflecting any interest, fees, payments, and credits since a particular date that you may be able to recognize or verify with records.

>> Provide the name of the creditor to whom you owe the debt.

>> Tell you that this is an attempt to collect a debt and that any information obtained will be used for that purpose.

>> Inform you that you have 30 days after getting the letter to notify the collector *in writing* (the "in writing" bit is very

important) that you dispute that the debt is valid. If you do not respond within that time, they can assume that the debt is valid and they can attempt to collect it.

>> Include information about your debt collection rights, including instructions on how to dispute the validity of the debt *in writing* within 30 days, the collector will obtain verification of the debt and mail it to you. If you've been sued, they may send a copy of the court judgment.

>> Provide you the name and address of the original creditor if you request it within that 30-day period. Your request has to be *in writing*.

The collector clearly has some specific requirements. The one thing you need to do if you don't agree with the debt is write a letter. Under the law, a phone call isn't enough.

Here are the things debt collectors *may* do (meaning, they're allowed to, but they may not do it, depending on how you work with them):

>> **Contact you directly.** However, if you tell the collector not to call you again or to contact your attorney instead, and you give the collector the attorney's contact information, they have to stop. If you give them your attorney's information, the file usually goes straight to a collection attorney. Lawyers like to talk to lawyers.

>> **Contact you by phone between 8 a.m. and 9 p.m., unless you agree to other times.** The collector may contact you outside those hours only if you give your permission to do so.

>> **Call you at work.** However, if you tell the collector that your employer prohibits such contact, the collector must not call you at work.

Check out www.dummies.com/go/creditrepairkitfd5e for a sample letter you can send to request that the collector not call you at your place of work.

>> **Contact you by mail.** However, the collector can't put information on the outside of the envelope that indicates a collection attempt or send information on a postcard.

>> **Contact you through social media.** Their messages to you must be private and not viewable by the general public or by your friends or followers. They must tell you that they're a debt collector. Finally, in every message, they must give you a simple way to opt out of further communications from them on that social media platform.

>> **Contact others to get information about where you live and work.** The collector can request only contact information. The collector can't say that he or she is calling in regard to an owed debt. The sticky part is that if the collector calls a friend or partner and they ask who the collector is, the collector can state his or her name and the name of his or her employer.

>> **Supersize your statement.** Only charges that you agreed to under the original terms of your loan may be added to your bill. You can find a list of them in the account terms, in the fine print. These charges could include lots of fees, huge interest rate hikes, and the costs of collection. The reality is that the amount being collected probably won't match what you saw on your last statement.

>> **Ask for postdated checks.** Depending on the state in which you live, the collector may be entitled to ask for postdated checks. Look into your state's guidelines. Although your state may permit collectors to ask for postdated checks, providing one is not in your best interest (see the nearby sidebar "Postdated checks: Good for the collector, bad for you"). The law also prohibits collectors from cashing the check before the date on it, if it's postdated.

>> **Tell the credit bureaus that you're behind on your payments after you've been sent a validation notice.** A delinquency that shows up on your credit report stays there for seven years and lowers your credit score.

>> **Hike your interest rate.** However, you may be hit with a penalty rate if the original contract specifies it. You can't pay the current bill, so why would the creditor increase your interest rate to 20 percent or 30 percent? It's because you're a higher risk than the creditor thought, and it could help them recover a bit more of what you owe.

>> **Repossess your purchase.** Repossession is almost always a bad deal for you because the creditor determines the value of the repossessed item and can charge you for costs incurred in reselling it, too. Here's another shocker: You may have to pay income tax on the difference between what they sell the repossessed item for and what you owe.

>> **Sue you in court.** The collector may ask a judge for a judgment against you in a court of law. Depending on your state's laws, this judgment can be a prelude to garnishing your wages or placing a lien on your home. This kind of civil judgment isn't part of credit reports any more, but it could still pop up to hurt you in other public records and consumer reports reviewed by businesses.

>> **Change the terms of your agreement.** Some collectors may allow you to make up what you owe over time by adding an amount to future payments. Some, to their credit, offer hardship programs, but usually only if you ask. Be sure to get any changes to your agreement *in writing*, particularly if communications are strained. You need documentation to ensure that the agreement is honored.

>> **Accept or offer a debt settlement option for less than the full amount owed.** If a lower amount is agreed on, the collector usually wants the settlement at once and in a single payment. The debt is reported negatively on your credit report as "settled" or "settled, paid for less than originally agreed." Depending on the amount of debt forgiven (usually a $600 threshold), you may get a Form 1099-C from the creditor in the mail at tax time. The IRS considers the forgiven portion of the debt as income and requires you to pay taxes on it.

TIP

Go to www.dummies.com/go/creditrepairkitfd5e for a sample letter you can send to request a settlement.

Knowing what collectors can't do

Debt collectors are *not* allowed to

>> **Threaten you.** In writing or over the phone, collectors must use businesslike language. Threatening, abusive, or obscene language is not allowed.

- **Be annoying.** An annoying collector — isn't that redundant? This rule means that collectors aren't allowed to make repetitive or excessively frequent phone calls to annoy or harass you. Yes, any call from a collector is annoying, but the legal definition is a bit more strict. A collector may not call you more than seven times within seven consecutive calendar days. They also may not call you within a period of seven consecutive calendar days after having had a phone conversation with you about the debt.

- **Be deceptive.** No "trick or treat, smell my feet!" Collectors can't pretend to be anything other than what they are in order to get you on the phone.

- **Lie about the consequences.** Collectors can't claim that you've committed a crime or that you'll be arrested if you don't send payment. The United States doesn't have debtors' prison.

- **Make idle threats.** Collectors can't threaten you with illegal actions or actions that they have no intention of carrying out. If they don't intend to take you to court, they can't threaten to do so.

Deciding whether to answer the phone

You may find yourself reluctant to answer the phone for any number of reasons. You may have had a hard day at work, you may be overtired, or you may not be feeling in control of your emotions at the moment. If you've been contacted by the collector and you've already explained that you're doing your best and that's all you can do, having the same conversation again and again may feel frustrating and unproductive, especially if the collector is on the overbearing side. Don't answer the phone if you know that you won't be able to have an effective conversation.

REMEMBER

Keep in mind, however, that although caller ID and voicemail can help you screen calls (and may help save your sanity), they won't help you avoid or solve your debt problems. If collectors can't reach you by phone, they'll try to find another way to contact you. Snail mail still works, and email, texting, and social media are also options. You don't have to pick up the phone this time, but you will need to communicate at some point.

Preparing to answer collection calls

When you decide that it's time to bite the bullet and talk to the collector, make sure you're prepared. Write down the key points you want to cover in your conversation with the collector. Having a plan in mind helps you stay on track and in control of the call. It also helps you not to over-promise and under-deliver, to avoid losing your temper, and to know when to hang up if the call gets abusive. If you start to feel overwhelmed or backed into a corner by the collector, get outside professional help. You can find out about getting help in Chapter 9.

REMEMBER

Even though you may feel nervous, guilty, or angry, you aren't the first or only person to have gone through debt collections. It happens all the time, and you *will* get through it.

If you're late on some bills, expect to get a call from a collector sooner or later — typically when you're 30 to 90 days late or more. If you decide to pick up the phone, here's what you need to do:

>> **Get the caller's name and contact information.** Use the collector's name during your conversation.

>> **Ask for proof of the debt.** Mistakes happen, and crooks call to try to get money from people all the time. (See the later section "Asking for proof that the debt is yours" for more information.)

>> **Explain what happened.** Provide a very short explanation of why you're behind and what, if anything, you're able to do about the debt.

>> **Make a payment offer.** See the later section "Negotiating a payback arrangement."

>> **Don't agree to a payment schedule that you can't keep.** Be realistic, or you may find yourself agreeing to a plan you know you can't follow through on. (See the later section "Keeping your promise.")

>> **Get it in writing.** If you come to an agreement, ask the collector to put it in writing so it's clear to both parties. If the collector won't do so, write the letter yourself (keeping a copy for your records) and send it to the collector by certified mail (return receipt) so you have proof that the collector received it. If the collector provided an email address, make a copy of the letter and send it that way, too. *Remember:* Putting things in writing is important.

Knowing what not to say

Saying the wrong thing in a conversation with a collector may be unproductive and can turn the conversation into a hostile confrontation that could end up causing you more harm. No matter how adversarial your caller seems, here are some definite don'ts:

>> Don't let yourself get drawn into a shouting match.

>> Don't make threats. It's illegal for them to threaten you and not helpful for you to threaten them.

>> Don't say that you're getting a lawyer if you don't intend to.

>> Don't say that you're going to file bankruptcy if you don't plan to.

>> Don't lie for sympathy (for example, saying "I got sick and couldn't pay the bill," if you were actually on vacation at the beach). If you're caught stretching the truth, even once, people will have a hard time believing you again. The law prohibits collectors from lying to you. Lying to them will only strengthen their case.

Taking Charge of the Collection Process

The best way to deal with the collection process is to face your debts head on and as quickly as possible. Debts don't improve with age, and they certainly don't go away if you ignore them. In fact, as debts age, they get bigger, uglier, and harder to pay. Unresolved debts also have an uncanny knack for resurfacing when you're least prepared to deal with them.

Accounts that are 30 to 90 days *delinquent* (overdue) are usually handled by people who work for the company from which you bought your product or service, or *inside* collectors. If you're contacted by an outside or third-party collector early in the process, chances are the company hired the collection agency because of its tact and effectiveness rather than its skill at offending people. Outside collectors are covered by the FDCPA and must abide by those rules (see the later section "Keeping Collectors in Check"). The creditor and its own internal collection department aren't governed by the FDCPA.

The biggest difference between an inside and an outside collector is that an inside collector may want to keep you as a customer in addition to collecting the money due. However, if the company determines that you're unlikely to make your payments, your customer status becomes less and less of a factor in the way the company attempts to work things out with you.

REMEMBER

Calling your creditors before they call you is always better. Contacting them first places you in a much different category than if they're the ones doing the dialing. Good faith is on your side (but even that fades if you don't deliver on your commitments). Plus, when you call first, you can be prepared and ready for business instead of having to respond to an unexpected call.

This section explains what to do to give yourself the greatest chance of success when dealing with collectors.

Asking for proof that the debt is yours

When you get a call or a letter claiming that you have a past-due financial obligation, make sure to verify its accuracy. Even if you're sure that you owe the money, ask for details: which account it pertains to, what the bill was for, how old the debt is, when the statement was mailed to you, and so on. Asking these questions never hurts. Why? Here are two good reasons:

>> **Mistakes happen.** Creditors make mistakes, so asking for a little proof is reasonable. You're not denying that you owe the debt; you're just making sure that you owe this particular debt, making sure the information matches yours, and making sure that the creditor has the right customer and the right account.

>> **Scammers are out there.** These people will call, email, or write and say that you owe money. Maybe you do, but not to them. They may even have proprietary information that persuades you that they must be legitimate. Get the facts in writing through the U.S. mail before you act. Having the information mailed to you opens scammers up to mail fraud charges.

REMEMBER

FDCPA rules say that you have 30 days to respond to a collection attempt, and you're both smart and well within your rights to dispute a debt. Here's how you do it: Send the collector a letter via certified mail with a return receipt. In the letter, ask the collector to provide proof of the debt. Keep copies of everything you send. When you dispute the debt, the collector must stop all activity and provide you with proof of your obligation before reinitiating contact.

Disputing a bill stops collection activity, but it doesn't stop the clock. Your debt continues aging during the process. It's usually in your best interest to try to resolve matters as quickly as possible when you're sure that the debt is yours and the collector is legit.

Knowing when debts fade away: Statutes of limitations

The United States is the land of the present, the here and now. Our culture and our laws enable you to overcome mistakes of the past so you can have a brighter future. This philosophy applies to old debts, too. Every state has a *statute of limitations* (SOL) that limits how long the courts can be used to collect a debt. After a debt is between 2 and 15 years old (depending on your state of residence) without a payment having been made, it disappears as far as the courts are concerned.

To find out exactly what the SOL is for your state, contact your state attorney general's office or check out www.money management.org/blog/understanding-the-statutes-of-limitations-on-debt. Debts that are too old can't be enforced in a court of law. It doesn't stop them from trying, but the statute of limitations severely limits a collector's ability to recover the debt.

REMEMBER

A debt may be too old to collect under the SOL, but if it is less than seven years old, it will stay on your credit report and severely affect your creditworthiness until it drops off.

Here's what to do if you think you may have an old debt that qualifies for SOL treatment:

>> **Verify the last time you made a payment.** Here's another instance where keeping good records works to your advantage. Making a payment can reset the clock on the SOL. Proving that you haven't made a payment can help protect you from unlawful actions by the debt collector. Today's online banking apps can also be your friend. You may have payment records at your fingertips just by logging into your account. If not, call your bank. Depending on your bank, you may be able to access checking-account payments from long ago. You don't want to see any recent payments.

Say it has been 6 years and 51 weeks since your last payment, and the SOL for your state is 7 years. If you make a payment, the 7-year period could start all over again. Expect more calls or letters from the collector as the SOL gets closer. They may put on more pressure to get you to send in any amount they can get as the SOL closes in.

>> **Contact your state attorney general's office for your state's age limit for SOL status.** They can tell you exactly what applies where you live to help you decide if it's time for you to see a lawyer if you believe that your debt may qualify.

>> **Get a real legal opinion.** When it comes to the law, we don't trust our friends or cousins, and neither should you. See a lawyer even though it may cost you some cash. This is a legal matter, and they call them *law*yers for a reason. They have their own rules and can help you win that game or tell you it will cost more to play than it's worth. When it comes to courts and the law, it's always in your best interest to get professional guidance. Many lawyers will meet with you the first time for free and can tell you if you have a case.

>> **Have the attorney write a letter.** Lawyers have their own language and can help you get the point across to the collector in legal terms. Just be sure the letter includes documentation of the debt's age, proof that it's over the SOL limit, a statement that you don't intend to pay a penny, and if the attorney is taking over for you, a note that all future contact must go through the attorney. No collector will bother to try to collect an uncollectible debt from a lawyer who knows better. And collectors can't go around the attorney after you notify them that you have a lawyer, or they can be sued. The last thing the collector wants is to be sued by the person from whom they were previously trying to collect.

Negotiating a payback arrangement

When you and the collector agree that all the particulars of the debt are legitimate, it's time for you to make an offer to resolve the obligation, whether the cause of the delinquency was an unintended error or unfortunate circumstances. You can make an offer to repay the amount over a period of time. Say you owe $1,000. If you offer to pay $50 per pay period for the next 20 weeks, that plan may be acceptable. Or you can offer to pay $25 per pay period until your next raise in three months, at which time you'll pay $75 per pay period. Offering the amount you're able to pay is always better than waiting for the collector to demand a certain amount.

You want to convey your concern and reassure the collector that you're sincere in your commitment to pay. But that doesn't mean you shouldn't try to negotiate some concessions. For example, you may ask the collector to

>> **Keep the matter between the two of you.** If, for example, you're able to pay off your obligation and you're only 30 to 60 days past due, ask the collector not to report your oversight to the credit bureaus. When the collection is still with the creditor's in-house collection division, your chances of it not be reported to the credit bureaus are better. When the debt is so late that it has been sold or transferred to a third-party collector, they'll be less likely to agree not to report it. Taking care of the unpaid debt early is always better if you can.

>> **Lighten the late fees.** It doesn't hurt to ask if they'll waive any late fees. Be sure to tell them that, if they do, you'll be happy to get off the phone so you can run to the post office to mail your check. Most — but not all — will agree if they're getting the balance due without delay.

>> **Reduce your interest rate.** Think it's not the ideal time to try to get a better interest rate? Actually, it is. The collector wants what's called a *promise to pay* from you to resolve your situation. So ask for a break on the interest rate in order to help you pay the debt faster. On a delinquent credit card account, for example, you may be looking at a 30 percent default interest rate. The lender knows that adding this much to a strained budget increases the chance of a longer and more costly default or even a bankruptcy if you feel you have no way out. Lenders are often willing to help if you're sincere.

TIP

If you're under extreme financial duress, go a step further and ask if they have a hardship program. You may have to meet some qualifications, but if you do, your interest rate may drop dramatically, perhaps even to zero, and may lower your payments for six months to a year.

If you feel that any repayment plan is unrealistic and may push you over the financial edge, work on a spending plan. After you establish your goals, identify your sources of income, and tally up your living expenses, you'll know what you can actually afford for debt service.

POSTDATED CHECKS: GOOD FOR THE COLLECTOR, BAD FOR YOU

At some point in the collection process, a collector may ask you to send postdated checks. The logic here is that, with the postdated check, you demonstrate a firm intention to honor your payment agreement, and the collector doesn't have to call you to remind you to send in any payments you may have agreed to. This scenario also covers the collector in case you "forget" to send a check at the appointed time.

This practice is akin to putting a piece of bacon on your dog's nose and telling him not to eat it. Giving a collector a postdated check is almost always a bad idea because the collector will likely be tempted to cash the check too early, even though he or she isn't allowed to under the FDCPA. If the collector cashes the check early and the money isn't in the account yet, the check will bounce, and the collector will be upset. If the collector cashes the check early and the money is there but the collector gets it sooner than you planned, all your other checks may start to bounce. That can make things even worse for you. You will be responsible for the bounced check. Bouncing a check (called passing an insufficient funds check) has its own set of laws and consequences.

TIP

If working out a repayment plan is too intimidating, if you're dealing with multiple collectors, if you just can't seem to communicate on money matters, or if you just want help getting started, a reputable credit counseling agency can help you create a spending plan. See Chapter 9 for help finding an agency.

Keeping your promise

When you've reached payment agreement, it's essential that you keep your end of the bargain. From the collector's perspective, you've already broken your original agreement to make payments. Breaking a second agreement places you squarely in the not-to-be-trusted category.

REMEMBER

To make sure that you and the collector are clear on what you promised, put everything you agree to in writing. Keep copies of the names, addresses, and phone numbers of everyone you talk to and include a written copy of your agreement with the payment. Ask for an email confirming the arrangement. This is a reasonable request. A letter is a little more challenging because the delivery time may cause you to delay acting on your promise while you wait for the mail to be delivered. That can slow things down a week or more. (They don't call it snail mail for nothing.) It's important to the collector that you act quickly, so confirm all agreements in a thorough note with names and times (don't forget to keep your copy) and send it off with your payment — certified mail, return receipt requested, if you want even more documentation.

Identifying Escalation Options That Help

When you're dealing with a debt collector, you may arrive at a sticking point and recognize that the person you're speaking with doesn't have the authority to do what you're asking. Instead of stopping at that frustrating dead end, you're better off tactfully suggesting that you'd like to talk with someone who has greater authority and is empowered to make decisions. This is known as *escalating* the issue. The following sections show you how to do so, as well as how to contact other people who may be able to help you if the manager can't accommodate you.

Asking to speak to a manager

Collection representatives may have several reasons for not warming to your proposed payment plan. They may

>> Not believe that you're offering your best effort to repay

>> Have a quota to fill, and your offer won't do it

>> Have strict rules regarding permissible payment options

>> Be having a bad day and just don't feel like being helpful

A manager has more flexibility and may have a bigger-picture view that can accommodate your best offer. By asking to speak to a manager, you take the pressure off the little guy and free him to move on to another customer while you and the boss work things out. If you present the situation as though you're helping everyone, you may have an easier time escalating the problem to management.

You can say something like this:

> I understand that you've done your best to try to resolve this issue satisfactorily. Thank you for helping. But I'd like to speak to someone who has the authority to make exceptions, waive policy, or take my offer to a higher level. It's not fair of me to ask you to go against company policy and take the payment I'm offering, so please let me speak to a manager.

If the collector refuses to let you speak to a manager, say that you'll call back on your own and ask someone else. Thank the collector for trying and say goodbye, nicely. Going over the same ground with the same person quickly wears thin. And being polite can go a long way, especially if the person on the other end of the line isn't.

Approaching the creditor

Stuck with the collection agency and unable to make headway? Taking a step backward may help you move forward. Your original creditor may be willing to cut a deal with you even after sending your bill to an outside collector. Much depends on how you left things with the creditor. If you left with bad feelings or you lost it with a customer service representative, you may not be welcomed back. But if the transition from inside collections to an outside agency was just business for the creditor and not complicated with personal anger or animosity, the creditor may still be willing to talk with you. Just don't wait too long, or you'll find the creditor has moved on.

So, why would you want to approach the creditor directly? If you're not getting anywhere with the debt collector, the creditor may be willing to work something out with you. After all, the creditor just wants the money you owe.

TIP

Creditors either place a debt for collection (and pay a commission based on results) or sell the debt outright. The former scenario is more common unless your debt is really old. If your debt has been sold, calling the original creditor won't do any good. The collection agency is then the legal owner of the debt, and you need to work with them. But this bit of bad news has a silver lining. You may well have more room to negotiate in a debt-sale situation because debts aren't sold at full value, so a smaller-than-owed payment may still be very profitable for the collector.

Medical collections are treated a bit differently from other kinds of charged-off accounts. Anything less than a year old or under $500 or already paid will not show up on your credit report. That's something to consider when negotiating.

TIP

A number of changes have occurred when it comes to collections for small amounts. Things like parking tickets, library fines, and debts less than $50 or so have been removed from credit reports. If a collector is trying to get you to pay up for a low amount, check your credit history first. You still legally owe the debt, but if it's not in your report, it could help you prioritize its importance in working with collectors.

Fighting harassment

Getting harassed by a collection agency? You're not alone, and you have a couple of options for help from the government. You can file a complaint with the Consumer Financial Protection Bureau (CFPB). It maintains a complaint database and can help you work with the collection agency to resolve your issues. You can also file a complaint with the Federal Trade Commission (FTC), which watches over the collection industry and enforces the FDCPA. Some consumers have even taken collectors who violate the law to court, and some of them have won very large settlements. Don't get your hopes up, though. The reality is that winning a big lawsuit is very rare. But you have the right to expect the law to be followed and to be treated fairly and with respect.

TIP

To file a complaint with the CFPB against a collector who is harassing you, visit www.consumerfinance.gov/complaint. They usually follow up with the collector about your complaint. Being contacted by a government agency is almost guaranteed to get the collection agency's attention. To contact the FTC, visit www.ftc.gov or call 877-382-4357. The FTC won't follow up on your specific case, but your complaint helps others by allowing patterns of possible law violations to surface. The CFPB uses its complaint database in the same way. Enough complaints against the same collector and the CFPB or the FTC may act.

Here are some other things you can do about harassment or abuse:

>> **Keep your cool.** Always be professional and as calm as you can manage, and never raise your voice.

>> **Take notes during each call.** Be prepared with facts and dates, and know what you're going to say before you say it. Being prepared can give you an advantage. The collection agency definitely knows what it's going to say before it calls you!

>> **Get a name.** Always get the name of the person calling you, and ask for full contact information, including the name of the company and the office manager. Do so *before* you get flustered or frustrated and things get out of hand.

>> **Just say no.** If a collector goes too far or breaks a rule (threatens, yells, uses obscene language, and so on), you can tell the collector to stop and call back when he or she can act in a businesslike manner. Keep a record of the call and the behavior. As always, make a note of the interaction. A record of the call with the time, date, name of the individual, and what was said is always in your favor.

>> **Complain to the original creditor.** Even though you aren't in good graces at the moment, a complaint here can result in action. No business wants an abusive collector scaring away past or future customers. The original debt holder may take the debt back and deal with you directly if you make a good case.

TIP

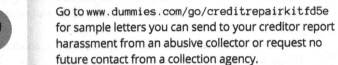

Go to www.dummies.com/go/creditrepairkitfd5e for sample letters you can send to your creditor report harassment from an abusive collector or request no future contact from a collection agency.

>> **Complain to the boss.** You were smart enough to ask for the manager's name when the collector first contacted you, so use it. Your complaint may be the one that gets the abuser fired. No collection agency wants to be sued because of a bully who can't be professional.

>> **Tell the collector to deal with your lawyer.** This is a double-edged sword. After you tell the collector to contact your attorney, all contact with you ends. Usually, the collection agency sends the debt to its own lawyer.

Communicating with Customer Service Before Collection Starts

Communicating effectively isn't always easy, and many people don't even know where to begin. If you're not sure where to start, keep reading. When dealing with creditors, communication can be even more difficult because of the associated guilt, anger, and other emotions; basically, your emotions can set you up for conflict and communication breakdown.

From your perspective, the situation looks like this: You're a responsible adult who has been a good customer for a long time. A series of unfortunate, unexpected, and undeserved events has descended upon you like a plague. You've tried for months to overcome your payment problems before asking for help. You can't seem to catch up. You're at the end of your rope, dangling at the edge of a cliff. But with some help, you know that you can pull yourself out. The process is similar to the one outlined in the earlier section "Preparing to answer collection calls" but the tone and your options are different.

From the customer service rep's point of view, the scenario looks like this: You made a promise and broke it. Everyone else is required to pay their bills on time, so why shouldn't you? You may be overspending and living beyond your means. You need to catch up on your payments as fast as possible. If you don't come through, the collector's job performance and business will suffer, and if the collector gets fired, he or she will be unable to pay his or her own bills.

REMEMBER

See how two people can see the same scenario so differently? It can be very hard to see things from a different perspective, but we know that you'll be more successful in getting the outcome you want if you're able to see the situation from the other side. For whatever reason, you haven't been able to keep all the promises you made. That doesn't mean you aren't a good person. Always remember: The issue is about money and numbers for the collector; it's not personal. But from a financial perspective, it does indicate that doing business with you may be risky.

So now it's *your* job to explain why the customer service rep should accommodate you. Is resolution possible here? Yes — if you do your homework, offer a solution, and follow through on your promises. Where do you start? What do you say? To minimize negative perceptions, be proactive from the start and follow the steps outlined in this section.

Contacting your creditor promptly

Putting off unpleasant tasks is human nature. However, when it comes to requesting assistance from your creditors, the earlier you make the request, the better. From the creditor's point of view, three types of customers exist:

>> Good customers who pay as agreed

>> Good customers with temporary problems who are willing to work things out

>> Bad customers who won't pay what they owe without being "encouraged," if at all

You'd like to be the first type of customer, but sometimes bad things happen to good people and you slip into the second group. What's really important, however, is not finding yourself lumped into the third group.

REMEMBER

The best time to let your creditors know that you're in trouble is as soon as *you* know and have a solution to offer. Don't wait until you've missed a payment if possible — or one payment at most — on that credit card or auto loan. Don't wait for the phone to ring or a letter to come and *then* give your story. Get in touch *before* the payment is late if you know you aren't going to be able to make it. By taking charge early, you give yourself a much greater chance that negative information won't find its way onto your credit report, where it could haunt you for years! Read on to find out what to say.

Explaining your situation

You may choose to contact customer service by phone, in writing, via email, or through the creditor's website. In some cases, you may even communicate through an intermediary like an attorney or a credit counselor. (More about those two options comes in the later section "Keeping Collectors in Check.") Whatever method you use, you need to explain your situation as clearly, effectively, and objectively as possible. Do everything you can to take your emotions out of it. Assure the creditor that, despite your temporary difficulties, you intend to get back on financial track as quickly as possible.

But what do you want to say? What can you do to increase your chances of getting the help you need and deserve? Here are some elements to communicate (using a phone conversation as an example):

>> **Introduce yourself and ask for the person's name.** Why? Because doing so adds a human dimension to the dialogue and may help personalize your call. Don't say "you" or "you people." You should write the name down, because you're probably stressed out and may forget it easily. Plus, when you call again, you'll have a name to refer to.

>> **Begin the conversation on a positive note.** Say something nice about the company and your relationship with it. For example, "I've been a customer for years, and I've always had great products/service from you."

>> **Briefly (in a minute or so) present the facts.** And just the facts. For example, you lost your job, you have no savings, and you have only unemployment insurance for income. Skip the gory details and the emotional commentary.

Offering a solution

After you've succinctly laid out the situation, propose a solution that works for you, *before* you turn control of the conversation over to the customer service representative. Your goal is to make it as easy as possible for the rep to agree to what you need, and the best way is just to ask for what you need! This is a critical and very positive step in the communication process. The customer service rep may actually be pleased that you've come up with a workable plan. Doing so not only increases the chance that you'll get what you want, but may also shorten the call if the rep can agree to your request, thereby making the rep look like a very productive employee. Plus, by keeping more control over the outcome, you have a much better chance of getting a repayment plan that actually works for you. (You may even be able to negotiate a concession or two in your favor; see the earlier section "Negotiating a payback arrangement.")

TIP

Whatever your proposed plan, be sure to cover these bases:

>> **Assure the rep that you're already taking steps to resolve the problem** *now.*

>> **Offer a realistic estimate of how long you need to rectify the situation.** Not "soon" or "I don't know."

>> **Propose a specific payment amount and plan that you can manage.** Don't ask the creditor to suggest an amount. You won't like the answer.

>> **Offer specifics.** Avoid saying, "I can't afford the $300-a-month payment right now. You're going to have to accept less." That's not a plan. Instead, say, "I need to reduce the monthly payment to $150 for the next four months. I could even pay $75 twice a month. Then, in four months, I believe I can return to $300, which only extends the length of the loan by two months." Now *that's* a plan. It shows that you're sensitive to the creditor's situation and that you're making a fair effort to make good.

>> **Don't overpromise.** You may feel intimidated or embarrassed, and it's only natural to want to give the creditor what the creditor wants. Don't be surprised if the creditor pushes back and asks for more. Be firm and don't budge

on your offer, if possible. In the end, though, note that the creditor won't be happy if you promise a certain payment and fail to deliver. If you get stuck, ask to speak to a manager, who may be able to approve your offer.

TIP

If you prefer to handle things in writing, check out the partial payment hardship letter and the offer to return a secured item letter at www.dummies.com/go/creditrepairkitfd5e.

Covering all the bases

REMEMBER

After you propose your plan and agree to terms, ask for a letter outlining the new agreement to be mailed or emailed to you so that there's no chance for a misunderstanding. If that doesn't seem to be forthcoming from your contact, or if you don't receive written documentation of the new terms within a few days, follow up yourself, stating the agreement in writing. Always make sure that any agreement you reach with the collection agency is put in writing.

Keeping Collectors in Check

Debt collectors are people, too. Some are thoughtful and considerate, and are just trying to do a tough job that affects people who have fallen on hard times. Other debt collectors see people with debt problems as deadbeats and get a strange satisfaction from bullying them into paying the debts they owe. Many in the collections field see their role as an extension of customer service to customers in trouble. They'll try to work with you. Unfortunately, there are those who get a power trip from their role and use it as an excuse to use unfair and abusive collection practices on people they think are vulnerable.

Regardless of which kind of collector you find yourself talking to, being prepared before you get on the phone is key to controlling the conversation. The following sections explain who you can call to help you with collectors. (Find out more about dealing with the collection process and collectors in the earlier section "Preparing to answer collection calls.")

Calling in a credit counselor

On your own, you may be able to get to a customer service manager, but the manager can't get around policy that is set by corporate headquarters. Very often, the top people at a collection agency set a special collection policy that applies only to the legitimate credit counseling agencies with which they've established a working relationship. When professional credit counselors get involved, they may be able to deal with a special department that handles only credit counseling accounts and is much more sympathetic than the line collector or manager you can talk to. So, in one leap, you escalate your account to high-level corporate policymakers.

REMEMBER

Talk to a credit counselor from an independently accredited nonprofit agency. Chapter 9 explains how to pick one from a crowded field. The cost to find out what an agency can do for you is zero, free, nada, and the professional analysis of your financial dilemma and your options can be invaluable. As an intermediary, the credit counselor can deal with your creditors on your behalf and may be able to administer a favorable workout plan (often referred to as a *debt management plan*) while you follow a fairly strict budget.

REMEMBER

Fair Isaac's FICO score doesn't take points away for using a credit counseling agency. In some cases, a statement will be added to your credit report that you're repaying a debt through a counseling agency. For some lenders, that's a positive. It tells them you're taking action to get control of your personal finances.

Referring the matter to your lawyer

A good lawyer can work wonders with the more complex legal situations people face from time to time. Like showing up to a gunfight with the second-fastest gun, hiring a so-so lawyer isn't worth the effort. The best attorney for you is one who specializes in debt law. The drawbacks: Lawyers are expensive, and after *you* start down a legal path, so do the collectors.

Get an attorney who specializes in representing debtors. These lawyers know the process, have the right letters on file, and may even know the collection agency or company. Besides sheltering you from having to deal with collectors directly, an attorney helps slow down the freight train of events heading your way. He or she knows what is acceptable to the collector, collection lawyer, and judge (if things get that far). Plus, in today's complex debt sale and resale environment, an attorney can review your loan documents to make sure that your debt is enforceable.

Freeing Up Money to Pay a Collector

It feels like everyone wants a piece of you, or at least a chunk of what little money you have. Where are you going to come up with the money to pay what you owe? The following sections explore ways to reduce expenses and free up some funds to satisfy those creditors and collectors.

We're not going to lie to you: Cutting expenses is no fun! But after you've done it successfully and you have a bit of money to make payments, you'll feel much better. The short-term sacrifice of retooling your spending and changing some old habits will prove to be well worth the effort when you're able to reduce or even eliminate your debt challenge. And establishing new money habits can make the long-term future much brighter.

Utilizing a spending plan

The best way we know to get the most out of every dollar you earn and set yourself on the road to credit recovery is to develop a detailed *spending plan*. A spending plan puts you in control of your finances, allowing you to identify how much money you have to spend on bills and necessities and decide how much money to spend on the stuff you want from what's left. A spending plan tells you just how much available cash you have to meet your obligations and allows you to set some aside to have fun, too. You've probably heard it called a *budget,* but when you look at it as a spending plan, it's less intimidating and actually empowering. More important for this chapter, your spending plan lets you know how much you can afford to offer a collector or creditor to rid yourself of problem debt. For more on developing such a plan, turn to Chapters 3 and 4.

Creating a spending plan is technically easy but emotionally challenging. By putting it in writing, you'll make a critical step toward determining what you need to change! If you still feel overwhelmed, Chapter 9 offers advice on choosing a good credit counselor who can help you with this process for free. (Believe it or not, there *are* people who love putting together spending plans.)

Cutting the fat from your monthly spending

The simplest way to cut expenses is much like cutting calories when you're on a diet. When slimming down, you eat the stuff that's lower in calories and skip the cake. When cutting expenses, you do things that cost less (use more coupons at the grocery store and plan meals to match what's on sale) and lay off the expensive stuff (cancel that reservation to the hot new restaurant in town).

TIP

We mention food for a reason. Eating out is one of the biggest entertainment expenses for American families. If you add up your monthly expense for restaurant food, you may be shocked. Even that $4-a-day latte on the way to work adds up to more than $1,000 a year. Instead of eating out, eat in more often, and pack a lunch for work or school. Make eating at home fun by involving the entire family in preparing some of the dishes you'd order at that fancy restaurant. You could see your monthly spending on food shrink by as much as 25 percent to 50 percent.

REMEMBER

You're not giving up doing something you love forever; you're only giving up these things until you resolve your current financial situation.

The important part is to honestly review your monthly expenses and determine whether you can trim back. The hardest part about creating a spending plan can be setting your emotions aside and looking objectively at the numbers.

The savings from cutting back on expenses may seem insignificant at first, but they add up quicker than you realize. And before you believe you can go another day without a triple latte, you'll have reached your goal. See Chapter 5 for more tips.

Avoiding Collectors Altogether

If you're reading this chapter, not paying your bills on time may be what got you into a bad-credit situation in the first place. But making on-time payments for the amount agreed every time the bill is due is the most important thing you can do to keep bad credit from getting worse. This section lays out specific ideas to help you pay your bills on time and keep creditors off your back.

Getting organized

Nothing is quite as frustrating as getting hit with a $25 or $35 late-payment fee on your credit card statement when you're trying to cut expenses. The good news is that a late payment doesn't necessarily cost you any more than the fee. Thanks to the Credit Card Accountability, Responsibility, and Disclosure Act of 2009 (CARD Act), you no longer have to worry about whether your interest rate will go up if you're one day late with a payment. Unlike a late fee, which is a one-time expense, a higher interest rate would make you pay more every month going forward. The CARD Act requires a payment to be 60 days past due before the penalty interest rate kicks in. You'll still probably have to pay a late fee, though. Unlike an interest increase, a fee for making a late payment can be charged as soon as it happens.

Getting organized is by far the best way to avoid unnecessary late payments. Here are some options for getting organized:

>> **Set up automatic bill payment.** Using online banking tools to make at least the minimum payment due lets you set it and forget it. You don't have to worry about missing a payment — it's automatically deducted from your bank account. The catch is that you have to make sure you have the cash in your bank account before the payment is due on your debt.

>> **Pay bills as soon as you receive them.** If you aren't comfortable with automatic payments, make a pact with yourself to get the mail, sit down immediately, and write checks or go online to pay any bills you receive *that day*.

>> **Mark a calendar with the due dates for all bills.** Allow at least a week for bills that you mail and a few days for bills that you pay online. Place the calendar where you'll see it every day so you don't miss any due dates. Better yet, set a reminder in your phone calendar so it alerts you when it's time to pay the bills. Technology is your friend when it comes to paying bills! And don't forget to include paying the phone bill in your calendar.

>> **Set up a filing system.** Place bills in folders or in due date order, marked with the day of the month that they need to be paid. The trick is remembering to place the bills in the folders or organizer and to check the folders on a daily or weekly basis. You can do it with paper or using a computer with scanned or downloaded documents. Either way, be consistent in gathering and filing the documents every month.

Experiment, find a solution that works for you, and get those bills paid!

Stopping the paycheck-to-paycheck cycle

If you live paycheck to paycheck, you may find it difficult to pay all your bills on time and in full every month because money is so tight, especially when an emergency crops up and you have to pay for it out of money allocated for another bill. Consider these tips:

>> **Start a savings account.** What does starting a savings account have to do with living paycheck to paycheck? Plenty. Without emergency savings, you won't be able to stop living paycheck to paycheck. When you have savings set aside, that unexpected expense is no longer an emergency, and you don't have to take on debt to pay it.

>> **Ask your creditor to change your due date.** You can request that your due date fall later in the month, or earlier, when you have the money to pay the bill in full and on time.

TIP

Check out www.dummies.com/go/creditrepairkitfd5e for a sample letter you can send to make this request.

>> **Look to your job to free up extra cash.** If you want to increase your cash flow and can't get a second (or third) job, you may not have to look far. Here are a couple of things you can do regarding your current job:

• **Check your payroll deductions.** If you get a hefty tax refund each year, see your employer and add withholding allowances on Form W-4 to increase your take-home pay. But if you'll end up writing a check to the IRS, don't do it.

TIP

For assistance in figuring out the right number of withholding exemptions you should take, see the IRS Withholding Estimator at www.irs.gov/individuals/tax-withholding-estimator.

• **Free up some money in your retirement plan.** Don't take money out of the plan; doing so would result in some ugly penalties, and a lot less for your retirement in the long run! But you can temporarily reduce or suspend your contributions to help close the gap. Just have a plan to make them up later.

Chapter **11**

Reducing Credit Damage in a Crisis

With millennials opting for smaller spaces and generations rooming together, many things have changed about the economics and potential risks of homeownership. What about staying in a home that's worth less than what you paid for it? What are your options if it's worth less than what you owe on the mortgage? And what are the risks to your credit if you have a default? What used to be a no-brainer decision has become more complicated than anyone could have imagined. Millions of people are asking these questions today. This chapter helps you find the answers. You find information on legal obligations, taxes, credit, and the long arms of credit scores and reports.

This chapter is an important one for everyone, including home-owners who are under financial stress, people challenged with medical debt or student loans, or those struggling with the fall-out from natural disasters. Money, credit, self-esteem, and the very roof over your family's head are at stake when a disaster occurs. Here you find the advice you need to make the best decision for your situation. Getting help and getting it early is critical. Fortunately, help *is* available, and this chapter guides you through the process of getting what you need.

Assessing the Damage from a Mortgage Meltdown

Credit score misinformation is everywhere. What you don't know can and will hurt you if what you don't know is that your credit report and score have been seriously damaged. If you're trying to assess the damage to your score from a mortgage melt-down or even just a mild mortgage sunburn, having the best information available is important.

Today, credit score simulators can provide you some indication of the impacts of negative events on your credit score. Regardless of which credit score is being used (FICO or VantageScore), you can get a fairly accurate picture. The major credit reporting bureaus (Equifax, Experian, and TransUnion) and many financial institutions offer credit score simulators as part of your customer experience with no fee associated (see https://wallethub.com/best-credit-score-site for more information). All these simulators allow you to use real-life scenarios to gain insight into the impacts certain actions may have on your score. Because they're just a simulation, they don't impact your real score so you can see the positive and negative impacts before you take any actions.

TIP

For an infographic from FICO showing the effects of various types of scenarios and the impacts on your credit score, go to www.dummies.com/go/creditrepairkitfd5e. Mortgage defaults, foreclosures, repossessions, and bankruptcy have some of the most significant impacts, underscoring how important it is to resolve any problems as quickly and amicably as possible.

REMEMBER

The terms *default, delinquency,* and *negative event* tend to mean the same thing. Strictly speaking, being *delinquent* (late on a payment) leads to a *default* (based on the legal terms in your mortgage documents). Both are negative credit events that you don't want to experience.

REMEMBER

People with great credit who default on a mortgage see a greater credit-score point drop than those whose credit isn't so great. Why? Because a good score has to fall farther in order to end up at the lower point level that indicates serious credit problems. In general, the higher your starting score, the longer it takes for your score to fully recover from the damage.

Delinquencies and some actions that result in your home being taken back by the lender *(deed-in-lieu)* or sold under distress (as in a *short sale*) cost you big points. However, there's no significant difference in credit-score impact between a short sale, a deed-in-lieu, and a settlement. Mega point drops in your credit score tend to occur when the lender loses money in addition to your being in default, such as in the event of a short sale or a foreclosure, both of which cost the bank money. But the worst and longest lasting of all injury to your credit occurs when you file for bankruptcy. Unlike the other, lesser defaults, a bankruptcy can stay on your credit report for up to ten years.

In addition to credit score penalties, you need to take the collateral damage into consideration:

>> Although a score may *begin* to improve sooner, it can take up to seven to ten years to *fully* recover.

>> Fannie Mae (the Federal National Mortgage Association) is the nation's largest mortgage buyer. It buys and then resells mortgages on Wall Street, helping to keep mortgage interest rates low. Fannie excludes borrowers who've gone through a foreclosure from obtaining a Fannie-backed loan for seven years.

>> Fannie Mae won't accept a mortgage from a person who has had a mortgage delinquency in the last 12 months.

>> If you can't get a Fannie Mae loan, you may have to take a nonconforming loan, which may require expensive mortgage insurance premiums and, for those with lower credit scores, higher interest rates and a larger down payment.

Understanding How Mortgages Differ from Other Loans

Mortgages differ from other consumer loans partly because of their size — a lot of money is on the line — and partly because they're backed by what historically has been the gold standard in collateral: your home. With more at risk, the stakes are greater. Furthermore, mortgages are not only underwritten differently from other types of credit but also have a different collection process, generally called the *foreclosure process*. When you default on a mortgage, the lender *forecloses*, or terminates the mortgage, and your house is taken away from you.

From a credit-score and credit-reporting standpoint, mortgage defaults and foreclosures are among the most serious negatives out there, with the exception of bankruptcy.

Obviously, a foreclosure puts a serious hit on your credit score and history. To help you minimize this hit, this section gives you an overview of how mortgages differ from typical credit and how mortgages and credit go hand in hand. Here you can find valuable information to help you understand when a late mortgage payment can quickly cause you problems and what you can do to get help.

Spotting a foreclosure on the horizon

A lender has a lot of money on the line with your mortgage, and the longer you're delinquent, the greater the risk that the lender will lose money on a defaulted loan. The result is that a mortgage lender or servicer has a much lower tolerance for delinquency than, say, a credit card issuer. For example, as long as you're less than 180 days past due on a credit card, it's not the end of the world. Generally, you can just pay the minimum due along with a late fee and pick up where you left off. If you're really lucky, you may get the lender to waive the late fee and not report the delinquency. For a mortgage, however, being just 60 days late puts you well on your way to the edge of a cliff, and you may not even be aware of it.

WARNING

The key number to avoid in a mortgage delinquency is 90 days late. After 90 days, unless you get some help or work out an arrangement, the mortgage servicer generally requires the entire amount that is overdue (the *arrearage*) to be paid at once and may not accept partial payments. A 90-day mortgage delinquency on a credit report is very serious. To make matters worse, many people don't understand when the 90 days is up. The time frame isn't as simple as you may think, so the next section covers it in detail.

Mortgage servicers don't call you at work or at night, and they don't yell or threaten you over the phone. On the contrary, the tone of their messages (often letters) is concerned, low-key, and polite. If you ignore these messages, you could lose your home. But if you know where to get help, what to ask for, and what to avoid, your situation can change for the better.

Counting to 90

If you're 30 or 60 days late on your mortgage and you make a partial payment, the servicer usually credits your account with the payment. If you cross the 90-day mark and then send in a month or two's worth of overdue payments rather than the entire amount due, however, the servicer may send the money back and let the foreclosure clock keep ticking.

REMEMBER

After you're late on your first payment, your grace period disappears. (Your *grace period* is the period of time specified in your mortgage loan agreement during which a default can't occur, even though the payment is technically past due.) The grace period applies only to loans that are up-to-date, or current. The following example illustrates how this works.

Say your loan agreement states that your due date is March 1. Assuming that you have a typical two-week grace period, your payment actually has to be in by March 15. If you don't submit your payment by March 15, you miss that window of opportunity and lose your grace period. Your April payment is now due April 1. April 15 is no longer an option. In other words, no more grace period in April. If you pay April's payment on or before April 1, you get your grace period back for May and thereafter, as long as you continue making your payments on time.

If you lose your grace period, the counting of the number of days you're late begins on the 1st of the month rather than the 15th. So, if you don't send in a payment on March 15, April 1, or May 1, then on May 2, you need to catch up on the payments for March 1, April 1, and May 1, plus any fees and penalties (which can be hundreds of dollars or more), all at once. This sum is a huge amount for someone in financial difficulty. If you don't pay, then the formal foreclosure process can start on May 2, and you may incur fees for collection costs, attorneys, title searches, filings, and more. After the foreclosure process begins (it's up to the mortgage servicer when this process actually begins), the mortgage servicer can *accelerate* the loan, meaning that it can ask for the entire loan balance — not just the late part — to stop the foreclosure.

Knowing Where to Turn for Help with Your Mortgage

If you're having trouble making your mortgage payments, time is of the essence. Getting your mortgage issue resolved quickly is critical. Note that the mortgage company doesn't want your house; it just wants to keep your loan *performing/up-to-date/current* (different terms for the same thing). But also note that the mortgage company doesn't care whether it has to take your home. If the rules say to foreclose, the mortgage company will foreclose, without hesitation and without remorse.

Following are a few ideas on where to turn for help (along with some tips on who *not* to turn to!). The essential point, however, is not to wait but to take action. You can work directly with your mortgage servicer, but the servicer may offer you only what it thinks is the easiest solution, not the one you need, because the servicer doesn't know your situation in detail.

Finding good help for free

A number of housing counseling agencies are available to help you work out a solution. You should use a third-party intermediary that's approved by the U.S. Department of Housing and

Urban Development (HUD). These intermediaries are cheap, experienced, and knowledgeable and can help guide you through what can seem like an insurmountable problem. They're experts at getting the right information on the right forms and to the right person at the mortgage servicer — no easy task!

TIP

Although the contact information may change over time and new players are continually offering this service, you can look for resources through Fannie Mae's website (www.fanniemae. com) or HUD's website www.hud.gov); contact BALANCE at 888-456-2227 or go to www.balancepro.org; or contact 995Hope at 888-995-4673 or go to https://995hope.org. For the fastest service, call or go online for a virtual visit before you visit an office. You can also get good help by contacting the National Foundation for Credit Counseling at www.nfcc.org or 866-557-2227. Many credit counselors are also HUD-certified housing counselors. See Chapter 9 for additional sources of help.

Working with your mortgage servicer

If you're unable to make a mortgage payment on time, you can contact your mortgage company for help. If you believe that this may be the beginning of a serious problem that needs serious attention, ask for the *loss mitigation department,* which may be referred to as the *workout department* or the *homeownership retention department.* This department is able to go the extra mile to help you and can deal with complex issues better than the standard collection department, which usually offers only to make catch-up payment arrangements.

TIP

To find the contact information for these departments, you can look in your mortgage loan documents, on your monthly statement, or in the correspondence you've received from your mortgage servicer. When you call, get names and extension numbers so that you can try to keep a single point of contact and continuity. Doing so may not be possible, but knowing who you talked to, when you talked, and what you agreed on is important in case matters get really serious. Take good notes!

Keeping the call simple is a blessing to everyone concerned, so you should do some homework before you call and have a written, well-thought-out proposal prepared that meets your needs and helps solve your problem. Be sure to include what concessions you need and for how long. You should also write down what happened, what changed, and how to contact you or your counselor if you're working with one. Writing down the facts and options before you call helps you keep from drifting during the conversation and keeps everyone focused on the task at hand. When you ask for what you need, be sure to ask what other options may be available beyond the one that's offered.

TIP

If you want some free help on figuring out what specific help you need to ask for, contact a counselor at 995Hope (888-995-4673 or https://995hope.org) or BALANCE (888-456-2227 or www.balancepro.org).

WARNING

If you can't resolve your issue quickly or if you get transferred to multiple people, get expert help quickly. Time is precious, and mortgage servicers can easily pass the buck until you find yourself in a foreclosure situation. See the preceding section for information on where to find free help from experts.

Avoiding help that hurts

REMEMBER

Some people make a living, and a good one, on the backs of folks in trouble. People who offer to help you with a mortgage problem for a fee are only trying to help themselves. So, proceed with caution and consider the following tips as you evaluate any prospective source of help:

>> Don't decide anything while in a panic.

>> Be sure that you're dealing with a HUD-qualified nonprofit organization. Look them up at www.hud.gov.

>> Don't make payments to anyone other than your mortgage servicer or its designee.

>> Be wary of any organization other than your mortgage servicer that contacts you to offer help. It's fine if you call them, but not if they call you!

>> Never sign a contract under pressure.

>> Never sign away ownership of your property.

>> Beware of any company or person who guarantees that they can stop a foreclosure or get your loan modified.

>> If English isn't your first language and a translator isn't provided, use your own.

>> Get a second opinion from a person or an organization that you know and trust.

WARNING

If you're having trouble paying your mortgage, getting a high-risk, expensive second mortgage won't help. It will only keep you from finding real solutions by wasting critical time and money.

If you receive an offer saying that you've been preapproved for a loan, don't get too excited. It only means that you've been preapproved on a very cursory level and only for the offer, not the actual loan. Don't waste too much time chasing preapproved offers.

Considering Alternatives to Going Down with the Ship

If you're having trouble making your mortgage payments, you may have a host of options to help you avoid the expense and upset of losing your home through a foreclosure. Even if you can't or don't want to keep your house, you can still lessen the damage to yourself, your family, and your credit by taking positive action.

REMEMBER

Before you take any action, assess your situation as dispassionately as you can. If stress and anxiety make that impossible, seek help first from a third-party professional such as a nonprofit HUD counselor (see the earlier section "Finding good help for free") or an attorney. Your situation may not be as bad as you think it is, or it may be worse. What's important is to know for sure where you stand. You need what's called *loss mitigation counseling*, which is help to develop a solution that enables you to afford to keep your home or lessen the damage caused by a foreclosure.

This section gives you some loss mitigation options to protect your credit.

What to do first

If you already have a plan to resolve your problem, catch up, or at least resume payments in three to six months, consider the following suggestions:

>> **Find a good nonprofit housing counseling agency.**
We recommend the Hope Hotline (888-995-4673), 995Hope (888-995-4673 or https://995hope.org), Money Management International (888-645-2227 or www.moneymanagement.org), BALANCE (888-456-2227 or www.balancepro.org) or another nonprofit credit counseling agency that has a HUD-approved housing counseling program. Expect an assessment of your overall financial picture and whether you can realistically afford your mortgage payments.

>> **Ask your mortgage servicer about a repayment plan.**
The servicer sets up a structured payment plan (sometimes called a *special forbearance plan*) that gets the mortgage back on track in three to six months by making up past-due amounts in addition to your regular payments. Get all the terms in writing so that you're both clear on the terms. The sooner you do so the less damage to your credit report and score.

>> **Check the HUD** (www.hud.gov) **and Fannie Mae** (www.fanniemae.com) **websites for resources and help.**
Both sites have excellent referral resources, information on programs that might be right for you, and warnings to keep you from falling for scams.

>> **Don't wait until it's too late!** Talk to your lender about your need for assistance, and do it soon. Some servicers have programs for those who are not yet delinquent and other programs for borrowers who already are delinquent. For the greatest number of options, get started as soon as you know that you have a problem making your mortgage payments as agreed, and be sure to ask for all the options your servicer may have for you.

What to do for more serious problems

For problems that may take longer than three to six months to remedy, ask for mortgage loan forbearance or loan modifications.

A *forbearance* temporarily modifies or eliminates payments that are made up at the end of the forbearance period. This is where the lender allows you a period of time (usually three to six months), during which time you can make lower or no payments. This option also prevents your credit from being damaged by a string of late payments.

A *repayment plan* is a payment arrangement agreed upon by the lender to accept partial extra payments from you until the delinquent amount is repaid. For example, if the monthly payment is $1,200 and the mortgage is three months delinquent, the lender may allow the borrower to pay $1,800 per month for six months. However, if no agreement is made, lenders will generally reject a partial payment.

A *loan modification* permanently changes one or more terms of the original mortgage in a way that addresses your specific needs. If this option seems intimidating, use a HUD-approved agency to deal with the servicer and offer solutions on your behalf. Clear communication is key here.

REMEMBER

Modifications need to be in writing and approved by both the servicer and the borrower. Don't be surprised if the servicer asks for a fee to cover the costs of processing a loan modification.

What to do to end matters

Even when you can't solve your problem or just can't stand it anymore, you're better off staying in control of the process rather than just giving up. Doing so can lessen credit damage and expenses and keep your dignity — and maybe your sanity — intact.

The following are some of the many options available. And don't forget that another reason to use a free professional mortgage counselor is that newer options may be available to you as well. Be sure to check out the resources mentioned in the earlier section "Knowing Where to Turn for Help with Your Mortgage."

>> **Selling your home:** You may be able to sell your home in a short sale if you have no equity left or a pre-foreclosure sale if the value of the house still exceeds the amount due on the mortgage.

>> **Short sale:** You get your lender to allow you to sell your home for less than the mortgage value. This option is generally cheaper for the bank and less stressing for the homeowner than a foreclosure. Because it is good for the lender, you can negotiate a bit. Ask that the loan deficiency be reported to the credit bureau as a zero balance rather than a charge-off.

>> **Pre-foreclosure sale:** A pre-foreclosure sale arrangement allows you to defer mortgage payments that you can't afford while you sell your house. It also keeps late payments off your credit report.

>> **Deed-in-lieu of foreclosure:** If the home can't be sold, you can sign the title over to the lender and move out. To qualify for this option, you usually can't have a second mortgage, a home equity loan, or another lien on the property.

>> **Stopping payments as part of a plan:** Not our favorite option, but if your plan is to save money for rent or for the larger down payment you'll need for a new place to live, then setting aside the money you would have paid for your mortgage can accrue several months or even years of savings. The price can be high in credit damage and stress, however. See the later section "Strategic default: Stopping payments."

Managing a foreclosure

REMEMBER

If you're being foreclosed on, you still may have the option to talk to the servicer and try to work things out, buy more time to come up with a solution, or at least make a more dignified exit from your home. But again, timing is very important, so don't wait!

>> **Get a HUD-approved counselor involved and review loss mitigation options with your servicer.** Most want to help. (Check out the earlier section "Knowing Where to Turn for Help with Your Morgtgage.")

>> **Remain in contact with the servicer's loss mitigation staff until you get a solution you can live with.** If they don't offer workable suggestions, ask to speak to managers and vice presidents or higher. This is not a time to stand on protocol or accept "I'm sorry" for an answer.

>> **See an attorney.** Ask for options. Review all the mortgage and foreclosure documents to be sure they were properly drawn and executed. The technical phrase used here is *truth in lending compliance.* Ask about bankruptcy options and timing so that you know all options available to you.

Strategic default: Stopping payments

A *strategic default* is an intentional mortgage default based on a plan or strategy. Here's an example: A person has a home whose value has fallen so far below what is owed on the mortgage that he will never realistically recover enough equity to break even on the home. Because the house will never be worth what is being paid, the homeowner stops paying the mortgage. This option is more popular in states with *nonrecourse mortgages* (meaning that the house is the sole security for the mortgage loan, and the homeowner isn't responsible for any shortage beyond what the house brings at sale). However, you need to understand some of the possible consequences:

>> **Credit score:** Any defaulted payments (delinquency) and foreclosure will show up on your credit report and lower your credit score. How much your score will be reduced depends on your score *before* the default and other credit activity. A lower score means you may have more difficulty when trying to get approved for credit in the future. If you're able to be approved, you may end up with a higher interest rate.

>> **Housing:** After foreclosure, buying a new home can be difficult. With a foreclosure on a credit report, you may

have to wait three years before you can qualify for a Federal Housing Authority (FHA) mortgage (one year on rare occasions) and two to eight years before you can qualify for a *conforming mortgage* (the most common type of non-government loan), depending on the lender.

>> **Deficiency balance:** This is the difference between what the lender sells your home for after foreclosure and what you owe on the mortgage. In some states, called *recourse states,* the lender can sue you for the deficiency balance, which may allow them to garnish your wages or take other collection actions against you. In nonrecourse states, the lender generally cannot sue you for the deficiency balance, although there may be some exceptions. For example, nonrecourse protection may not apply to a refinanced loan or second mortgage.

Other factors to consider include how much longer you would like to stay in the home and how far underwater you are. If you're $25,000 underwater and your home suits your long-term needs, it probably makes sense to just stay put and wait for the market to recover. But if you're $100,000 underwater and your job or family situation requires you to move quickly, you may find strategic default more appealing. At the same time, it may not be your only option. For example, you may be able to rent out your home or get your lender to approve a short sale, where you sell your home for less than what you owe on your mortgage.

Thinking about your goals and the implications of strategic default can help you decide if it's the right choice.

TIP

For a chart that shows each state's timeline for foreclosure based upon the last payment installment, go to `https://single family.fanniemae.com/media/6726/display`.

Strategic default is a high-credit-damage strategy, but it may be cost-effective depending on your situation and plans involving loans or credit use in the future.

Strategic default is an unfortunate reality for many of the long-term unemployed. Thousands of homeowners are stopping payments on homes that they can no longer afford or that are deeply underwater. The argument goes: After all, this is business, and businesses routinely stop paying on debts that they can't afford or that are worth less than they owe. You probably have been told that you have to pay your bills, honor your obligations, and keep your promises, but many home buyers are taking a business rather than a personal approach to their homes and finances.

Most mortgages detail what happens if you don't pay. Either you pay or your home is taken away. So the question arises: If you tell the bank to go ahead and take the house, are you meeting your obligations? From the bank's perspective, clearly you're not. From your family's perspective, however, the answer may be different.

Some states require all mortgages to be *nonrecourse*, meaning that the lender has recourse to the defaulted property and nothing else.

REMEMBER

Staying in a home you can't afford can deprive your family of your precious savings, empty your retirement accounts, and eventually ruin your credit when you finally default. Many people are willing to put up with the price of any stigma or guilt in order to ensure a faster recovery with more money in their bank accounts.

Dealing with Deficiencies

When all is said and done, you may still owe some money. If your home sells for less than the amount you still owe on the mortgage, plus fees, then you may have what's called a *deficiency balance*. For example, say you borrow $500,000 to purchase a home, but you fall behind on payments or walk away from the home, and the bank forecloses. The home ultimately sells for $400,000. The $100,000 that the lender loses on the deal is called a *deficiency*. A first mortgage holder may or may not forgive this amount. Second mortgage holders often go after the borrower for deficiencies.

Your lender can get a deficiency judgment lien against your personal property and any other real estate that you own, giving it a security interest in that property. This means that the bank could foreclose on other real estate if you have enough equity for the bank to think that it might get enough money to make the effort worthwhile. However, just because the lender gets a deficiency judgment does not mean that it will try to collect. The lender may opt to write off the debt and issue you an IRS Form 1099-C. If this happens, you might owe taxes on the forgiven amount.

REMEMBER

If a lender comes after you for a large deficiency, consider speaking to an attorney about the benefits of filing for bankruptcy versus trying to work out a payment agreement with the lender. This can help ensure you're making the best possible decision for your situation.

The most important thing is to realize that your problems may not be over when you leave the home. You may need to deal with the IRS if you don't qualify for mortgage debt forgiveness under its rules.

The following are some potential, and we stress *potential*, situations you may face and what you can do to deal with them:

» **The lender may ask for a note.** Although this practice isn't current among first mortgage holders, we want you to be aware of it for the future, or if your second mortgage holder loses money on your loan. This note isn't written on monogrammed stationery; it's a promise to pay an unsecured amount to cover the mortgage deficiency after the sale. Use an attorney if your lender mentions this to you.

» **The lender may send a demand letter.** A mortgage lender may send a demand for payment of any deficiency following the sale of a home. The lender uses a *demand letter* if it doesn't want to give you an unsecured loan for the balance due. In essence, the problem is all yours, and you need to work out a way to pay the balance. Again, if this happens, get an attorney to advise you.

» **The lender may forgive what you owe.** More likely among first mortgage holders, forgiveness isn't required. This gesture is nice as far as it goes, but the IRS counts forgiven debt as income. Forms 1099-A and 1099-C, which are normally used to document unreported income, are also used to report forgiven debt. The amount of the forgiven debt becomes taxable income in most cases.

Debt reduced through mortgage restructuring, as well as mortgage debt forgiven in connection with a foreclosure, may qualify for this relief. If you spent the forgiven debt money to pay a car loan, credit card bills, or for any non-real estate purpose, it's not covered, and you'll get a tax bill for it. Debt on second homes, rental property, and business property doesn't qualify.

TIP

If you are a foreclosed borrower faced with a sizable 1099-C, you still have hope. If you file IRS Form 982, Reduction of Tax Attributes Due to Discharge of Indebtedness, and you're insolvent at the time of the forgiven debt, the IRS may forgive the liability. (You can find IRS Form 982 at www.irs.gov/pub/irs-pdf/f982.pdf.) Again, see your attorney for the details.

If you receive a Form 1099-C from your mortgage lender for the current tax year, or if you filed a tax return for the prior tax year that included income from mortgage loan forgiveness, this option may be for you. If you meet the requirements of the Qualified Principal Residence Indebtedness (QPRI) exclusion, you don't have to report the forgiven principal as income on your tax return. The QPRI exclusion may allow an exclusion up to $1 million (up to $2 million for married couples) of forgiven debt from their taxable income.

>> **The state you live in makes mortgages nonrecourse.** If you live in certain states, you may get a break relating to personal mortgage deficiencies. Some states have passed laws saying that you're not responsible for any mortgage deficiencies.

Preparing for "Credit Winter"

After a foreclosure, your credit will be severely damaged — in some cases and for some purposes, for years to come. Knowing that post-foreclosure credit is hard to come by, you're wise to give some thought to how you'll cope with the credit fallout that may seem like the equivalent of a nuclear winter.

When you realize that you may be getting in trouble with your mortgage, you can do some things to protect your access to credit in the "credit winter" that often follows a foreclosure. Like the biblical farmer who put aside grain for the lean years to come, you can store up some credit in advance. Here's how:

>> **Review your credit cards to make sure that you have enough credit available.** Open new credit cards before you become delinquent on your mortgage. Doing so ensures that you can lead a more normal credit life while your credit is recovering. Plus, using and paying off multiple cards each month provides new streams of positive data to help repair your damaged credit report.

>> **Establish a personal line of credit at your local bank or credit union that is not secured by your home.**

>> **If you're planning to make a large financed purchase such as a car (purchase or lease), major appliance, or furniture down the road, consider making it before you become delinquent on your mortgage, while your credit is still strong.**

>> **Prepare a short explanation (called a *consumer statement*) of why you defaulted and what you've done to make sure it won't happen again, and have that statement placed in your credit report.** It's like an exit statement that explains why you left your last job in the best possible light. This explanation may be useful if you need to find a new job that checks your credit report, are up for a promotion at work, or are looking for new housing.

Curing Medical Debt

For any health decision, it's always important for you to understand your rights. Whether it's patient privacy, informed consent, or otherwise. State and federal laws provide a variety of protections when it comes to healthcare. However, it's always important to be your own advocate or ensure you assign it to someone who has your best interest.

Receiving a medical bill in the mail doesn't impact your credit score, but if you don't pay it and it goes to a collection agency, it will likely be reported to the bureau. This is when it impacts your score. The challenge is that you may not know when the healthcare provider is sending it to a collection agency because it could be different from provider to provider often from 60 to 180 days or some time in between.

Understanding reporting and scoring rules

Because of the amount of time it can take even a well person to review and challenge a hospital bill and then to wrangle with an insurer over coding or coverages, the three major credit bureaus standardize medical debt reporting and protect consumers' credit reports from being unduly affected by medical debt. Equifax, Experian, and TransUnion do not report paid medical debts on consumer credit reports and those less than a year old. They also don't report any medical collections under $500.

Medical debt can stay on your credit report for seven years, so an unpaid medical debt on your credit report can weigh heavily on your score if it's sent to a collection agency and is over a year old. Curing your medical debt can often be the difference in a change to your score, especially as you deal with the health of you and your family.

Reviewing your options for paying medical bills

Take specific and timely action to negotiate your medical bills, ideally before the treatment or procedure, but you can also contact the provider afterward and discuss options. The No Surprises Act (www.cms.gov/nosurprises/Ending-Surprise-Medical-Bills) may help. It limits the amount you pay out of pocket to a level closer to what you would pay if the healthcare provider were in network. The act defines this limit using a recognized market amount or qualifying figure (like the average fee for the service).

TIP

Consider setting up a repayment plan — many healthcare providers would rather work out a plan with you than refer it to a collection agency. If you don't have healthcare insurance and have to pay out of pocket, you may also find resources to check

costs on procedures in your area. Healthcare Bluebook (www.
healthcarebluebook.com) and FAIR Health Consumer (www.
fairhealthconsumer.org) allow you to research average costs
of specific procedures in your area. This can also be helpful when
negotiating prices for procedures.

Discovering how insurers get your medical information

In June 1995, the Federal Trade Commission (FTC) announced
that it had reached an agreement with the largest insurance
provider to provide the same guarantees and protections from
unfair treatment in credit and employment investigations for
consumers applying for health, disability, and life insurance as
they provide to millions of consumers under the Fair Credit
Reporting Act (FCRA).

The establishment of the Medical Information Bureau (MIB)
effective October 2, 1995, required that all insurance companies
that are members of the MIB abide by the FCRA. What does this
mean? That you have to be informed when a consumer report (or
information included in the MIB) played any part in the insurer's decision to deny coverage or to charge a higher rate. The
insurance company must notify you of the name and address of
the consumer reporting agency that provided the report, which
in this case, would be the MIB. As a result, you're entitled to
receive a free copy of your report from the MIB, if requested
within 30 days, to verify the information is correct.

Any health, disability, and life insurance provider that is a member of the MIB must give notice to you if they received information from the MIB concerning you, it was used to alert the
provider for possible further investigation of your insurability,
and the application for the insurance was rated or declined in
whole or part because of the information obtained from that
investigation.

MIB also provides assistance to finding lost life insurance or
unclaimed funds if a loved one has passed away.

TIP

To request your consumer report from the MIB, go to www.
mib.com.

Monitoring insurance claims for errors

Centralized, comprehensive statistics or reporting regarding errors in medical insurance claims don't exist, but some studies have shed some light on the subject. One audit study from Equifax in 1988 found that 98 percent of hospital bills contained mistakes. The audit of thousands of bills from more than 5,000 public, private, and university hospital bills were reviewed, and an average bill at that time was $39,000, while the average mistake was $1,488. Yikes! Other more recent studies and articles indicate estimates of 30 percent to 80 percent of bills contain errors.

REMEMBER

You may be one of those people who hate opening medical bills that come in the mail, but this is an area that requires an extra level of diligence. Go through the entire bill and ask questions to make sure you understand the charges.

Dealing with denied medical claims

Be aware of your options if you have denied medical claims. If your medical claim has been denied, you may want to consider the following:

>> **Contact your healthcare provider and advise them of your situation.** If you can't pay, you have options. And if you don't have medical insurance, contact the hospital or provider. Most hospitals are required by the IRS to provide benefits back to their communities. Eliminating your debt can certainly qualify as one of those benefits!

>> **If your insurance claim is denied, file an appeal.** This includes writing a letter to your insurance company. The deadline for submitting an appeal is noted in your denial letters. You may have to ask your doctor for assistance if she disagrees with the insurance company or reach out to your insurance regulators for help. For help with filing an appeal, go to www.healthcare.gov/marketplace-appeals/getting-help.

>> **If you cannot be an advocate yourself, find a medical billing advocate who can provide you the help you need.** The Patient Advocate Foundation is a national

nonprofit organization that has provided mediation and arbitration services since 1996. It offers assistance to patients dealing with the effects of chronic, debilitating, or life-threatening illnesses. Its free services include resolving insurance-access issues, helping patients with employment issues, and assisting with medical-debt crises. Reach the organization at 800-532-5274 or www.patientadvocate. org. You also may want to check out

- **Healthcare Advocates, Inc.** (www.healthcare advocates.com), which knows the industry, laws, and regulations to help you get the best health care.

- The **Alliance of Claims Assistance Professionals** (www. claims.org), which is a nationally recognized association of independent Claims Assistance Professionals (CAP). It provides medical claims assistance and patient advocacy to individuals and businesses and is fee-based. Each business determines its own scope and cost of services.

Managing Student Loans

Student loans can be a great way to establish a good credit history, as long as you pay them as you agreed. In 2023, the U.S. Department of Education's Office of Federal Student Aid reflected more than 43 million student loan borrowers in the United States totaling more than $1.77 trillion in outstanding debt.

Graduating from college is an exciting time, a time when you can begin a career and potentially move to another location. In many cases, you have a grace period (usually 6 or 9 months, depending upon the type of loan) before you have to begin repayment. Some circumstances — like active-duty military service, loan consolidation, leaving school, or dropping below half-time enrollment — may affect the grace period.

Default timelines

For student loans, the first day after you miss a payment, the loan becomes past due or delinquent, and it remains delinquent until you pay the past-due amount or make other arrangements.

If your loan is delinquent for 90 days, your student loan will be reported to the three major national credit bureaus.

A delinquent loan becomes a defaulted loan after it remains delinquent for a certain amount of time. A William D. Ford Federal Direct Loan or a Federal Family Education Loan defaults after you've failed to make scheduled payments for at least 270 days.

TIP

If you feel like you won't be able to make your student loan payment, contact your loan servicer (https://studentaid.gov/help-center/answers/article/how-to-find-my-loan-servicer). You may be able to defer your payment based upon the Federal Student Aid definition for discretionary income. If your income is up to 150 percent of the poverty guidelines for your state and family size, deferral may be an option. You may also be able to qualify for an economic hardship deferral if you're receiving welfare (Temporary Assistance for Needy Families [TANF]) or you're serving in the Peace Corps.

Other types of deferments include cancer treatment deferment, graduate fellow deferment, in-school deferment, military and post-active duty deferment, parent plus borrower deferment, rehabilitation training deferment, and unemployment deferment. Go to www.usa.gov/financial-aid for details.

If deferral isn't an option, you may want to consider modification of your repayment plan. A graduated repayment plan usually starts with a smaller payment and then graduates to a higher payment for ten years or up to 30 years, if consolidated.

Loan forgiveness programs

Depending on your situation, you may be able to have your student loan(s) forgiven. In other words, you may not have to pay them back. There are many ways to qualify, but Public Service Loan Forgiveness is the most common (https://studentaid.gov/manage-loans/forgiveness-cancellation/public-service).

Other forgiveness programs exist for:

>> **Teachers:** https://studentaid.gov/manage-loans/forgiveness-cancellation/teacher

>> **Government employees:** https://studentaid.gov/manage-loans/forgiveness-cancellation/public-service

>> **Nonprofit workers:** https://studentaid.gov/manage-loans/forgiveness-cancellation/public-service

>> **Doctors, nurses, and other medical professionals:** https://studentaid.gov/manage-loans/forgiveness-cancellation/public-service

>> **Disabled people:** https://studentaid.gov/manage-loans/forgiveness-cancellation/disability-discharge

>> **Repayment under an income-driven repayment plan:** https://studentaid.gov/manage-loans/repayment/plans/income-driven#idr-forgiveness

>> **Those whose school has closed:** https://studentaid.gov/manage-loans/forgiveness-cancellation/closed-school

>> **Those whose school has misled them:** https://studentaid.gov/manage-loans/forgiveness-cancellation/borrower-defense

>> **Federal Perkins loan borrowers:** https://studentaid.gov/manage-loans/forgiveness-cancellation/perkins

>> **Victims of forgery:** https://studentaid.gov/manage-loans/forgiveness-cancellation/forgery

>> **Those who have declared bankruptcy:** https://studentaid.gov/manage-loans/forgiveness-cancellation/bankruptcy

>> **Those who have died:** https://studentaid.gov/manage-loans/forgiveness-cancellation/death

Loan programs and rules are constantly changing. For the most up-to-date information on managing your loans, go to www.usa.gov/financial-aid.

WARNING

The Consumer Financial Protection Bureau (CFPB) advises borrowers to be aware of servicer issues now that the three-year payment pause has expired. Long hold times, delays in processing income-driven repayment plans, and inaccurate or untimely billing statements may be encountered. If this happens to you, let the CFPB know by calling 855-411-2372.

Where to get help

We always recommend a discussion with a nonprofit credit counselor, because they're trained to know how to help you create the best plan for your situation. Contact the National Foundation for Credit Counseling (800-388-2227 or www.nfcc.org) to find a nonprofit credit counseling agency near you.

If you need help with managing the repayment of your student loan, go to the Office of the U.S. Department of Education at https://studentaid.gov/manage-loans/repayment#.

Federal student loan borrowers who are having trouble making their monthly payments should check out the 2023 SAVE plan (https://studentaid.gov/announcements-events/save-plan#other-updates), which can lower payments and reduce interest in addition to providing other benefits.

If you're a totally and permanently disabled veteran, check out www.disabilitydischarge.com.

Avoiding Car Repossession

When you finance a car or truck, the lender holds certain rights on the property until you make your final loan payment. This means that if you default on the contract by missing payments, they have the right to *repossess* (take back) the vehicle.

If you're having financial trouble, contact your lender immediately. Don't wait until you've missed a payment or two. Depending on the state where you reside, the lender may not need a court order or provide advance warning to repossess the vehicle. In some cases, they may repossess after just one missed payment!

Before the vehicle is repossessed, review your spending plan or contact a nonprofit credit counseling agency (see Chapter 9). See whether there are any areas of your budget where you can cut back. Maybe you can get a second job or a part-time job to add to your income. If you can't make changes that will enable you to afford the payments, you have a few options:

>> You can contact your lender and ask for assistance.

>> If the vehicle's value is more than you owe on the loan, you may want to consider selling the vehicle.

>> You may decide to give the vehicle back to the lender. This is called a *voluntary repossession*. Not only can a voluntary repossession save you the repossession fee, but the lender may also agree to waive the deficiency balance and not report it as a repossession on your credit report. (Get these promises in writing!)

Don't be afraid to contact your lender. In almost all cases, they don't want the vehicle — they want you to repay the loan. So, the earlier you make this contact, the better. If you wait until after you've missed a payment, it may be too late. If you've looked at your cash flow and know what you have to work with, you can begin to negotiate. Explain your situation — whether it's temporary or permanent, and how much money you have (if any) to go toward the payment. Your options for resolution may include the following:

>> **Making no or reduced payments for a period of time:** When that time is up, you either increase your future payments until you repay the balance due or add the amount you owe to the loan and make extra payments at the end.

>> **Refinancing your loan:** If your credit rating is good and the value of your vehicle is greater than the loan balance, you may be able to refinance the loan with a better interest rate or longer payment term, which would reduce your monthly payments. For example, if you have two years left on your loan, you may be able to get a new loan where you have five years to repay, which will reduce the payment because of the longer time frame.

Repossession: What you can do

If you can't make a payment arrangement with your lender and you don't make your payments, eventually the lender can hire someone to repossess the vehicle. If that happens, you have a few options:

>> **Reinstating the contract:** Depending on your state and the contract, you may have the right to *reinstate* the contract (pay all past-due installments, including late fees and costs the lender has incurred in repossessing and storing the property).

>> **Redeeming the car:** You may be able to *redeem* the car (pay off the whole debt for the car in one lump sum, including late fees and costs the lender has incurred in repossessing and storing the property).

REMEMBER

Not all states have these options, nor do all contracts, so check with your lender on what options may be available to you after a repossession.

Dealing with auto loan default deficiencies

If you can't reinstate the contract or redeem the car (see the preceding section), the lender will sell the car at a wholesale auction. Whether you or someone else buys it, you'll be responsible for the deficiency balance if the vehicle sells for less than the loan amount. A *deficiency balance* is the difference between the amount that you owed on the loan and the price the vehicle sold for at auction — plus repossession, storage, and auction costs.

With car repossessions, there is almost always a deficiency balance. Some lenders may sue for this sum, while others may try to work with you to repay it or even forgive it. If the lender does forgive it, the IRS will consider that amount income and will assess taxes due on the forgiven debt.

In some circumstances, the lender may decide that the deficiency balance is uncollectible and "charge off" the loan as an unsecured debt. This generally means that the lender will claim it as a loss to its business. However, you should be aware that the dealer may still sell this "uncollectible" debt to a collection agency, which will then seek you out to collect on the loan.

Coping with So-Called Acts of God and Other Things That Aren't Your Fault

It seems as though, just when you think you can get your finances together, something else comes along beyond your control (for example, a natural disaster, a pandemic, or a terrorist attack). The good news is that, often, when disasters occur (and depending upon significance of the impact), programs are set up to assist those in need.

You're more than likely dealing with many other important things after a disaster, but timely action is key. Missing payments can significantly impact your credit score, even if you were injured, your home was destroyed, or you lost your job. If you're having financial difficulty as a result of the disaster, or you think you'll have trouble keeping up with your financial obligations, don't wait until after you've missed your payment to contact your lenders or creditors. Even the IRS may have access to additional hardship options. These are specific actions that can help put your mind at ease during these difficult times.

Creditors can add information or special codes when they report to the credit bureaus to grant special treatment to victims of natural disasters. In the past, those codes neutralized positive and negative information on your score, which may have resulted in your score being reduced. Recently, the VantageScore was modified so that missed payments for these victims are neutralized so your credit score isn't impacted if you aren't able to pay your bills during this time.

TIP

Monitor your credit reports for fraudulent activity after a natural or declared disaster. After the declaration of the pandemic, the three national credit reporting bureaus made it possible for you to request a free credit report each week.

TIP

Check out www.experian.com/blogs/ask-experian/how-does-a-natural-or-declared-disaster-impact-my-credit for helpful links and tips on coping with a disaster.

4

Successfully Managing Your Debt and Credit for Life

Create (or restart) good credit for first-timers, immigrants, students, and military service personnel.

Give your credit score a boost by identifying your credit style and achieving balance with your spending and savings.

Chapter **12**

Starting or Restarting Your Credit in Real Life

C redit isn't an American invention. It's been around in one form or another since ancient Roman times. Modern consumer credit, however, is as American as apple pie. Taking off after the GIs returned from World War II, credit has been among the most prolific of financial services. Life without it is almost unimaginable today, but if you're among those starting over or just getting started, getting the credit you need may be easier said than done. Those starting over because of divorce or death can find the process to be a stressful endeavor, while credit newbies such as recent immigrants and high school or college graduates may wonder where to start. You may find yourself feeling like you're looking through a shop window but can't find the door to get in.

This chapter is your point of entry. Take your seat at the table and help yourself to a big piece of the American dream: credit.

Debunking Misinformation about Banking and Credit

REMEMBER

Depending on your culture or what your friends and family may have told you, you may not have an accurate understanding of how credit really works. However, with a few tips, you'll find that using credit can increase your enjoyment of life and all it has to offer. The following list debunks some commonly held misconceptions about banking and credit:

>> **Banks aren't safe places to put money because they can fail, causing you to lose all your money.** Not so. All depository institutions (like banks) are insured by the full faith and credit of the U.S. government for up to $250,000 per depositor. No one has ever lost a penny of money that was insured in an FDIC or NCUA federally insured depository account.

>> **Bank accounts are unsafe because currency can decrease in value or become worthless overnight.** When you deposit money into a U.S. bank, it's deposited in dollars. The dollar, though subject to fluctuations in value, is the most stable and trusted currency in the world. So it's safe!

>> **The government may nationalize your bank and your account.** If the last financial crisis taught people anything, it's that the government wants to support, not own, banks.

>> **You need to be rich to be treated well at a bank.** Not so. Adding new customers is a top priority for banks, and the size of your account, no matter how small your deposits may be, doesn't determine your value as a customer. Banks know that many big depositors start out small and increase their deposits over time. If a bank doesn't respect you on your terms, take your money to a competing bank.

>> **Using cash is safer than using credit or debit cards.** A lost or stolen card is protected against misuse by another person (most have a liability of $50 or less); lost or stolen cash is gone. Plus, purchasing with cash never builds the credit history you need for a credit score.

>> **You can't build a credit history if you have only a consular ID or a green card and not a Social Security number.** Not true. You can establish a credit history and use credit without a Social Security number.

The following sections explain why you need credit and why it's safe. We hope that this information eases any anxiety you may have.

Why you need credit

What's your definition of the good life? A good job, a safe place to live, a car, some financial security, and a good education for your kids? The reality of life in the U.S. is that having good credit is important in accomplishing goals like these.

Let's start with that good job. Chances are that at some point you'll have to compete with others for a good position. Many employers check your credit history to see whether you're reliable or you have distracting financial issues at home before making an offer. People can lie about their experience (ADP Screening and Selection Services says that about half of applicants lie on their resumes), and they can pretend to be nice during an interview, but a good credit history is tough to fake. As one employer put it, "When you think about it, people who have good credit keep their promises and are responsible, so it makes sense that if their credit is good, they may be more honest." So, all other things being equal, the job may go to the candidate with the best credit history.

The same thing happens when you try to rent an apartment, buy insurance, apply for a college loan, or vie for a promotion at work. In all these circumstances, the person making the decision may check your credit history as part of the qualification process. Being underbanked and relying on cash may knock you out of the race. It pays to understand how to build good credit and use the banking and financial system to your advantage.

Why credit is safe

The credit industry didn't become the huge and powerful entity that it is today without addressing the question of safety. The federal government has put many regulations and safeguards in place over the last several years to ensure the safety and fair treatment of credit users. As a result, you have access to one of the fairest and most market-driven credit systems in the world. The following laws play a major role in protecting borrowers in the U.S.:

>> **The Fair and Accurate Credit Transactions Act (FACT Act or FACTA)** gives you lots of rights when it comes to how your credit is reported and what you can do to correct mistakes. It also gives you rights and remedies in the event of identity theft.

>> **The Fair Debt Collection Practices Act (FDCPA)** spells out what third-party bill collectors can and can't do when they try to collect a debt. If they step over the line, you can sue them.

>> **The Equal Credit Opportunity Act (ECOA)** prohibits credit discrimination on the basis of race, color, religion, national origin, sex, marital status, age, and whether you get public assistance. Creditors may collect this information, but they can't use it to decide whether to give you credit or how to set your credit terms.

>> **The Credit Card Accountability, Responsibility, and Disclosure Act (CARD Act)** protects you from unfair credit card billing practices. Major protections spell out notification requirements, grace periods, fees, interest rate changes, restrictions on student cards, and more.

>> **The Dodd-Frank Wall Street Reform and Consumer Protection Act** established an independent consumer financial protection bureau within the Federal Reserve to protect borrowers against abuses in mortgage services, credit card services, payday lending, and credit counseling.

>> **The Truth in Lending laws** ensure that you won't find any hidden surprises when you borrow money. All the costs of borrowing must be spelled out for you before you sign a contract.

Obtaining Credit: Starting Out on the Right Foot

You're ready to begin building your own credit, but you're not quite sure where to start. They say that a journey begins with a single step, which just goes to show how wrong people can be. The journey actually begins when you have a destination in mind. Then, after packing your lunch and other essentials, you take that first step. You build up a credit history over a period of time. How much time depends on how active you are and which scoring model is used to rate your credit file.

Don't fret, though. This section walks you through the steps to help you begin your credit journey down the right path.

Establishing a credit file without a Social Security number

You don't need a Social Security number to start building your credit report. In fact, a frequent misconception is that to establish a credit history, and thereby a credit score, you need a Social Security number, a driver's license, or a voter registration card. None of these items is required to establish a successful and envious credit record.

REMEMBER

When a credit bureau receives a new data line, the bureau matches the data with the following items, in the order shown:

1. Your name
2. Your birthdate
3. Your address
4. Your Social Security number

No number? No problem. The bureaus can use plenty of other matching points to get your information into the right file. But being consistent is important! For example, make sure to spell your name exactly the same way every time you apply for or use credit.

Setting goals before you set out

Figuring out what your goals are prior to seeking credit is an important step, especially for the underbanked and those new to credit. Writing down your goals enables you to see what you need to do financially to achieve success.

To begin setting goals, you (and your partner, if you have one) should follow these steps:

1. **Set aside some uninterrupted time to dream about the future you want.**

TIP

Allow at least an hour, and set an end point so that you finish before you are exhausted. You can always come back to this step later after some reflection.

2. **Write down some short-term (one year or less), intermediate-term (one to five years), and long-term (more than five years) goals.**

Typical goals include beginning to save this year, beginning to save next year, getting out of debt in a year, and rebuilding bad credit. Other goals may be to get some financial education on topics such as investing, children's college savings accounts, and retirement accounts.

Writing down your goals serves two purposes: It clarifies what you're talking about, and it makes your goals seem more real.

3. **Make a list of the actions you need to take to reach each goal.**

For example, if you want to get a better apartment and a new job, how do you do so? Good credit can help. A smart first step is to get a free copy of your credit report at www.annualcreditreport.com and make sure that it's accurate (see Chapter 7). Dispute and remove any inaccuracies or out-of-date items to improve your credit. Consider adding utility payment histories and banking information using programs like Experian Boost (www.experian.com/consumer-products/score-boost.html) and UltraFICO (www.fico.com/ultrafico). Then make sure to make your payments on all your accounts on time. It's simple, but it works. Part 1 has more suggestions about budgeting and goal setting.

4. **Track your progress.**

Reviewing your progress toward your goals periodically is not only an incentive to keep up the good work but also an opportunity to celebrate your interim successes.

Establishing a relationship with a financial institution

The saying "That's as good as money in the bank" means that it's as good as it gets. Having money in the bank is a good thing; it is the situation you want to be in. If you don't have a relationship with a bank or credit union, we can't stress enough how important this relationship is to your ultimate success. You want to develop a relationship with a bank by setting up at least a savings or checking account, not just so you have a place to take out a loan or get a titanium credit card to impress your friends, but because you need a place to put the money you earn but don't spend right away. Saving is essential to your success.

WARNING

Spending everything you make or using credit to supplement your income is a recipe for disaster. There's no substitute for savings when life throws you a curveball. Chapter 10 has details on what you can do when times get tough. But without savings, even life's little bumps are enough to hold you back on your journey to financial success.

Why you need to save

Everything is going okay. The money that comes in goes out, and your debt is under control. You may be a little short at the moment and your credit card balances may be building, but you figure that will end as soon as you get that promotion in six months. Then your car muffler falls off and costs $500 to repair, your tooth breaks at lunch and you need $1,200 for a crown, and your roommates tell you that they're moving out and you have to pay the rent on your own. Where does the money come from if you have no savings?

You can use credit if you have any left. But if you do, you may be paying a high interest rate and getting closer to your card limit, your credit score may be dropping, and your minimum payment may now be huge.

Without access to credit or savings, you have fewer choices. You may have to carpool, have the tooth removed rather than crowned, and be forced to move to less-expensive housing. That's why you need savings; credit and good luck are never enough for you to be financially successful.

How to get started saving

Fortunately, starting to save is easy and painless once you get going. The key is not to focus on how you're going to save six months' worth of living expenses, which could test even a saint. (For your information, St. Matthew is the patron saint of money managers.) What you should do is start with a small savings program but make it automatic.

To get started saving, take the following steps:

1. **Go to a nearby bank or credit union and ask about automatic deposit savings and checking accounts.**

    You probably don't have much to put away, at least right now, but that's okay. Limited funds are no excuse for not saving. Tell the bank that you don't want to pay any fees because you'll be using automatic deposit. If the bank charges a fee, go to another bank or credit union. Banks and credit unions usually waive all fees for people who save regularly through payroll deductions.

2. **After you open two accounts, one checking and one savings, go to your human resources or payroll department at work and say that you want your pay automatically deposited into these two accounts.**

    For example, you want all your take-home pay minus $5 (or more if you can) put into checking and the remaining $5 (or more) put into your savings account. At the end of the first pay period, you will have saved $5. Not a huge sum, but you're starting a habit that will grow and add up with time.

    TIP

    If direct deposit isn't available through your employer, you can have your bank automatically transfer money monthly from your checking account to your savings account as soon as your paycheck is deposited.

3. **When you get that next raise or promotion, have half the increase automatically deposited into your savings account.**

   Now you're making a smart financial move — increasing your savings by putting away the extra money from your raise before you have an opportunity to spend it! Do the same thing for tax refunds and other windfalls. In no time you'll have a cushion that can get you over life's bumps without stretching your credit or damaging your credit history!

REMEMBER

To secure your financial future, stop cashing paychecks and start automatic savings. You owe it to yourself, your family, and your future.

Using prepaid and reloadable cards

While you are building your credit, you may want to consider using prepaid and reloadable cards as alternatives to using cash. They're neither credit cards nor debit cards; rather, they exist somewhere in between. You deposit money onto the cards at locations throughout the nation and then use them as you would a credit or debit card. But they don't build your credit history or score.

REMEMBER

The following list outlines the major advantages of prepaid and reloadable cards:

>> You can use money without getting mugged for the cash in your pocket.

>> You need no credit record or credit check — just your name, address, and phone number and the ability to pay a one-time fulfillment fee. Non-U.S. citizens can provide an alternative form of ID, such as a driver's license, passport, or alien registration. Funds may post to your account within 30 minutes.

>> Prepaid cards offer convenience, easy availability, guaranteed approval, and other features that can make them ideal substitutes for credit cards.

>> You can use prepaid cards online, over the phone, and in many other places, just like a credit card or debit card.

>> Prepaid cards can help with financial discipline and the building of good financial habits.

Fattening up your credit file

If your credit file is underweight, you're not alone. Today, up to 62 million U.S. adults — nearly 22 percent of credit-eligible consumers — come back from credit inquiries to the major bureaus either as no-hits or as *thin files* (files with too little data in them to receive a credit score).

If you fit this category, don't worry. You can take action to build your credit muscle. The following options work well for credit newbies and underbanked individuals.

Continue using your foreign credit card if you have one

You may be surprised to find out that foreign credit history doesn't carry over and can't be imported into your U.S. credit file. However, you can still use your impeccable overseas credit experience to your advantage. You can either continue to use your foreign credit card or get a letter from a multinational bank extolling your virtues so that the local underwriters will approve you for an American credit card that is reported to the American credit bureaus.

TECHNICAL STUFF

Global scoring is expected in the future; in fact, FICO claims a proven global score that's accurate in every country in the world except France (*quelle surprise!*). However, while the global score is being used in many countries, it isn't used in the U.S. yet.

Ask that an alternative score be used to score your application for credit

FICO Score XD is a one-time snapshot that obtains positive and negative landline, cellphone and cable data from the National Consumer Telecom and Utilities Exchange (NCTUE), and public record and property data from LexisNexis Risk Solutions to generate a score for those who may have a thin file (very little data) or only stale information in their credit reports.

Take out a passbook loan

A *passbook loan* is a loan the bank makes to you using your own money. It may sound strange, but if you open a passbook savings account at a bank or credit union and then borrow the money back, the bank gladly charges you interest (low interest, thank heavens) and reports your loan repayment history to the credit bureaus. You use your money in place of credit for the loan until you can build enough credit to get an unsecured loan. Faster than you can say "Super Prime," you're adding positive history to your file and improving your score.

TIP

Check with your bank or credit union to make sure that it reports the loan to at least one, and preferably all three, of the major credit-reporting bureaus. If it doesn't, request that it do so. If the bank is unwilling to report the loan to at least one of the bureaus, take your business elsewhere.

Get a secured credit card

A secured card is a cross between a credit card and a prepaid card. After you establish a savings account and build up the balance, you can ask the bank to give you a credit card backed by your deposit in the bank. You may qualify for a credit line in excess of the amount you have in savings.

Many credit issuers eventually move you to a traditional credit card after a period of successful payment. The best part is that, unlike most prepaid cards, many secured cards are reported to the three major credit bureaus and can help you build a history and a credit score. Shop around for the best terms; many secured credit cards have high interest rates and fees.

Here's how to get and use a secured card:

1. Contact your bank or credit union to find out whether it offers secured credit cards, or look online for an issuing bank.

TIP

Watch out for annual processing or maintenance fees. You can get secured credit cards for free — you just have to look around for banks or credit unions that offer them.

2. **Deposit the funds to be used as security for the card.**

   Be sure that the account is FDIC or NCUA insured.

3. **Use the card for purchases, making sure that you can pay the balance each month.**

   You don't need to use the card a lot. Just make a few purchases each month.

4. **Make on-time payments every month.**

Avoiding high interest, fees, and scams

Unfortunately, being new to something leaves you vulnerable to abuse by people who know the rules better than you do. Abuses perpetuated on immigrants and credit newbies have been around forever and aren't about to go away. This section lists several that you're likely to run into, along with some guidelines on how to handle them.

Payday loans

When you have a job, no savings or credit, and an unexpected expense, what do you do? An entire industry has arisen to answer this question. *Payday lenders* charge a very high interest rate or fee for a short-term loan guaranteed by your next paycheck. The fee is based on the amount of your paycheck, and you must supply the lender with a signed check for the date the loan is due.

It's not unusual for a person seeking such a loan to need additional money after the lender cashes the postdated check. This can start a vicious cycle of high-fee, high-interest loans rolling over or piling up with no practical way to pay them off. Payday lenders don't report your loan experience to the credit bureaus, so you receive no credit history–building benefit. If you must use a payday lender, look for one that's a member of the Community Financial Services Association of America (www.cfsaa. com). Members subscribe to a code of conduct and may offer extended repayment terms if you can't pay back a loan as scheduled.

Refund anticipation loans (RALs)

Refund anticipation loans (RALs) are high-fee loans secured by your tax refund that may, and the operative word here is *may*, get you your refund a week or so earlier than having it direct-deposited after filing your return electronically. The real down-side of these loans is that the person who sells you the loan has an incentive to inflate your tax refund to get you to take out a higher loan.

If your actual refund is less than what you borrow, you owe the difference plus a hefty interest rate. A much better idea is to open a bank account and have any refund direct-deposited. You get it fast, free, and with no surprises.

Check-cashing for a high fee

Going to a check-cashing place instead of a bank or credit union is like shopping at the most expensive store in town in the worst possible neighborhood. Check cashers are often located in places that are rife with crime. Why? Because everyone coming out has a pocket full of cash. A bank or credit union with which you have an account won't charge you to cash your check, and you don't have to take all the cash with you when you leave — you can deposit it in your savings and checking accounts.

Instant credit rating

WARNING

Credit repair companies may offer you a new identity or a repaired credit rating for only a few hundred dollars. Don't spend the money. The new identity is often illegal, and the instant credit repair doesn't exist.

Foreign bank accounts

WARNING

Occasionally, you may receive a letter or email saying that you've been chosen (lucky you!) to help a rich foreign person get some money into the U.S. and that you'll receive a fat percentage of the amount for your small trouble because you're trustworthy. Most of these communications come from Nigeria, but they can originate anywhere. Don't do it!

Overcoming Credit Fears and Mistakes

Everyone makes mistakes, even lenders and credit bureaus. A mistake needn't be a big deal if you deal with it quickly.

As a person new to credit and maybe even new to the United States, you may be a tad scared of having to deal with credit and the problems that can come along with it. Bill collectors aren't above using threats of deportation or imprisonment if they think that doing so will help them collect a bill. The truth is, they can't legally do either. You won't be deported and you won't go to jail, no matter what they say. How do we know for sure? Well, these companies only get paid for collecting the money due their employers. If they actually deported you or put you in jail, they wouldn't get their money!

If you're a credit newbie or have had a problem with your credit (including checking overdrafts), keep these basic tips in mind for dealing with mistakes:

>> **Don't delay.** Credit and debt problems don't improve with age. If you're proactive and make an effort to resolve a problem before you receive a call, you'll get a much better reception and improve your chances of a favorable resolution.

>> **Open your statements when you get them and challenge anything you don't understand or remember.** You can correct errors, but often there are time limits. And what may look like an error may turn out to be the beginning of an identity theft.

TIP

If you overdraw your checking account, be sure to contact the bank as soon as you find out. The objective is to work out a solution before the bank reports the overdraft to one of the specialty credit bureaus. Having this kind of a negative mark on your report can make it difficult or even impossible to open a checking account for up to several years afterward.

TIP

At www.dummies.com/go/creditrepairkitfd5e, you can find a sample letter to send to your creditor when you see an error on a billing statement.

>> **Do everything in writing.** You may resolve simple problems over the phone, but to protect your rights in a dispute, you need to make your case in writing. If you really want a problem fixed, do it in writing and keep good records.

>> **Keep track of contacts.** Keeping notes on who promised what to whom not only keeps you from making more mistakes but also tells the other person that you know what you're doing. So when the manager says that this is the first time you've called, you can say, "You are mistaken; I called on these occasions, and I spoke to these people, who told me these things."

>> **Keep cool and calm.** Nothing can derail your effort to resolve an error faster than raising your voice. After you escalate the volume, you'll be directed to someone who does "loud" professionally, or you'll be politely ignored. Either way, you lose. Call back if you need to, but don't lose control.

>> **Safeguard your identity.** Newbies to credit often come from a culture of sharing. Whether you shared with your family in Mexico or you shared with your roommate at Harvard, the time for sharing information and credit is over. Identity theft is a serious and growing crime that can take years to unravel and cost thousands of dollars to fix. In brief, guard your personal identification, mail, computer passwords, and bank account information. Shred financial mail. If you invite people into your home, be sure to put away your financial statements and checkbook. You wouldn't leave $20 bills all over the floor and furniture. The same applies to financial information.

Chapter 7 has more information on what to do if you run afoul of the credit-reporting system. If you do end up owing more than you can pay and you have to deal with collectors, Chapter 10 has the advice you need.

Qualifying for First-Time Cards and Lending

This section looks at how credit impacts two major and basic consumer credit instruments that most people need when they get started on life's journey: credit cards and loans. You may think that you know how these instruments work, but things have changed because of regulations like the CARD Act and the 2008 financial meltdown that threatened banks with failure due in large part to lax underwriting standards.

Getting a credit card

Getting credit for the first time used to be easy. All you had to do was drive to your nearest gas station and fill out an application for a gas card and then wait for the mail to arrive with your new plastic. If you were a city dweller who didn't drive, the trip may have been on foot to a department store, which would often grant credit on the spot. Both types of credit were relatively easy to get, and they reported your credit history to the three bureaus so that you built a credit history quickly. More and more department store and gas cards are tightening their standards to reflect credit conditions.

You can try for cards issued by banks that use a national transaction network such as Visa. Though these cards are more versatile and powerful than their earlier counterparts, they're also harder to get. Getting that first card now requires a new approach.

To begin with, you need a credit history. But how do you get a credit history without credit? Three of the most popular ways are to use someone else's credit, supply your own data, or use a secured credit card.

Using other people's credit

In most instances, when you use another person's credit, the other person is a family member or a person with whom you have an emotional attachment. Why? Because using someone else's credit can be dangerous to that person if you mess up. Only someone who really likes you is willing to risk helping you get started.

You can piggyback on another person's credit in two ways. The most popular way is to be added to the person's account as an authorized user. The other way is to have the person cosign for you.

>> **Becoming an authorized user:** Being named an *authorized user* on someone's credit account enables you to have his or her credit history reported on your credit report while you use a card for which the other person is solely financially responsible. The card statement goes to the account owner, he or she pays the credit card company, you pay the card owner, and the card's credit history is reported in both your and the owner's files.

WARNING

Problems with this approach can arise if you overcharge and the account owner has to ask you for more money than you have available, which can cause a rift between you.

WARNING

>> **Cosigning:** Cosigning on an account is often a recipe for disaster, and we usually don't recommend it. The cosigner's credit history doesn't show up on your credit report. Instead, all that shows up is your own payment history. The statement for a cosigned account doesn't go to the cosigner, so unless you share the information, the cosigner has no idea what's happening to the account. Often, the cosigner first hears of a problem when a collector calls and demands an overdue payment. Unfortunately, if you make late payments, the delinquency history appears on the cosigner's credit report, and negative information stays on the cosigner's credit history for a full seven years.

If you decide to go the cosigning route, you as the borrower should commit to paying this bill before almost any other. You also need to have the courage to keep your cosigner informed of any changes in your financial picture, especially if you may be late on a payment.

Supplying your own data

In the past, the only way information could get to your credit report was via a creditor. Using products like Experian Boost (www.experian.com/consumer-products/score-boost.html) and UltraFICO (www.fico.com/ultrafico), you can add your own information drawn from utility payments or banking accounts. See Chapter 7 for more information on adding positive data to your credit reports.

Using secured cards

A secured card looks and works just like a credit card but is backed by a cash deposit at the bank that issues the card. Typically, your deposit qualifies you for a credit card with a limit equal to that deposit amount. As a result, limits on secured cards tend to be low, but the real value here is to establish a credit history so that you can get an unsecured card and reallocate your deposit to a better purpose, like your emergency savings account.

TIP

You can find and compare secured cards on a number of websites such as www.bankrate.com and www.creditcards.com. You want to balance services, fees, and interest rates to find the best card for you.

Using savings for credit

Most banks and credit unions are happy to lend you your own money. If you accumulate some savings in a passbook account, you can use the savings to secure an installment loan of the same or a lesser amount. Needless to say, with 100 percent collateral in cash for the loan, the interest rate should be very low. Make sure that the loan is reported to the credit bureaus so that you build your credit as you pay the money back.

Chapter **13**

Putting Yourself in Control of Your Credit

Profitability is credit issuers' top priority. They shovel out credit offers by the truckload based on cursory reviews of your relative creditworthiness. Sure, some of the things they tell you may actually apply to your specific situation (for instance, you may indeed have earned the right to exclusive privileges and benefits), but the only thing you can be sure of is that the offer is designed to enhance lender profitability. Whether you need the credit product in question, or whether it's even remotely advantageous to your life, that's up to you to figure out.

This chapter is all about helping you take the control of your credit away from the issuers. It unmasks the plans others have for your financial future and introduces you to the tools you need to chart your *own* course to success. You also figure out how to perk up your credit score; gauge your credit style; and balance your spending, savings, and credit use.

Determining Your Credit Style

Lenders, particularly banks, divide their credit card customers into two main categories: *transactors* and *revolvers*. Identifying your type is important in the process of picking a credit product that fits your lifestyle.

Transactors

Transactors, also referred to as *convenience users,* are pretty straightforward in their credit use. You fall into this category if you use your credit cards primarily for convenience in place of cash. Doing so reduces your need to carry a wad of bills with you. You pay your balances in full every month and avoid fees and interest charges.

TIP

If you think that you may be a transactor, focus on the incentives that a card offers you for using it, like airline tickets or hotel stays, rather than a low interest rate. No balance means no interest, so who cares if it's 19.8 percent over prime; if you don't carry a balance, the interest rate is irrelevant to you.

Be sure that you use the card enough to benefit from it. For example, if you choose an airline mileage card that requires you to charge $25,000 annually to get a free ticket, and you plan to spend only $10,000 a year on the card, it may not be a good choice.

Revolvers

Revolvers frequently carry a balance from month to month. If you're one of these more desirable customers (from a lender's point of view), you consider your credit card a line of credit to use to pay for purchases over time. You make your payments on time, and often pay the minimum or more, but you rarely pay the balance in full. You pay interest every month and may not look too carefully at what the interest costs you over the long haul. Your bank could only love you more if you missed a payment or two and racked up even more interest and penalty charges!

A revolver's best choice is a card that offers a low interest rate. A low rate does a lot to help keep your balance down because your interest charges are included in the minimum payment you make each month. If your rate is high and you make minimum payments, you carry debt for much longer. Shopping for a zero-percent-interest card makes sense, but expect to change cards more often, as these rates usually apply for limited periods.

Be careful about incurring a 3 to 5 percent fee for transferring the balance from an old card with an expiring rate to a new one. Changing cards often has a negative effect on your credit score (see the list of score components in Chapter 6).

Other types

In addition to the usual card user categorizations, you may find one of the following helpful in identifying yourself:

>> **The quicksand charger:** You qualify as a quicksand charger if you spend on impulse and don't notice that you're slowly sinking into debt. Using credit without knowing how or when you'll be able to pay the bill is a bad habit that usually leads to an unhappy ending.

Use short-term installment loans for expenses that you plan to carry for six months or more. The fixed payment helps you pay off the debt more predictably, and the additional type of credit use can help your credit score. Plus, every time you apply for a new installment loan, you get a free reality check from your lender.

>> **The clueless charger:** If you continue to find unpleasant surprises on your credit card statements (like unexpected balance transfer fees and penalties), you may be a clueless charger. Students and other credit newbies tend to find themselves being taken advantage of because they don't understand how their cards work and lack a plan for using credit.

Read and understand the terms that come with your credit card. Believe that you have to make payments on time as your card agreement says, and not what other clueless chargers may tell you. For example, you can and eventually will be sued in court if you don't make the minimum payment required by the card issuer, even if the lesser payment you're making is all you can afford. Get some financial education from a responsible provider. Lenders and credit counseling agencies can help you make an affordable plan to get out of debt.

>> **The great pretender:** With apologies to the Platters, who released the hit song "The Great Pretender" in 1955, this category includes millions who extend their income or lack thereof by using credit as if it gave them additional money to spend. A $10,000 credit limit does not mean you can now afford to spend an additional $10,000! This approach may help you make ends meet in the short term, but it is often a disaster in the end.

REMEMBER

The tighter your finances, the tighter you need to control your use of credit. Start with a budget, trim your expenses, increase your income, and use credit only when you know that you can pay it off in a reasonable length of time (90 days or less is best). If you can't say when you will be able to pay off a charge, don't charge it. It's better, and cheaper, to cut back now rather than later, when your credit is trashed.

Balancing Spending, Savings, and Credit Use

An orchestra is beautiful to hear. A gourmet meal is a delight to eat. What makes each experience a pleasure is balance. Whether it's the balance of instruments or the balance of ingredients, each component must be in harmony with the others. If the balance is wrong, the outcome can be a disaster.

The same idea of balance applies to your finances. Your spending, savings, and credit use must work together for the most pleasing results. The following sections show you how to take baby steps toward achieving that all-important balance.

Spending on your terms

If your spending is under control and you have money for periodic expenses, chances are you've built a strong foundation for your financial house, and your credit will be safe and strong when you need it. Say your car has a mechanical problem; where does the money come from to fix it? If you plan your spending, then you should have a category for periodic auto maintenance and repairs. So the money comes from there and not your available credit on a credit card.

REMEMBER

When you use credit, you use tomorrow's money — money you haven't yet earned and may not earn. Look at it as using tomorrow's money today. When tomorrow comes, how are you going to pay if you've already spent tomorrow's money yesterday? The more you shelter your credit from surprises or overuse by planning where and how to spend your money, the stronger your credit history, credit score, and financial future will be.

Saving for emergencies

If a spending plan gives you a firm foundation on which to build, then emergency savings provide the roof for shelter. Saving for emergencies and goals is essential to financial success. One more time: If you don't save, you'll fail, becoming more and more vulnerable to money shortages caused by factors beyond your control. Anything from a car expense to a layoff to an economic shock caused by a pandemic or natural disaster along with the stress they bring is much worse for you and those who depend on you if you don't have a substantial emergency savings stash.

TIP

Of course, you don't *want* to live paycheck to paycheck, but perhaps money is tight and you're wondering how on earth you can possibly save anything, much less enough. Here are a few essential ways to save your hard-earned moola:

>> **Make saving painless.** Use direct deposit to put money from every paycheck into a savings account. Start small with what little you can afford — even $5 a week. The amount doesn't matter.

>> **Make saving a habit.** Automatic deposits build slowly. Your confidence in seeing savings where there were none before will build faster. Soon you'll have enough saved to handle a small emergency or even just a part of one.

>> **Add to savings with money you don't have yet.** Make a commitment to put half of new raises, tax refunds, and other windfalls like birthday money into the account. This is money you never had, never counted on, and won't miss.

Using credit to enhance your life

With your spending under control and money in the bank for emergencies and expected big-ticket items, you can use your excellent credit to get the best offers. You get the best terms on loans and credit cards thanks to a solid credit history and score. Even better, you free up thousands of dollars for trips, school, and other expenses when you get the lowest interest rates on mortgages, car loans, and more. Great credit also gives you lower insurance rates, access to better housing, and even an edge at work. Hiring and promotional decisions often involve credit report reviews. Your good credit can give you a competitive edge over other applicants or coworkers who have blemished credit.

Remembering the Importance of Planning

Lenders, credit grantors, insurers, landlords, and employers are constantly measuring your credit performance, and the cost of a substandard performance can be higher interest rates and fewer opportunities. These players and others use your credit profile as a gauge of your potential for success or failure, so having a plan and goals for your credit makes real sense.

The following sections reveal the plans that others have for your money and introduce you to the steps you can take to take control of your funds so that you don't fall prey to plans that benefit only credit issuers.

Zeroing in on the plans others have for your money

People constantly try to get you to spend money that you don't really need to spend. Just think of the credit offers you receive. These offers may ebb and flow with the economy and lenders' appetites for new customers, but inevitably they continue to show up from banks, investment companies, and even strangers. Rest assured that the issuers design these offers to be great for them without knowledge or regard for your particular situation. If you answered many (or all!) of the offers you receive, your credit score would take a hit each time your report was reviewed for an offer, and you'd get a further score reduction every time you were approved for new credit. The issuers don't care that their plans are winning at the expense of your credit.

If credit issuers' hidden goals seem a bit nebulous to you, consider what happens when you set foot in your local grocery store. The fact that the milk is located on the opposite side of the store from the door is no accident. This setup forces you to walk through the entire store, past an array of tempting products, to get to the one thing you need. The potential for an impulse buy is greatly enhanced, to the delight of the store owner and at your expense.

WARNING

The bottom line is that if you have no plan for your finances and others do, you're more likely to fail and they're more likely to win.

Developing your own plans

To avoid being a pawn in some credit issuer's chess game, you need to craft a plan for your finances. Specifically, you need to identify what you want to spend money on (goals), develop a spending and savings plan that reflects your goals, and then determine how credit fits into those plans. The key tasks are as follows:

>> Set and prioritize your financial goals.

>> Take simple steps to create a workable plan.

>> Adjust your plan as you go along.

The same process applies to your credit, but with a few differences. Yes, you need to set credit goals, but they can be simpler. For example, perhaps you want to buy a home in three years. If you had to wait until you saved up, say, $300,000 to purchase your dream house in cash, you might be ready for assisted living before you moved into your first home. Borrowing on future income to move in today makes sense and may well improve the quality of your life for years to come. You need to save for a down payment, and you need to have good credit to get a good mortgage interest rate and terms. This won't happen overnight, so you need to plan to make it happen.

TIP

Setting goals is easy. Just keep these steps in mind:

1. Do a little prep work.

Set aside an evening or a weekend afternoon, sit down alone or with your partner, without distractions, and look into the future. No need to pull out a crystal ball; simply describe what you want your future to look like. Consider the short term (generally from a few months to a year), intermediate term (two to five years), and long term (five years and beyond). Your goals may include such things as getting a car, buying a home, having a family, saving for college or weddings, and going on a fabulous vacation. In no time, you'll be imagining all those things you've always wanted to do.

2. As you identify goals, write them down.

Documenting your dreams is important because doing so makes them seem more real. Better yet, cut out or print out pictures that illustrate your goals — maybe a picture of a cruise ship or a tropical island surrounded by blue waters, or just you relaxing without fiscal worries.

As part of your planning, find out where you stand by obtaining free copies of your credit report and ordering your credit score; you find out how to do both in Chapter 7. Review your report for inaccuracies and then dispute any errors or out-of-date items you find using the pointers in Chapter 7.

After you take care of the inaccuracies, you can use the correct information in your report as a starting point for building the credit you want. Make adjustments to your credit usage based on your credit-score report's four statements about how you can improve your credit, called *reason statements.* They may indicate that you have too many active cards or that you have too much credit available. Both situations can hurt your credit.

Next, use your spending plan to determine which of your goals (say, buying a home or taking a cruise) need to be funded using credit. Then find out the credit criteria for a low-interest mortgage rate and determine what kind of credit card you want to use on your cruise. Consider a card that gives you points toward a cruise as an incentive. Now you're making decisions about which credit offers to accept or turn down instead of just accepting the preapproved offers that show up, whether or not they fit your needs.

REMEMBER

When you match your spending goals to a credit or lending need, you take charge of your own finances.

5

The Part of Tens

Steer clear of steps that are likely to backfire as you manage your debts.

Decide whether to stay in your home or leave, and reduce credit damage in the event of a foreclosure.

Understand your options for repaying your student loans.

Chapter **14**

Ten Debt Don'ts

When you are worried about the amount of money you owe to your creditors and confused about how to handle your debts, it's easy to do things that you later regret.

Although there are plenty of ways that you can trip up when you are struggling to keep up with your debts, this chapter warns you about ten common mistakes consumers make. We hope that our warnings help you avoid some headaches and hassles.

Ignoring Your Debts

When you feel overwhelmed by your debts, you may be tempted to stuff bills and notices from your creditors in a drawer, and you probably don't return creditors' calls. Bad idea!

WARNING

Sweeping your debts under the rug just leads to higher bills because interest and late fees keep coming. You end up at greater risk for being sued by your creditors, having your car repossessed, losing your home (or being evicted if you're a renter), and having your utilities shut off. So no matter how much it hurts, open those bills, return your creditors' calls, and put a plan in place for dealing with your debts.

Falling Behind on Car Payments

If you don't stay current on your car loan, you risk having your car repossessed. Repossession can happen without any warning after just a single missed payment. One day you have your car, and the next day you don't. If you need your vehicle to earn a living, losing it could spell disaster for your finances. At the very least, it makes life more difficult for you and your family.

Managing Money Without a Budget

It's foolhardy to think that you can get out of debt without using a written household budget to help you reduce your spending and manage what you do with your money. No tool is more fundamental to managing your debts and to ensuring that your limited dollars go toward paying your top priority debts and living expenses.

TIP

Review your written budget each pay period to make sure it continues to reflect the state of your finances and so you can decide if you want to revise your budget — allocate more of your income to savings, for example. If you haven't already done so, be sure to read Part 1 for more about budgeting.

Paying Creditors Just Because They're Aggressive

When money is tight and you don't have enough to pay all your debts, never make decisions about which ones you'll pay based on which creditors hound you the most. The ones that bother you the most may be the creditors you should pay last.

REMEMBER

Base your decisions instead on the consequences of not keeping up with a particular debt. The bigger and badder the consequences, the more important it is to pay the debt. For example, if you don't pay your mortgage, you could lose your home; if you fall behind on your car loan, your vehicle will be repossessed; and if you don't pay your federal taxes or your child support, you're at risk for a wide range of possible consequences, none of them pleasant.

On the other hand, say that you don't pay your credit card debts. Yes, the credit card companies may eventually sue you to get the court's permission to garnish your wages, seize some of your assets, and so on. But that process takes time — unlike a car repossession, for example. And if your debts are not large, a credit card company may decide to write off what you owe as bad debt. Furthermore, you can use bankruptcy to get rid of credit card debt, but filing for bankruptcy won't erase your obligation to pay your mortgage, car loan, federal taxes, or child support.

Making Promises That You Can't Keep

When a creditor contacts you about a past-due debt, or when you contact the creditor to negotiate a way to catch up on past-due payments and stay current on future payments, never agree to pay more than you truly believe you can afford. Base your decision on your household budget.

WARNING

When you don't have enough money in your checking account to pay what you owe to a creditor, don't give the creditor a post-dated check, gambling that by the time the date of the check arrives, the money you need to cover it will be in your account. There is nothing to stop the creditor from depositing the check before its date, which could cause the check to bounce. If that happens, you have to pay an insufficient funds fee to the bank, and you have to pay a fee to the creditor as well. On top of that, if you can't come up with the money you need to make good on the check, you may be prosecuted for passing a bad check.

If you over-promise and then begin having problems living up to the agreement, you lose credibility. That makes it difficult (perhaps impossible) to negotiate any additional concessions. Also, if you default on the agreement you made with a creditor, you may find that the full amount you owe — not just the past-due amount — becomes due immediately.

Continuing to Use Credit Cards

It's a no-brainer! If you're having problems keeping up with your credit card payments, don't rack up more credit card debt. If you can't afford to pay for something with cash, don't buy it.

TIP

Help yourself out by leaving your credit cards at home. For even greater protection, put your credit cards in a plastic bag of water and then place the bag in your freezer. If you're tempted to use your cards, by the time the ice has melted, you may think better of it.

Borrowing Against Your Home

WARNING

When you're having problems making ends meet, don't put your home on the line. You may be tempted to borrow against the equity you've built up or to use your home as collateral to get another type of loan. Don't. If you can't afford to keep up with your loan payments, you could lose what is probably your most valuable asset.

Working with a For-Profit Credit Counseling Agency

Always work with a nonprofit credit counseling agency (as explained in Chapter 9), not a for-profit agency. A for-profit credit counseling agency is in business to make as much money as possible off your financial woes. Therefore, you cannot trust that its recommendations are in your best interest. Some for-profit agencies may tell you to do things that make them money at your expense and that could get you into legal hot water.

Getting a High-Risk Loan

Some for-profit credit counseling agencies try to loan you money, claiming that the loan is a way out of your financial morass. Other creditors, like finance companies, also claim that their loans will help you deal with your debts. Always beware of loan offers that are made by nontraditional lenders, especially offers that require you to use as collateral your home, car, or some other asset that you don't want to lose.

WARNING

Although loans from nontraditional lenders may sound tempting, steer clear. If you read the loan paperwork carefully, you find that the loans are a very expensive source of cash and that the terms actually set you up to lose your collateral.

Asking a Friend or Relative to Cosign a Loan

If you cannot qualify for a loan from a traditional lender because of the state of your finances, think twice before you ask a friend or family member to help you get the loan by cosigning for it. If someone you know is the cosigner and then you fall behind on your loan payments, the lender will look to your friend or family member for the money you owe. Not only may paying your loan put your cosigner in a financial bind, but it also may very well ruin your relationship.

Chapter **15**

Ten Ways to Deal with a Mortgage Meltdown

For most people, a house is more than just a building you live in. It's a place you worked hard to earn, plan a life, grow a family, and make memories. It's a home. Sometimes those dreams don't come true and that mortgage can become unsustainable. But misinformation, stress, and denial can make it hard to accept the writing on the wall when you're in trouble with your mortgage.

Lenders may take a soft approach to early mortgage delinquencies, hoping you can get back on track. Unfortunately, when you can't get back on track, they can take a hard line on foreclosures. If you owe a past-due balance on a credit card, you'll get phone calls and letters that feel like harassment. Mortgage holders aren't nearly as aggressive when you're late on your payments. After all, they have security for their loan: your home. To them, that dwelling you live in is collateral that can be sold to recoup their losses.

This chapter outlines ten things you need to know and do after you realize you aren't going to be able to pay back the mortgage but before you leave or are asked to leave your home.

Knowing When You're in Trouble

You aren't in trouble if you owe more than the value of your home. You aren't in trouble if your roof leaks and you can't afford to fix it (although that may be an early warning sign). You may be in trouble if you can't pay your real estate taxes, but chances are, your unpaid taxes won't result in the bank calling. But you are *definitely in trouble* if you are late on your mortgage payments and have a feeling you're on the edge of a cliff and at any moment could fall off and into the foreclosure abyss.

If you're late on a single payment, you can probably just catch up. There may be a late fee, a hike in interest rate, or a penalty. At that point, it's financially advantageous for your lender to say, "Thank you, but this fee is a reminder to not be late again." On the other hand, if you've fallen several months behind, your mortgage lender might say, "No thank you!" Why would they do that? It's complicated, but basically, here's how it works: Because most mortgages are packaged into securities and sold in bulk to investors, the default terms for all the mortgages in the "package" must be spelled out in great detail and generally be the same. The result is a rigid set of rules that were made up in advance and have very little flexibility when applied.

It's not that your lender is an unfeeling automaton. As people, they do care. But legal agreements and contracts spell out what they must do. If you're more than 90 days late and you try to make a payment or even two, there is an excellent chance that your money will be refused and returned to you. You may need to make up *all your payments at once* to get any payment applied to your mortgage. A day late is indeed a dollar short when it comes to home mortgages. To further complicate matters as only bankers and lawyers can, the 90-day payment cliff does not include your grace period (typically 15 days). See Chapter 11 for more information about crossing the 90-days-late line, and check out www.hud.gov/topics/avoiding_

foreclosure/foreclosureprocess for more details on the foreclosure process.

REMEMBER

If you're late on your mortgage, it's vital that you open and answer your mail. The notices you receive generally offer good information about your options. The sooner you seek help, the more options you'll have to save your home.

Knowing How Your State's Laws Treat Foreclosures

Every state has its own foreclosure laws. It is important to know how your state's laws work so that you don't inadvertently cross a line or miss an important date. You can find summaries of the laws for all states at www.foreclosurelaw.org. The following sections outline a few critical differences.

Nonrecourse or recourse

REMEMBER

If your lender is foreclosing on your mortgage, whether you live in a "recourse" state or a "nonrecourse" state makes a big difference.

>> In general, if you live in a nonrecourse state, you can't be held liable for any deficiency between the amount you owe and the amount your home sells for in the foreclosure.

>> If you live in a recourse state, the lender may get a deficiency judgment against you in court. For example, if you owe $200,000 on your mortgage but your home nets only $150,000 at the foreclosure sale, the deficiency is $50,000. You would then be responsible for paying that "deficiency" of $50,000.

But knowing which states are nonrecourse states isn't enough. Some states define certain loans as nonrecourse if, for example, they were used only to purchase a home but as recourse debts if part of the proceeds of the loan were used for some other purpose, like paying off credit card debt. Other states limit the amount of the deficiency to the fair value of the property versus the sale price. Still other states have a one-action limit. For example, New York makes lenders choose between the acts of foreclosing on the property and suing to collect the debt.

Consult a housing counselor certified by the U.S. Department of Housing and Urban Development (HUD) or an attorney to get definitive information about the rules for your state.

WARNING

State nonrecourse rules don't apply to the IRS. If you lived in your home for less than two years, you may not qualify for the $250,000 individual home sale exclusion, so you may have a capital gain or phantom income from a foreclosure. See your tax professional for advice.

Judicial or nonjudicial

REMEMBER

It is important to know whether your state handles foreclosures on a judicial or nonjudicial basis.

>> If you live in a nonjudicial foreclosure state, your lender does not have to go to court in order to foreclose on your home. This means that the foreclosure can proceed more quickly.

>> In judicial states, foreclosures go through a court. These are called *judicial foreclosures* and may take longer to finalize.

REMEMBER

Time is your enemy in a nonjudicial state. Lenders are required to give very little notice of foreclosure sales, and once the foreclosure process begins, you may have no further options.

Deciding Whether to Stay or Go

This decision used to be a no-brainer. It was a matter of pride. People would do everything they could to keep their house. The stigma of losing the roof over your head was a big one. Today, though, the decision is often less about emotion and more about the math. Faced with seemingly unrecoverable deficits, some homeowners crunch the numbers and decide to save time, money, and stress by letting the foreclosure process run its course. Some move out, and others stay until the home sells to a new owner or the bank forces them to leave. The following sections describe your options.

Walking away

Strategic default is a new term in the language of mortgages. When the housing bubble burst in 2008, some properties went so far *underwater* (more is owed than the home is worth) that it seemed that it would take years or even decades for the home to regain the value of its mortgage — or it never would. More recently, rate hikes in adjustable mortgages may result in some borrowers choosing to stop making payments, even if they can afford to make them, because they see their house as just another investment, and a bad one at that. Walking away is known as a strategic default.

WARNING

Potential drawbacks to strategic default include deficiency judgments, significant credit score damage, problems buying or renting in the future, the personal impact of a major life failure, and to a much lesser degree these days, stigma in the eyes of others.

Working with the lender to exit

A more lender-friendly version of a strategic default is the deed-in-lieu of foreclosure option. Rather than go through a long and expensive foreclosure process in order to obtain title, the lender agrees to accept the deed to the property. This option may also incur a deficiency judgment for the difference between the fair market value of the property and the total debt owed. You'll still see damage to your credit scores and possibly a "deed-in-lieu" notation on your credit reports.

Another option in this category is a *short sale*, which involves selling your home for less than what you owe. If you choose this option, you may be subject to a deficiency judgment, depending on the terms you work out with your lender and the laws in your state. A short sale will have an equally serious effect on your credit scores, but don't look for the term *short sale* on your credit report. It's an unofficial phrase that was created to more gently describe settling your loan, and your lender will report the mortgage as "settled."

Staying the course

If you decide to do all you can to stay in your home, several courses of action are open to you. The major ones include the following:

>> **Loan modification/refinancing:** The two main types are the Home Affordable Modification Program (HAMP; https://home.treasury.gov/data/troubled-assets-relief-program/housing/mha/hamp) for Freddie Mac and Fannie Mae mortgages and conventional refinancing for others. A conventional mortgage servicer or lender may modify your loan to make it more affordable, but each one has its own programs and guidelines. Speak to your servicer about HAMP. If your loan is owned or guaranteed by Freddie or Fannie and you are ineligible for conventional refinancing, HAMP can change the type of your loan from adjustable to fixed, to a longer fixed term, or to a lower interest rate and can add past-due payments to the principal balance to be repaid over the full mortgage term.

>> **HUD Foreclosure Avoidance Counseling:** HUD offers free counseling to anyone who may be faced with foreclosure. They may be able to help you find alternatives to losing your home, or help with special loan programs to modify or refinance your mortgage or reduce your monthly payments to help you keep your house. To find a HUD counselor near you, visit https://apps.hud.gov/offices/hsg/sfh/hcc/fc/index.cfm.

>> **Assistance because of a natural or declared disaster:** Hurricanes, fires, earthquakes, tornadoes, volcanoes, and global pandemics can put lots of people in situations beyond their control. During times of disaster, federal and state governments, lenders, and credit reporting agencies may offer special relief programs. If you've been affected by a disaster, check with your lender about payment accommodations, such as forbearance or deferment, to help you maintain your mortgage payments through a period that is beyond your control.

Tightening Your Spending to Stay in Your Home

Whether your financial life has a ding or two or is upside-down, tightening your budget can help you free up sorely needed cash and get back in control of your situation. If you don't have a budget, now is the perfect time to make one. (See Part 1 for details on budgeting.)

Making a budget is basic but effective. Begin by listing all your expenses and then list your income. Look carefully at both sides of the equation, make some cuts to expenses, and look for ways to add to your take-home pay (like reducing your tax withholding) or increase your income with a part-time job. For example, if the bank forecloses, you'll lose your cable TV anyway. Cutting cable now may give you the extra cash that helps keep you in your home.

TIP

Technically it's not a spending cut, but you can also try to sell some stuff to raise cash for a mortgage payment. You've probably seen the "Cash for gold!" signs. Selling old and unused gold or jewelry is something you may want to consider. Having a yard or garage sale, downsizing to one car, and selling your violin should also be on your list. You get the idea. Lightening your load of stuff may buy you the time you need to catch up.

Prioritizing Your Spending to Build Cash

No matter what you choose to do in the event of a mortgage crisis, you're going to need some cash. It may be to pay an arrearage. It may be to come up with first and last month's rent and a damage deposit on a new apartment. Either way, you need to tighten your budget (or create one; see the preceding section). Yes, this step is basic, but as with everything in life, you have to start at the beginning. As described in the preceding section, list all your expenses and then list your income. Take a look at both sides of the equation and determine where you can make changes — by cutting expenses and/or increasing income (Chapter 5 has some ideas).

REMEMBER

Car repossessions can happen within weeks — not months — of missing a payment. So if you need your car to get to work, keeping up on your car payment is critically important.

If you can't make your mortgage payment, it's important to save as much of the money you're not sending to your lender as possible. If your payment is $1,000 and you can only scrape together $800, don't spend it on something else. Put the money aside to help ease your transition into a new place.

TIP

Want some help with creating a spending plan? Try a nonprofit consumer credit counseling agency member of the National Foundation for Credit Counseling (www.nfcc.org). Organizations like Operation Hope also offer money management programs. There may be a Hope Inside center near you (https://operationhope.org/how-we-help/credit-money-management).

Lessening the Damage to Your Credit

In a nutshell, if you stiff your mortgage lender with a loss in the form of a short sale or foreclosure, your credit will take a much bigger hit than if you come to an agreement to repay or forgive any deficiency. See Chapter 11 for more on what you'll need to negotiate.

For a person with decent credit and a FICO score in the 720 range, the difference in credit score deduction between a short sale with a deficiency and one without can be more than 50 points. See Chapter 11 for details on the damage to your credit and credit score that various mortgage problems can cause.

Knowing Who to Call

You know that you have the right to remain silent, and remaining silent can be wise in some situations, but not when you're facing a mortgage crisis. If you're behind on your payments, your lender will communicate with you by mail. The worst thing you can do is to remain silent, which could leave the bank no other option than to take legal action.

The best thing you can do is to open your mail and speak to your mortgage servicer at once. You should also contact an independent HUD-approved mortgage counselor (www.hud.gov/i_want_to/talk_to_a_housing_counselor) or your state housing agency. Avoid foreclosure-prevention companies like the plague they are. The best help is easy to find and available for free (see Chapter 9 for details).

Beware of Scams

It's easy to forget a lifetime of wisdom when the pressure is on and you are desperate for a solution. Knowing that you're vulnerable during a mortgage crisis, scammers will try to charge you money or even trick you into signing your deed over to them. Keep in mind that not everyone out there wants to help you; many just want to help themselves.

WARNING

Here are some quick scam signs to watch out for:

>> Never pay a fee in advance. The best help is free.

>> Never believe someone who guarantees that they can stop your foreclosure.

>> Be wary of anyone who contacts you and offers to help. Always get a second opinion from a person or an organization you trust.

>> Never hand your mortgage money over to anyone other than your mortgage servicer.

Beefing Up Your Credit

As soon as you default on your mortgage, your credit scores will take a nosedive. You likely won't be able to qualify for new accounts for quite a long time. Now is the time to take steps to improve your credit as much as possible so you can be in a position to move forward.

Pay down as much debt as you can, especially on your credit cards. If you're not making the mortgage payments, put some money toward your credit card balances. Lower credit card balances will help you bump up your scores and reduce your debt burden after the foreclosure proceedings have completed.

Try not to take on any more debt. Any purchases you make should be essentials. It's why having a budget is so important. Digging yourself deeper into debt when you can't pay what you already owe will only make things worse.

Take advantage of other new tools that can help bolster your credit scores, as well. Having things like your on-time cell-phone, utility, and video streaming payments added can help bolster your credit scores. Services like Experian Boost (www.experianboost.com) can be worth looking into. Just be sure you understand what you're signing up for. Although these kinds of services are free from a cash point of view, you'll likely get marketing offers to tempt you to open your wallet. Be prepared to say no thank you. You may sign up for alternative scoring systems like UltraFICO (www.fico.com/ultrafico), that incorporate information not included in credit reports. Lenders may consider that information in addition to the traditional scores to approve your application.

If you lose your house, you may find yourself renting. Studies have shown that doing so almost always helps build your credit. Talk to your landlord about having your positive rent payments reported or sign up with a rent payment service yourself. Here are a few options:

>> **ClearNow:** www.clearnow.com/creditreporting

>> **eRentPayment:** www.erentpayment.com

>> **PayYourRent:** www.payyourrent.com/residents

>> **RentTrack:** www.renttrack.com

You should know that there may be a nominal fee for these services to report your rent payments, so compare their offers to find the one that's right for your situation.

Consulting an Attorney

You have rights and you have legal options. Only an attorney can give you sound legal advice, so before your mortgage crisis gets too far along, spend the money to get a competent assessment of where you stand and what the law can do to help.

For example, a bankruptcy filing can stop a foreclosure in its tracks — probably not forever, but maybe long enough. A Chapter 7 or 13 bankruptcy may be a way to reduce other debt or the amount of your mortgage that exceeds the value of your home. It may be enough to get you back on track with your mortgage payments. Also, not all mortgage documents are properly drawn and executed. Have a lawyer review your files to see if they are unenforceable or flawed in any way.

REMEMBER

Bankruptcy is a last resort. It's the most serious financial decision you can make related to your debts. It's there for a reason, but that reason is that there is no other financial option.

TIP

A good lawyer who does a lot of foreclosure-prevention work can sometimes work minor miracles, maybe even delaying foreclosure for years, which can help you begin to build your savings account to pay for your next move, or maybe even keep your house.

Chapter **16**

Ten Strategies for Dealing with Student Loans

Student loans are hard to live with and, for many, hard to live without! Few question the value of a post-secondary education, whether it be in a technical field, for a skilled trade, or for a four-year (or more) degree. More education frequently yields a better, fuller life as well as more income. But with the cost of education rising fast and the job market always unpredictable, there is a growing disconnect between the cost and the benefit. This is demonstrated by the default rate of student loans, which has been on an upward trend.

So how do you get the benefits you want and need without the risk of owing more than you can pay? This chapter is just what you're looking for, with some advice to keep you moving in the right direction.

Knowing How Student Loans Are Reported

REMEMBER

The way that student loans are reported often catches people off guard. What most of us didn't know when we were in school is that, depending on how your education is funded, you may have a new loan every semester. That equates to up to two loans per year, or a total of eight smaller loans hitting your credit report instead of just one big one, even though you may pay them all with one check each month. When you start repaying the loans, each of them will reflect being paid on time (or not).

All this activity can build your credit score, but failing to pay can sink you big-time if you end up defaulting.

Another unique feature of student loans is that they are not normally dischargeable in a Chapter 7 bankruptcy. A student loan is a commitment that follows you until you honor it, regardless of how long it takes.

If you are not yet convinced that student loans are different from garden-variety credit card and auto loans, don't forget that in a Chapter 13 bankruptcy, they can grow even bigger! See the section on bankruptcy later in this chapter.

Dealing with the Collection Process

When you know the stakes are high, you'll want to handle any collection process quickly. The key to minimizing damage from a defaulted student loan is to address it right away. Don't procrastinate or ignore the letters and calls. Private student loans may charge off in as few as 120 days rather than the traditional 180 days for normal loans. Early action can enable you to handle loan issues quickly with the servicer rather than a collection agency. Servicers are more likely to work with you to come up with a solution that works for both you and the lender.

Federal student loans, in particular, may offer alternatives to help you get through a financially challenging period and avoid the prospect of default altogether. Contact your loan servicer at the first sign you may have difficulty and they can discuss alternatives with you. Here are two of those alternatives:

>> **Forbearance:** While in forbearance, your loan payments are temporarily suspended or reduced. However, interest continues to accrue, so be sure you understand the terms of the agreement. With forbearance, you probably won't be making any progress toward any loan forgiveness program available or paying back your line. As an alternative, consider income-driven repayment.

>> **Deferment:** When a loan is placed in deferment, your payments are suspended and interest usually does not accrue, although that isn't universal. If interest continues to accrue, you'll need to be prepared to repay it when the deferment period ends.

These tools may help you avoid defaulting or even becoming late with your payments if you act soon enough.

TIP

Before you call or write to the loan servicer (begin with a call and follow up in writing), organize your thoughts. Treat this as a very important job interview. Explain coherently why you weren't able to pay: medical issues, job loss, pay reductions, armed-service call-up, or family emergency. If you're calling to propose a payment alternative, have a number prepared and be able to justify it based on your budget. Call your servicer or the U.S. Department of Education information line at 800-872-5327, but be sure to do it before you miss a payment.

REMEMBER

Collectors are not obligated to offer you the best repayment terms you can get. They just want to get as much money from you as fast as they can. A loan servicer is much more likely to steer you to programs that will keep you out of collections, but you have to act fast.

Quick action also means that any delinquencies will be early, which typically gives you more options to get on top of the situation. The later you are, the fewer options are available to you.

Identifying the Best Repayment Option for Your Situation

A huge number of repayment programs are available, and they change all the time. Check out the big sites that deal with them, such as Federal Student Aid (https://studentaid.gov/manage-loans/repayment/plans) and FinAid (www.finaid.org).

If you qualify for student loan forgiveness, you may have to pay income tax on any amount that is forgiven.

TIP

Taking Your Loans to Bankruptcy

Because the value of your education can't be repossessed, a student loan generally can't be wiped out in a bankruptcy. And if you're not careful, you could end up increasing the amount you owe if you choose a Chapter 13 bankruptcy filing. Trying to get rid of student loan debt through a bankruptcy is difficult and perilous, but in some cases it can be done (check out https://studentaid.gov/manage-loans/forgiveness-cancellation/bankruptcy for more information).

Most debtors do not qualify to discharge (eliminate) student loan debt in a Chapter 7. The exception comes when you can prove to the court that repaying your student loans would cause you undue hardship. This provision is known as the *hardship exemption*. One size doesn't fit all, and the criteria can vary by court. Your best chance is if your income is very low or your loans are from a for-profit trade school.

Here are some factors the court may look for:

>> **Poverty:** Based on your current income and expenses, you can't maintain a minimal standard of living for yourself and your dependents if you are forced to repay your loans.

>> **Persistence:** Your current financial situation is likely to continue for a significant part of the repayment period.

>> **Good faith:** You have made a good-faith effort to repay your student loans.

REMEMBER

If you have a Health Education Assistance Loan (HEAL), your loan is more than seven years past due, and repayment would impose an "unconscionable" burden on your life, you may be able to get a discharge. A qualified attorney can advise you on your chances for a discharge.

Dealing with the Prospect of Default

Before you can be late on your loan, you have to have used up your grace period (the length of time you have after leaving school before you have to make your first payment). Determining when you have used up your grace period can be complex. Each type of loan may have a different grace period. For example, if you have a federal Stafford loan, your grace period is six months, while it is nine months for a federal Perkins loan. Federal PLUS loans can be based on when they were issued (see https://studentaid.gov/app/launchPLUS.action for more info). Check your loan documents or contact your lender to find out when your grace period runs out.

Here are some simple steps that may help keep you out of trouble:

>> **Keep in communication with your lender or servicer.** If you move, tell them. Being hard to find isn't a plus. If they send you a letter or an email, read it. Ignoring a potential problem only allows it to grow more serious.

>> **Find out which plans are available to you.** Federal loans are usually based on a ten-year repayment plan. If you can't or don't want to have that big of a bite taken out of your earnings, change your repayment plan. Extending your payments costs you less each month but more over time. You get to decide what's best for you. (See the earlier section "Identifying the Best Repayment Option for Your Situation.")

>> **If you have a private loan, contact your lender for forbearance options.** Private loans are different from federal loans and may not be eligible for income-based repayment or other federal plans, deferments, or forgiveness. Your private lender may offer other types of forbearance plans, but expect to pay for them. They may include interest-only payments for a set period.

>> **Look to community banks, credit unions, and state-based not-for-profit lenders for refinancing options of private student loans.** An example is the cuGrad Private Student Loan Consolidation program (https://consolidation. custudentloans.org). Available from many not-for-profit credit unions, it can be used to refinance and consolidate existing private student loan debt into one payment at a lower monthly rate.

Interest accrues on all types of loans during forbearances and on some types of loans during deferment, increasing your total debt.

Gaining Student Loan Forgiveness

In most cases, your loans are yours to have and to hold until you pay them back or expire trying. However, on some occasions student loans may be forgiven, canceled, or discharged. Following is a summary of the types of loan absolution that are available.

Different rules govern Direct Loans, Perkins Loans, and Federal Family Education Loans (FFEL). Be sure to know which rules apply to your loans.

>> **Total and Permanent Disability Discharge:** Like the name says, this discharge is for those who have been permanently disabled by military service or those receiving Social Security Disability. You also qualify if your physician

certifies that you couldn't work for the last five years, your impairment can be expected to last for at least five years, or you are expected to die.

>> **Death Discharge:** This one comes into play if you die. No life, no loan.

>> **Discharge in Bankruptcy:** See the earlier section "Taking Your Loans to Bankruptcy."

>> **Closed School Discharge:** Direct Loans and FFEL are forgiven only if your school folds.

>> **False Certification of Student Eligibility, Unauthorized Payment Discharge, Unpaid Refund Discharge:** To qualify for this discharge, your school has to have messed up in a major way, like approving your loan for a degree in law enforcement when you have a felony record disqualifying you as a law enforcement officer or giving money to an identity thief in your name.

>> **Teacher Loan Forgiveness:** This discharge may be yours if you have taught full-time in a low-income elementary or secondary school or educational service agency for five consecutive years. Only $17,500 of your subsidized or unsubsidized loans are forgiven. PLUS loans cannot be included.

>> **Public Service Loan Forgiveness (includes Teacher Loan Forgiveness):** If you work in a specified public service job or nonprofit and make 120 payments on your Direct Loans (beginning after October 1, 2007), the remaining balance that you owe may be forgiven.

>> **Perkins Loan Cancellation and Discharge:** Federal Perkins Loans may be cancelled if you perform certain types of public service or are employed in certain occupations. Generally, each complete year of service gets a percentage of your loan canceled. Occupational categories include volunteers in the Peace Corps or ACTION program (including VISTA), teachers, members of the U.S. armed forces (serving in areas of hostility), nurses and medical technicians, law enforcement and corrections officers, Head Start workers, child and family services workers, and professional providers of early intervention services.

TIP You can find more info at https://studentaid.gov/manage-loans/forgiveness-cancellation.

Lowering Your Bill While You're in School

There is no need to let the bill for your student loans grow while you're in school. Unless you have a subsidized loan, interest accrues and accumulates during the term of your education. Consider these strategies to reduce or eliminate your interest buildup:

» **Pay your interest as it accrues.** For students trying to save money on student loan debt, one solution is to make payments of at least the new interest that accrues during the in-school and grace periods. There are no prepayment penalties on federal and private student loans, so you can make interest-only payments. When making a payment, include a note asking for the payment to be applied to interest.

TIP If you have both subsidized and unsubsidized student loans, specify that the extra payment should be applied to the unsubsidized loans.

Paying off interest early not only saves you money, but also enables you to get used to working with your student loan servicer and helps you establish a relationship for successful repayment. It also gets you in the habit of making payments. Plus, you may get some tax benefits! As much as $2,500 in interest paid on student loans may be deductible on your federal income tax return. This may result in a refund that you could use to prepay a portion of your loan to lower the cost of your loan even further. Sweet! See IRS Publication 970 (www.irs.gov/publications/p970) for details. The tax break is income sensitive, so doing it while you're still a poor student makes even more sense.

» **Pay both interest and principal.** Doing so gives you all the benefits listed in the preceding section, plus it reduces your principal, which seriously lowers your future payments. A $5,500 loan might accrue $31 a month in interest. Paying the interest as you go could result in a savings of about $1,500. Paying on the principal will lower the debt even more.

» **Work a little to save a lot.** You don't need a full-time job to make a big difference in future loan payments. If you can earn only $57 per month (or $13.25 a week, or $1.89 a day), you can pay all the interest that will accrue on a typical $10,000 unsubsidized Stafford loan throughout four years of college and your six-month grace period. This means you can get your diploma owing only $10,000 instead of $13,060 (your principal plus interest). And don't forget, you may get a fat tax deduction as a bonus for deducting the interest you pay on your loans each year.

Keeping Up with Your Loans After You're Out

Keep in mind that federal student loans are real loans, just like car loans or mortgages. You must repay your student loans even if your financial circumstances become difficult. Your student loans cannot be canceled because you didn't get the job you expected or you didn't complete your education (unless you couldn't complete your education because your school closed, as explained in the earlier section "Gaining Student Loan Forgiveness").

You need to make payments to your loan servicer. Each servicer has its own process, so check with your servicer if you aren't sure how or when to make a payment. You are responsible for staying in touch with your servicer and making your payments, even if you do not receive a bill. It's your job to know who services your loan(s).

A lot of repayment plan options are available; see the earlier section "Identifying the Best Repayment Option for Your Situation." How much you have to pay and for how long depends on the plan you choose, so it's critical that you understand and act on your options. You should figure your real repayment amount under each plan before you pick one.

You may be able to consolidate your loans. Understand what consolidating means for you and how it may affect your future payments. You may also want to consider loan forbearance or deferment to temporarily reduce or postpone payments if you go back to school, join the military, or experience a hardship.

You may qualify for discharge, cancellation, or forgiveness in certain circumstances that are covered earlier in this chapter.

WARNING

Although student loans do offer generous terms, the danger here is that many young people just out of school don't have much experience budgeting and living on their own. You may find yourself in a real-live "grown-up" job with a salary that makes you feel like a millionaire, and you may start spending like a millionaire, too. Without tools such as a spending plan, you may quickly lose control of credit and debt responsibility and find negative items being added to your credit report.

Setting Limits During the Application Process

Beware of passion and peer pressure. Deciding your financial limits early in the game saves you from the emotions that are sure to surface as you narrow down your choices. Begin by setting a value for the education you're pursuing get in the field you plan to enter. Don't know your career choice yet? Then you should minimize loans until you do. Consider community colleges. Like buying a house before you know where you'll be working or what you can afford, buying an expensive education without knowing what type of job or salary you're likely to get is a mistake.

TIP

Shop around with different types of lenders, including the government, private nonprofit sources like your state student loan authority, private lenders, banks, and credit unions. Give extra points to those lenders that keep and service the loans they originate. Keep Parent PLUS Loans and cosigning to a minimum.

Getting Help If You're in the Military

The GI Bill (https://benefits.va.gov/gibill) offers substantial benefits to service personnel who have at least 30 days of active duty. More than one program is available, and programs typically offer tuition, books, and housing allowances. Be sure to check your eligibility before you take on any student loan debt. Here are three simple steps to consider:

>> **Reduce your interest rates.** Currently serving active-duty personnel are eligible to have interest rates lowered to 6 percent on *all* student loans taken out prior to active-duty military service under the Servicemembers Civil Relief Act (SCRA; formerly the Soldiers and Sailors Act). The SCRA provides protections for military members as they enter active duty and includes items such as rental agreements, security deposits, prepaid rent, evictions, installment contracts, credit card interest rates, mortgage interest rates, mortgage foreclosures, civil judicial proceedings, automobile leases, life insurance, health insurance, and income tax payments. It also provides benefits to dependents. Ask your loan servicer how to apply.

   Note: If you are in areas of combat or serving during national emergencies, you're eligible for a 0 percent interest rate. This rule applies to both federal and private loans.

>> **Opt for Income-Based Repayment (IBR) and Public Service Loan Forgiveness (PSLF).** These are two great options to repay federal student loans. IBR ties the amount of your monthly payment to your income and family size. PSLF can forgive any remaining balance on federal student loans after you make ten years of on-time qualified payments while working full-time in public service, like active-duty military service or service with the government or certain nonprofit organizations.

   Begin IBR as soon as possible so that every payment you make is a qualifying monthly payment. Make 120 qualified monthly payments, and the balance of your loan can be forgiven.

>> **Manage your private loans.** After you've chosen options for your federal loans, note that private loans don't qualify for IBR or PSLF. Postponing payments on private loans through deferment or forbearance may give you short-term relief if you're having trouble making ends meet. The terms and conditions of these payment plans vary, but for most private student loans interest continues to accrue after you suspend your payments. This means that your debt grows while you wait. You may be better off paying back your private loans if you can afford it. If you can't afford to repay your loans while you're on active duty, ask your servicer about interest-only payments instead of deferment or forbearance. This stops your loan balance from growing while providing you with some relief.

If you run into trouble keeping up with your payments, contact your Judge Advocate General for assistance.

TIP

Index

A

ACA (Affordable Care Act), 13
accounts
  about, 79–81
  credit reports for, 131
  history of on credit reports, 135–141
accounts summary, on credit reports, 133
active-duty alerts, 167
acts of God, 122, 242, 286
adverse action notice, 116, 144–145
Affordable Care Act (ACA), 13
Airbnb, 89
alarms, setting, 167
Albert app, 76
Alliance of Claims Assistance Professionals, 236
American Bar Association, 183
annual credit report, 126, 161, 250
apartment rental, credit reports for, 130
apps, budgeting, 74–77
arrearage, 219
assets, 39–40
attorneys, 183–184, 208–209, 291
authorized users, on credit cards, 261
auto loans, 10, 11
avalanche method, for paying off debt, 18–19

B

bad debt, 8
BALANCE, 176–177, 181, 221, 222, 224
balance transfers, 26–27
banking myths, 246–248

bankrate.com, 151
bankruptcy
  credit counseling for help with, 178
  on credit reports, 114, 134
  for student loans, 296–297
Barrett Values Centre, 53
bike-riding, 94
bill collectors, credit counseling for help with, 178
borrowing against your home, 278
bottled water, 93
budgets
  about, 45–46, 61
  checking, 29
  creating, 61–83
  determining categories for, 63–71
  expenses, 46–53
  financial goals, 58–60
  importance of, 276
  income, 53–57
  methods for, 62–63
  practicing creating, 81–83
  relaxing on, 96
  tools for, 72–81
bulk, buying in, 92–93

C

CARD Act (Credit Card Accountability, Responsibility, and Disclosure Act of 2009), 211, 248
cash benefits, 55
cash buffer, 82–83
categories, for budgets, 63–71
cell phones, 97
CFPB (Consumer Financial Protection Bureau), 201–203, 238–239

F

About the Authors

Steven Bucci: Steve has been helping people decode and master personal credit and debt issues for the last 20 years. For more than a decade, he has authored a popular weekly personal finance column for the financial mega-site Bankrate (www.bankrate.com). He also writes a weekly column on credit scoring that appears on CreditCards.com (www.creditcards.com). Steve is also a personal credit coach, speaker, and expert witness. He is a coauthor of *Credit Repair Kit For Dummies.*

Melyssa Barrett: Melyssa is vice president in data, security, and identity products at Visa, Inc. Her responsibilities include the development and management of identity products detecting and mitigating fraud to reduce identity theft, synthetic identity, and account takeover. Melyssa is also the CEO of Advanced Resolution Services, Inc., a subsidiary of Visa, Inc., and a consumer reporting agency. Prior to joining Visa, Melyssa held several positions at Citibank and worked in retail banking at Wells Fargo. She is a coauthor of *Credit Repair Kit For Dummies.*

Rod Griffin: Rod is senior director of consumer education and advocacy for Experian, where he manages the national consumer education and advocacy program in North America. With more than 20 years of experience in the credit reporting and information services industry, he is an expert on consumer issues, particularly credit reporting, credit scoring, and identity theft. In his role, Rod supports national financial literacy and financial inclusion partnerships and conducts training programs for clients, Experian employees, and consumer organizations across the United States. He is a coauthor of *Credit Repair Kit For Dummies.*

Mary Reed: Mary is a personal finance writer who has coauthored or ghostwritten numerous books on topics related to consumer money matters and legal rights. She is also the owner of Mary Reed Public Relations (MR·PR), an Austin, Texas–based firm that provides public relations services to a wide variety of clients, including authors, publishers, attorneys, financial planners, health-care professionals, retailers, hotels, restaurants, and nonprofits. She is the coauthor of *Managing Debt For Dummies.*

Eric Tyson: Eric is an internationally acclaimed and best-selling personal finance author and speaker. He has worked with and taught people from all financial situations, so he knows the financial concerns and questions of real folks. He is the author of five national best-selling financial books in the *For Dummies* series, including books on personal finance, investing, mutual funds, home buying (coauthor), and real estate investing (coauthor). An accomplished personal finance writer, his syndicated column is read by millions nationally, and he was an award-winning columnist for the *San Francisco Examiner*. He is the author of *Personal Finance in Your 20s and 30s For Dummies*.

Athena Valentine Lent: Athena is an award-winning financial columnist for *Slate* magazine. Her work includes items for BuzzFeed, Prudential, Experian, T. Rowe Price, The College Investor, and Money Under 30, to name a few. She also serves as a community liaison for FinCon, an annual conference for content creators and brands in the financial industry. She is the author of *Budgeting For Dummies*.

John Ventura: John was a best-selling author and a nationally board-certified bankruptcy attorney. He was also an adjunct professor at the University of Houston Law School and the director of the Texas Consumer Complaint Center at the Law School. John was the author of 13 books on consumer and small business legal matters, including *Law For Dummies*, 2nd Edition; *The Everyday Law Kit For Dummies; Divorce For Dummies*, 2nd Edition; and *Good Advice for a Bad Economy* (Berkeley Books). He is the coauthor of *Managing Debt For Dummies*.

Publisher's Acknowledgments

Senior Acquisitions Editor:
Tracy Boggier

Editor: Elizabeth Kuball

Compilation Editor:
Georgette Beatty

Production Editor: Pradesh Kumar

Cover Image: © PeopleImages/
Getty Images

PERSONAL ENRICHMENT

Staying Sharp
9781119187790
USA $26.00
CAN $31.99
UK £19.99

Facebook
9781119179030
USA $21.99
CAN $25.99
UK £16.99

Guitar
9781119293354
USA $24.99
CAN $29.99
UK £17.99

Investing
9781119293347
USA $22.99
CAN $27.99
UK £16.99

Beekeeping
9781119310068
USA $22.99
CAN $27.99
UK £16.99

Digital Photography
9781119235606
USA $24.99
CAN $29.99
UK £17.99

Meditation
9781119251163
USA $24.99
CAN $29.99
UK £17.99

Pregnancy
9781119235491
USA $26.99
CAN $31.99
UK £19.99

Samsung Galaxy S7
9781119279952
USA $24.99
CAN $29.99
UK £17.99

iPhone
9781119283133
USA $24.99
CAN $29.99
UK £17.99

Crocheting
9781119287117
USA $24.99
CAN $29.99
UK £16.99

Nutrition
9781119130246
USA $22.99
CAN $27.99
UK £16.99

PROFESSIONAL DEVELOPMENT

Windows 10
9781119311041
USA $24.99
CAN $29.99
UK £17.99

AutoCAD
9781119255796
USA $39.99
CAN $47.99
UK £27.99

Excel 2016
9781119293439
USA $26.99
CAN $31.99
UK £19.99

QuickBooks 2017
9781119281467
USA $26.99
CAN $31.99
UK £19.99

macOS Sierra
9781119280651
USA $29.99
CAN $35.99
UK £21.99

LinkedIn
9781119251132
USA $24.99
CAN $29.99
UK £17.99

Windows 10
9781119310563
USA $34.00
CAN $41.99
UK £24.99

SharePoint 2016
9781119181705
USA $29.99
CAN $35.99
UK £21.99

Fundamental Analysis
9781119263593
USA $26.99
CAN $31.99
UK £19.99

Networking
9781119257769
USA $29.99
CAN $35.99
UK £21.99

Office 2016
9781119293477
USA $26.99
CAN $31.99
UK £19.99

Office 365
9781119265313
USA $24.99
CAN $29.99
UK £17.99

Salesforce.com
9781119239314
USA $29.99
CAN $35.99
UK £21.99

Coding
9781119293323
USA $29.99
CAN $35.99
UK £21.99

dummies.com

dummies
A Wiley Brand